INVISIBLE AMERICA

INVISIBLE AMERICA

Unearthing Our Hidden History

MARK P. LEONE

NEIL ASHER SILBERMAN

A HENRY HOLT REFERENCE BOOK

NEW YORK

Henry Holt and Company, Inc.
Publishers since 1866
115 West 18th Street
New York, NY 10011

Henry Holt® is a registered
trademark of Henry Holt and Company, Inc.

Published in Canada by Fitzhenry & Whiteside Ltd.,
195 Allstate Parkway, Markham, Ontario L3R 4T8.

Library of Congress Cataloging-in-Publication Data
Invisible America: unearthing our hidden history/ [editors], Mark P.
Leone, Neil Asher Silberman.—1st ed.
p. cm.—(A Henry Holt reference book)
Includes index.
1. United States—Social life and customs. 2. Popular culture—
United States—History. 3. Material culture—United States.
I. Leone, Mark P. II. Silberman, Neil Asher.
III. Series.
E161.I58 1995   95-31067
973—dc20   CIP

ISBN 0-8050-3525-7

Henry Holt books are available for special promotions and
premiums. For details contact: Director, Special Markets.

First Edition—1995

Designed by Kate Nichols
Maps by Jeffrey L. Ward

Printed in the United States of America
All first editions are printed on acid-free paper. ∞

1   3   5   7   9   10   8   6   4   2

CONTENTS

PREFACE

Because this book is the result of such a long period of formulation, collection, and compilation, we believe that it might be useful for readers to have some idea of how the project came about. The process started in 1988, when one of the authors, Neil Asher Silberman, began occasional conversations with Russell Handsman, then research director at the American Indian Archaeological Institute in Washington, Connecticut. Silberman was by training and experience a Near Eastern archaeologist who had written about the political power of archaeology in the modern Middle East. Handsman was a North American prehistorian and historical archaeologist who was also deeply interested in the politics and ideology of archaeology; he had initiated a combined research and public education program to document the continuing presence of Native Americans in southern New England long after they had presumably been wiped out or driven away.

Both Silberman and Handsman were interested in developing new ways of conveying archaeological interpretation as well as different interpretations to the general public. Their occasional discussions eventually focused on the possibility of producing a new kind of archaeological guidebook—one that would examine American daily life and popular culture from a nontraditional point of view. The five hundredth anniversary of Columbus's first transatlantic voyage was then approaching, and Handsman and Silberman envisioned a book about the archaeology and material culture of post-Columbian America, in which native villages, Spanish missions, Anglo-Colonial gardens, Victorian houses, department stores, subways, and shopping malls would be the building blocks of a new story of five centuries of history in America. In contrast to the usual presentations of battles, famous men, and purely political history, this book, soon tentatively called *American Landscapes*, would concentrate on the rich material contributions of the largely forgotten American men, women, and children—farmers, workers, slaves, artists, and craftspeople—as they had been discovered and studied in recent years by historical archaeologists, folklorists, geographers, and social historians.

In Silberman's preliminary discussions with Kate Kelly of Prentice Hall, the idea became more focused: this was a story that could not be told only through narrative; scholars all over the country would be solicited to contribute specialized presentations about their particular interests and most recent discoveries. Thus came the idea of the "route map," a visual means of juxtaposing space, time, and substance through graphic clusters of artifacts or monuments linked to familiar landscapes through maps. Elements of popular culture and everyday life would be linked to larger patterns in American history. The scholars working in many different fields would provide vivid examples of the spatial patterning of material culture in America over the parts they knew of the past five hundred years. Examples would be of instruments of control and domination (public buildings, official monuments, city planning) and means of popular protest or resistance to the mainstream imperatives (vernacular architecture, unofficial local landmarks and tourist attractions, and folk art).

Early in 1989, Mark Leone of the University of Maryland at College Park became involved in the project. Because Handsman's professional commitments made it impossible for him to devote substantial time to the book, Leone agreed to assume a leading role. Leone had for years been deeply concerned with the examination of the implicit ideology of traditional archaeological interpretation; he was known for his use of critical theory to analyze messages conveyed to the public by open-air museums and historical restorations. In his ongoing excavations in Annapolis, Maryland, he and his students and colleagues had attempted to challenge traditional views of Colonial America and the Early

Republic by pointing out archaeological evidence for the rise of inequality and popular resistance to the dominant economic order.

Through the summer and fall of 1989, Leone and Silberman refined the projected contents of the book, settling on five main chronological periods, marked by the conventional dates of American history, yet giving them a decided point of view. The next step was to gather scholars—archaeologists, folklorists, popular culture specialists—and offer them a chance to present unusual or evocative studies of material and popular culture to the general public in the form of route maps. Silberman and Leone decided to divide the commissioning between them. Leone assumed responsibility for contributions for the theoretical introduction (Chapter 1), the seventeenth and eighteenth centuries (Chapter 3), and the era from the Federal Period to the end of the Civil War (Chapter 4). Silberman solicited contributions for the late fifteenth and sixteenth centuries (Chapter 2), the late nineteenth century (Chapter 5), and the twentieth century (Chapter 6).

The selection of the subjects in a book with such a wide chronological range can only be suggestive, not encyclopedic. Thus, Leone and Silberman then contacted dozens of scholars—some colleagues and close friends, others known only through published works or personal recommendations—searching for unusual and enlightening subjects, from the prehistoric periods to the present day. Each of the potential contributors was asked to submit the following elements:

- a map
- 4 to 5 illustrations of artifacts or landmarks with captions
- a "route map" commentary, explaining why the juxtaposition of artifacts or landmarks and geography was important
- some historical background material to be reworked in Leone and Silberman's formulation of introductory chapter texts

Between 1990 and 1994, the pieces came together, as titles and subjects of dozens of route maps were gathered, shaped, and accepted. The scholars who were eventually commissioned held conceptual approaches that varied widely, from critical theory to art history, historical sociology, popular culture studies, heritage management, and architectural history. Yet the layouts, ranging in date and types of material, from prehistoric hunter-gatherers to late-twentieth-century mall shoppers, all demonstrated that artifacts and landscapes of everyday life in America bear significance for understanding some of the deeper trends in American society. Although it is clear that other examples of material culture could have been chosen for each chapter and many more subjects could have been considered, the object was to show that archaeology, popular culture studies, and the study of folklore are ways of seeing both past and present, not merely the study of old things.

The next challenge for Leone and Silberman was the crafting of a larger narrative framework. Although the collection of route maps was on one level the composite work of many contributors with their distinct philosophical approaches, Leone and Silberman—as overall authors—believed that it was important to make sense of this admittedly impressionistic mosaic, to give it narrative coherence through a general introduction and introductory chapter texts. It should be noted that although these introductory texts are based on material supplied by the contributors, the attempt at synthesis and the specific conclusions are those of Leone and Silberman. The resultant text does not necessarily represent the views of individual contributors, which are expressed in their original form in the signed route maps.

The final, composite form of the book, eventually retitled *Invisible America*, should be seen as an experiment in creating a medium of historical and archaeological interpretation aimed at the nonscholarly public. Readers wishing to pursue the themes explored here in greater detail should refer to recent volumes of such periodicals as *Historical Archaeology, Winterthur Portfolio*, and *The Journal of American History*; to scholarly monographs from such academic publishers as Basil Blackwell, Routledge, and the University of North Carolina Press; and, of course, to recent books and articles written by our individual contributors. Our main purpose here has not been to provide detailed references to the specialist literature but rather to combine a wide range of scholarly contributions with an overall perspective and point of view that will offer the general reading public a glimpse at the themes and subjects that are becoming increasingly central to the study of American history today.

As will be made clear in the introduction and chapter texts that follow, we—Leone and Silberman—see American history as a never-ending dynamic between those who seek to dominate culture, economy, and society, and those who struggle to resist, all within capitalism. Questions about *Invisible America*'s choice of specific contents and its literary genre—whether it is a guidebook, history book, or atlas—seem to us to be far less important than whether it is useful in providing readers with some new ways to make sense of America's ground, America's things, and America's history.

We would like to extend our thanks to Kate Kelly who commissioned this book for Prentice Hall; to Carol Mann who handled the negotiations; to Gerry Helferich, our first editor; and to Mary Kay Linge of Henry Holt and Company who skillfully and enthusiastically helped us bring the manuscript to its final form. Early in the project, we were ably assisted in administrative matters by Lynn Jones and Tracy Shiflett. In the final, critical months of revisions and collection of material, Ellen Silberman took over virtually the entire administrative load. We thank her for her organizational skill in maintaining order in a mass of details and for her perseverance in tracking down elusive contributors and hard-to-find illustrations. She helped make this project, begun so long ago as an abstraction, finally become a reality.

Mark Leone also wishes to thank Nan S. Wells, his wife, for her long-term, thoughtful encouragement and Joseph Antonellis for his enthusiastic reading of an early version of the manuscript.

Mark P. Leone
Neil Asher Silberman
May 1995

1
HOW TO SEE THIS BOOK

WITH CONTRIBUTIONS BY

Janice Bailey-Goldschmidt

James A. Delle

John Michael Vlach

Mark Bograd

Pauline Turner Strong

Invisible America is a different kind of historical narrative: We have intended it as a way of challenging old-fashioned and conventional versions of American history. We intend to arouse questions in your mind about both present and past. Through the maps, pictures, and explanations that we will present, we hope that you can see that the historical development of the New World of North America and of the United States was not an inevitable march of "progress," that the course of events was in fact filled with alternatives, and that our history is dynamic, unstable, and often unpredictable. So instead of maps and illustrations of early explorers' voyages, of the orderly establishment of English colonies, or of the establishment and gradual spread of the United States westward, we present maps of European–Native American trade networks; house plans; and pictures of schools, factories, subways, and Indian reservations.

These are all important elements of our national, historical landscape that may help explain how we got to be here now. We will talk about Iroquois, Algonquian, Pueblo, and Sioux; about venerated national myths and monuments that should not be; about department stores, popular entertainment, and drive-ins; about slave revolts, immigrants, skyscrapers, and suburbia as parts of the reasons for being what we are and have come to be. We talk about these things not as incidental to our national character and heritage but as important elements of our social makeup that we often prefer, for good reason, not to see.

As you look through this book, we ask you to keep in mind how Americans have traditionally been taught history. Remember the old-fashioned school books with their succession of presidents and domestic policies, wars, battles, famous inven-

---

This famous 1845 painting entitled Osage Scalp Dance *by John Mix Stanley, expresses one of the most vivid—and misleading—images of conventional versions of American history. The Indian's raised tomahawk over the white woman and child represents the threat posed by savagery to the advance of civilization on the western frontier. In the contest of competing cultures, Indians are portrayed as savage and overwhelming, whites as helpless and innocent.*

An unrealistically romantic approach to our history is typified by this early-twentieth-century Wallace Nutting photograph of a colonial kitchen. As part of a conservative reaction to large-scale immigration and modernization at the turn of the century, the Colonial Revival—with its love of antiques and preoccupation with colonial genealogy—created an entirely artificial image of a past of stability, modesty, and quiet elegance.

tions, heroes, and dates? Of course, things have come a long way from the patriotic history books of earlier generations—books with such titles as *The Building of Our Nation* (1937) or *History of a Free People* (1954). If our national history still begins with Columbus, at least we now know that he entered a New World filled with millions of Native Americans, hundreds of distinct nations, dozens of regional cultures stretching across the continent and possessing a complex 12,000- to 20,000-year history. It will probably never be possible again to write a textbook about our national beginnings that mentions only Columbus and the Europeans. Native North America was and remains so large, vital, influential, and powerful in our history that its place is not only parallel to that of the discovering and arriving Europeans, it is an integral partner in the story.

Because we see the act of presenting the past in schoolbooks and museums as incomplete, often unreliable, and filled with misrepresentations, this book will take a different approach. It does not present the past as an even developmental flow that comes up to today showing American life and society becoming steadily better, healthier, richer, or wiser. Rather we hope it will show you some of

the ways our society has always acted, operated, and constructed its everyday reality.

We also intend to identify often overlooked traces of past lifeways, customs, and injustices that can still be found within and beneath the modern American landscape. This is where archaeology takes on an important role. Because museums and outdoor excavations have often displayed historical artifacts in sealed glass cases, we have become used to seeing the "past" as broken bits and pieces of pottery and metal, costumed mannequins, colorful dioramas, bits of text, skeletons, and old-fashioned weapons and tools. The implicit message of such "things" is that history is composed of extinct Indians, obsolete technologies, and simpler times. When we examine the paintings and reconstructions of the past in these museums, their unspoken message is that men did most of everything; that the boundaries were clearer between wilderness and civilization, between right and wrong; and that, except for its patriotic or entertainment value, the past is dead and gone. Our message challenges these understandings. We argue that Indians are not extinct; that women had and have a vital role. And we believe that the past continues to have a powerful impact on the present in places as diverse as the Pine Ridge Reservation in South Dakota; Annapolis, Maryland; the Mississippi Delta; and Paradise Valley, Nevada. At even the most famous and frequently visited historic sites we can discover hidden, overlooked, or ignored histories by reading traditional museum texts between the lines.

Part of the difference in our perspective comes from the fact that we do not see American society as a static mosaic, but composed of groups of people whose relationships to one another are constantly changing. Although we have often been taught to see Early America as mostly wilderness with small colonies that were backward or provincial versions of European society, we want to show that European society and its extensions into North America were not simply matters of colonization or pioneering but were characterized by dramatically different levels of wealth and power, which were interrelated in unstable ways.

Early America certainly had its share of wars, rebellions, exploitation, social tension, technological developments, and cultural institutions. This book illustrates the relationships between such groups as Native Americans and the Spanish in the Southeast in the 1500s; African Americans and Anglo Americans in the Mid-Atlantic area in the Federal Era; immigrant workers and industrial employers in the Northeast between 1880 and 1930. In this book, you can read about class rebellion in seventeenth-century Virginia; see the Civil War not only as a war against southern slavery but also as the triumph of northern industry. You may recognize that printing presses and schools were not just cultural or educational innovations but effective instruments used to destroy and replace Native American culture in the nineteenth-century South, East, and Midwest.

We hope to show that many of the most familiar elements of everyday life throughout American history effectively mask the deeper workings of our society. Indeed, the cultural institutions of our nation—schools, museums, popular literature—have presented our society as stable, functional, improving, and productive of a common good. That impression was—and still is—often produced in the public consciousness by the manipulation of the landscape, which includes architecture, public monuments, works of art, and countless other manifestations of popular culture. Therefore, this book will devote considerable attention to artifacts and other objects.

The traditional schoolbook and museum presentation of American history is not necessarily wrong, but we think it is time for a new popular presentation. Our goal is not to expose the evil, the wicked, or the depraved—those exist everywhere. Our point is to show the missing, the submerged, and the anonymous: where on the American landscape they can be found, what they made, and who they were. And at the same time, we will try to address the issue of their anonymity. Who caused all these people, places, and things to seem irrelevant?

AN ALTERNATIVE HISTORICAL SCHEME

We have divided this book into chronological chapters, examining social, economic, cultural, and political developments in five distinct eras of American history. Although clear-cut beginning dates and ending dates are often hard to determine, we have tried to show that certain stages can be discerned in the unfolding relationships between settlers and native peoples, farmers and city dwellers, employers and workers. The first part of each chapter is dedicated to showing the underlying stresses that existed in American society in each of these periods; in addition to peaceful relationships, accidental confrontations, and technological progress, we also describe unequal or hostile relationships, and attempts to control nature and peoples. It is important, though, to recognize that this book is not primarily about war, struggle, or violence; it is about the powerful tools that have been used by certain Americans in various periods of our history to shape and control our society.

In brief and almost telegraphic form, here is the story we plan to tell, covering five chronological periods whose dates will be familiar to most. We begin, predictably, in 1492, a year in which Europeans most manifestly did not discover America.

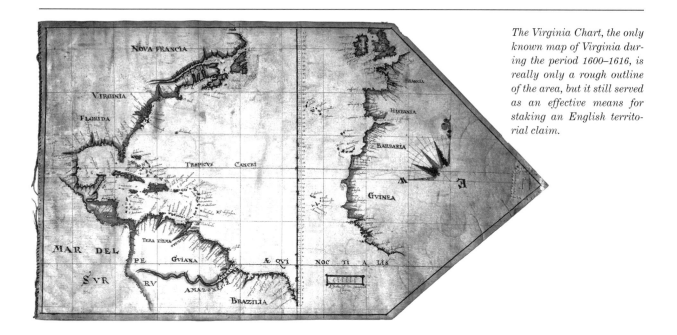

The Virginia Chart, the only known map of Virginia during the period 1600–1616, is really only a rough outline of the area, but it still served as an effective means for staking an English territorial claim.

They did find it, but not for the first time; the ancestors of Native Americans had migrated into the Western Hemisphere at least 12,000 years before. And Viking and perhaps other European navigators had crossed the Atlantic many times centuries before. The significance of 1492 is, as we see it, the date of the first demonstration of a technologically successful way of crossing the Atlantic over and over again in a way that was predictable, could transport many, many people back and forth, and, by far the most important, could make a profit in so doing. Since this profit was to be made through the confiscation of land and resources owned by others, many of those others frequently protested, rebelled, and went to war. This is one of the main conflicts that began in the period covered by our first chronological chapter—a struggle by Native Americans to preserve their culture that continues to this day.

Our second period begins with the year 1607 which is, of course, the date of the founding of the first successful English colony at Jamestown, Virginia. Within only a few years the English relationship with the surrounding native peoples was one of territorial claims, competition, or outright domination. Thus, as was the case with the arrival of the Spanish and the French, the establishment of British colonies in North America represented the

beginning of a new kind of economy. Yet, it is important that we do not confuse ethnicity— "Spanishness," "Frenchness," "Britishness"—with the common political and economic system that the early Spanish, French, and British colonies served. For, in addition to the conflicts with Native Americans, the various European powers competed with one another for control of New World resources throughout the long, strife-ridden era that came right up to and culminated with the French and Indian War, the American Revolution, and the War of 1812. What unified the Europeans is what we Americans still share with them: The common belief that land, resources, and sometimes people are commodities to be bought, rented, and sold for profit.

At least on the surface, 1780, one of the years of the American Revolution, is the date that represents the end of the colonial period in American history and it is where our third period begins. By the War of 1812, when the British retreated permanently to Canada and the Caribbean, the former British colonies in America had become culturally independent with their own developing industries. They had founded the economic, cultural, and political processes that we see in many of the layouts in the coming chapters, which highlight American industries, plantations, the role of

Children are among the groups who are seldom seen and whose voices are even more rarely heard in conventional versions of American history. Pictured here are three sisters of the Coplan family of Boston, painted by William Matthew Prior in 1854.

women, the importance of clocks, and even a new concept of childhood.

Most histories of the United States treat the Civil War as a watershed, and its end in 1865 marks the beginning of our fourth period. Yet no less important than the abolition of slavery and victory for the Union was the subsequent spread of mass production, mass consumption, and mass marketing, the movement of populations, and the triumph of the Union's overreaching ideology. By 1900, the North's ideas had been thoroughly accepted from coast to coast. Yet the ideas and economy usually associated with the North are not simply "Yankee" or northern; this economy is based on the mass production of consumer goods for profit, by entrepreneurs who invest or borrow money to set up factories and plantations, and pay others to supply both skilled and unskilled labor. Too often this economic system is defended, condemned, or caricatured as "industrial capitalism." We take a closer look at some of its rationales and effects.

Somewhere, or somehow, between 1865 and 1945, the era in which we are living began. We picked 1918, the end of World War I, as a starting point. Here we want to focus not only on mass production and the creation of a national market but also on mass communication, mass disaffection, mass rejection of older traditions, and the continu-

ous change of styles and cultural attitudes that is now proclaimed as positive virtues. We show how these developments manifested themselves in the construction of nationwide highways, shrines to popular heroes, fast foods, advertising, skyscrapers, and suburbs.

Within each of these five chronological periods we highlight some continuing themes that compose a dynamic that makes our story go ahead. First, we undergird our approach in each chapter with a discussion of some of the sources of social conflict and instability. We assume neither smooth social functioning nor inevitable upward development in order to understand American history. We see tensions between groups—those who have, want, do not have, do not want—as a way of understanding why and how American society has been transformed over time.

We also show some ways in which those tensions and conflicts were dealt with—often by the use of ideas, notions, or belief systems to disguise or rationalize each society's basic inequalities. The rationalizations are possible because each era's idealizations and misrepresentations about how the world works (called *ideologies* in our usage) can come to be accepted by most of the population as natural, God-given, or inevitable.

Ideologies include the belief that America is a special land of opportunity; that a woman's place is in the home; that children are like adults; that blacks were born to be beasts of burden; that Indians are better off as Christians or at least "civilized"; that bathing once a day is better; that vacations are natural; that paying people by the hour is efficient; that progress is inevitable; and that immigrants assimilate. That many familiar slogans painted on billboards, printed in textbooks, and embroidered on pillows are not necessarily so; that the "takens-for-granted" about how the world works are sometimes profoundly misleading (and often designed to prevent any meaningful change) is one of the main assumptions of this book.

Many elements of specific ideologies can be and have been very powerful. They convince us of our equality, and when we believe them, or when they were believed, they hide great inequality. Commonly accepted ideologies have masked the brutal-

Ideology can be clearly expressed in landscapes and architecture, as well as in abstract ideas and literature. Beginning in the eighteenth century, many public buildings in America were built in a classical style, resembling Greek temples. In this way, institutions important to the new system of mercantile capitalism were shrouded with the symbolic authority of antiquity. Seen here (top to bottom) are the Second Bank of the United States in Philadelphia; the Redwood Library in Newport, Rhode Island; and the Quincy Market in Boston.

ity of slavery; the suffering of poverty and exploitation; and the tragedy of the destruction of native cultures. They have also concealed the self-interest of their makers and the vacuousness of the statisticians and scholars who taught them, unknowingly or willingly. We want to show that societies like our own have the capacity to paper over differences, to disguise exploitation, and sometimes to make restricted opportunity seem like freedom. And we seek to contest the validity of an ideology that teaches us to rationalize wealth for the few as deserved failure for the many, and to see special privileges for the powerful as a blessing that will "trickle" down to us.

The dominant social, economic, and political order in the United States—the urge to invest and make a profit—is so dynamic and potentially exploitative that it is almost always being challenged by peoples, cultures, and social orders that stand in its way. Another of the assumptions behind *Invisible America* is that individual groups and classes of Americans have said or can say "no" to the effects of social, economic, and cultural domination. Most often their resistance has been ineffec-

tive in the long run, and it has almost always been unrecorded, ignored, or misrepresented by others so as to disguise the intent. Yet, the fragmentary and incomplete record of this resistance is valuable evidence of the social tensions, compromises, and conflicts that constitute a basic feature of historical change. Such resistances are often accompanied by their own ideologies, which were or are efforts to promote alternate social consciousness. This book is intended to allow you to recover instances where people said "no" to colonizing invasions, and later, to some of the harshest effects of industrial capitalism; who said it; how and why they said it. And how their resistance was most often either silenced or absorbed into mainstream society.

Some protesters directly challenged the status quo; others opted for a nonconfrontational approach. Across the United States in the early to mid-nineteenth century, thousands of Americans helped establish many utopian societies based on both religious and communitarian principles. Feminists in the nineteenth and twentieth centuries challenged traditional notions of family and home by designing houses and communities with central kitchens and

The pantheon of great Americans can reflect protest and reform as well as material prestige and power. This pen-and-ink drawing from the early twentieth century depicts the historical apotheosis of Elizabeth Cady Stanton and Susan B. Anthony, early leaders of the American women's movement.

group child care. Still other protests were voiced by everyday people in everyday ways. Workers in factories regulated the pace of their labors through slowdowns, sabotage, and absenteeism. Slaves resisted masters by hiding tools, learning how to read and write, and running away. For working people, saloons and songs often became sources of protest.

Why should we care about these voices from the past? We care because the protests had real effects. As one of the contributors to this book, Mark Bograd, notes on pages 26–27, many of the events we study in American history—both positive and negative—are better understood when placed in the context of a society filled with conflict and protest, in the constant interaction between those who dominate and those who protest. Protests carried with them in many cases either an independent ideology, like those of the Shakers or the Mormons, or a level of consciousness about themselves and their society, like that of the women's movement of today, which are separate from dominating ideologies.

These subordinate ideas and ideologies are significant for us because of their coherence and because they sometimes provide a clear-eyed view of the society—ours—that triumphed. The material culture of more recent protest is evident today even though we often do not recognize it as such. The rebellious clothing of flappers, greasers, beatniks, and hippies was turned into fashion and is now, in modified form, part of our national costume. The anthems of the civil rights movement and the songs of Woody Guthrie and Bob Dylan have become a part of the repertoire of school choirs and community groups. If we can recognize these voices for what they tend to say, they tell us that the status quo is not inevitable, and that protests virtually always exist. One of our challenges in this book is to recapture the original intent and content of these protests before they were absorbed into the mainstream and muted.

"OTHERS" AND OURSELVES: TOOLS TO ENCOUNTER PEOPLE

As Pauline Turner Strong points out on pages 24–25, European explorers, conquerors, and settlers laid claim to a New World through an ideology of "discovery," portraying the landscape as an unimproved, natural "wilderness" and the indigenous people as uncultured "savages" lacking social order, government, religion, or history—by virtue of their natural, perhaps even biological, simplicity. In doing so, Europeans invented an America and an "Indian" population that needed Europe for its religion, its forms of control, its technological expertise. The Europeans believed that only they, using their own ideology of discovery, could properly cultivate the American wilderness and its "savage" peoples. They called this process "progress," and saw their task as divinely ordained.

One of the most important tools used in this European process of identifying the strange or exotic as inferior was the travel or picture book. And since *Invisible America* is itself something of a travel and picture book, it may be worthwhile to describe the origins and development of this literary genre and to suggest some of the ways it might be transformed. As Janice Bailey-Goldschmidt explains in pages 22–23, the travel genre became enormously popular in sixteenth-century Europe—to dramatic effect.

She points out that although some worldwide economic networks and trade routes had existed prior to the fifteenth century as trade routes, the period from 1450 to 1640 was unique due to the growing dominance of Europe at the expense of the independence of such regions as Mexico, Peru, Japan, India, and China at its economic periphery. Indeed, European travel became an essential way by which the world came to be spatially perceived and, inevitably, divided up among competing European interests.

Why were the exotic peoples encountered by Europeans in the "New World" transformed into picture book, textbook, and museum constructs? The question is an important one, for the symbolic process through which some five hundred distinct indigenous cultures of North America became generalized as "Indians" and "savages" resembles in significant ways the process by which other groups have also been defined as inferior Others: Africans who were made into slaves; Jews who were pushed into marginal or despised economic pursuits; immigrant laborers who were hindered from assimilating into the mainstream culture; women, children, mental patients, and criminals whose movements have been restricted and who have been classed as lower forms of humanity. In each case, a dominant group affirmed its identity, legitimized its superior position, and justified processes of social control by opposing itself symbolically, literally, and politically to a group defined as lacking rationality, divine authority, technological competence, or self-control.

HISTORY AND POPULAR PRESENTATION OF THE PAST

This book is what might be called a history book, but we believe it has some important differences. To understand how, it is important to understand how our Western society has conceived of the past and history over the past few centuries. The process of European expansion—and the absorption of non-Western peoples and resources into the European economy—was accompanied by an attempt to "conquer" the past as well. Ever since the Renaissance, Western scholars have been constructing a universal scheme of history. In it, the pasts of all peoples have been incorporated into a single story, usually of triumph. And it is a triumph in which the technological, intellectual, and religious achievements of Europeans represent the culmination and crowning glory of the long saga of humankind.

In a way, this ethnocentric style of representing the past is not unusual. Virtually every society conceives of itself as the center of the universe—both main character and hero in the story of the world. The Sumerians, the Egyptians, the ancient Israelites, the Greeks, the Chinese, and the various Native American peoples who identified themselves as "the real people" (and of course these are only a few examples of hundreds) paid careful attention only to their own kings, triumphs, and achievements, leaving the doings of others in the semidarkness of barbarism that surrounded their own enlightened, civilized world. Such was the historical attitude of Europe, at least until the time of the Crusades. But with the expansion of European armies and increasingly complex trading connections into the world of Islam and, eventually, into the Americas, those other peoples and places—whom the Europeans sought to conquer—could not be left in semidarkness. Their destiny as subjects of European conquest had to be incorporated into the saga of European history in a powerful and convincing way.

Sixteenth-century European travel books lavished detail on the strange sights of the New World. Their exotic character underlined the hazards of foreign conquest, the natives' backward customs, and the consequent need for civilizing. This illustration by the English explorer and artist John White depicts the dining customs of an Algonquian man and woman, circa 1585.

Popular presentations of the past—in schoolbooks and at national parks and memorials—make subtle suggestions about what we should consider important in our shared history. In the recent restoration of the Ellis Island Immigration Station in New York Harbor, the main registry hall has been intentionally left empty, transforming a place once filled with noise, confusion, and immigrants' uncertainty into a hushed cathedral of citizenship.

So instead of conceiving history as an ethnic chronicle, the Europeans began to conceive of the past in almost geographical terms. Like the maps of previously uncharted territories neatly folded into a ready-made grid of latitude and longitude, European historians of the Renaissance began to incorporate the histories of all peoples into a chronological sequence of days, weeks, years, centuries, and millennia, in which the history of Europe could be coordinated and compared with the events that unfolded in those same periods of time in the rest of the world. Yet, despite the avowed intention of creating an objective, "true" version of history, the European chronicles saw the past from their own perspective. The very act of researching the history of others implied that those others' own versions of the past were somehow deficient or inaccurate. And like the maps and sea charts that facilitated the incorporation of space into the European world system, European methods of history making did the same with time.

In this book we hope to persuade you to question the absolute authority of popular presentations of history. If there is certainly no single "objective" vision of the present (just think of the wide range of opinions expressed today about political, economic, and social developments), can there be a single "objective" version of any moment in the past? It is our contention that even the most objective-sounding histories are stories that we create in the present about what happened in the past. They can never be literally "true" for at least two reasons. First, since evidence about the past is never complete (memories fade, records are lost, cities are destroyed), historians must fill in the gaps with their own imaginative reconstructions in order to tell a meaningful story. And since that work of imagining takes place in the present, with the conceptions and world view of the present, it injects into our history concepts and interpretations that could never have been present in the past.

Of course, history is always written in a contemporary perspective, and although it has become written with ever greater ideals of honesty and accuracy, it continues to embody contemporary ideologies as well as concrete images and beliefs: that American history begins with the voyage of Columbus; that North American Indians were uncivilized; that the Spanish were cruel conquerors; that the British were the first real settlers of North America. When we examine when and why these images were first put forward, and how far they depart from other possible interpretations, we can see how history is sometimes used to conceal aggression, justify genocide, and validate the imperial claims of certain European powers. History, in short, can be a powerful political tool.

SPACE AND MAPS

Because this book deals with America's changing social and physical landscapes and contains a number of maps, we invite you to see our maps as propositions, not as facts of nature. We invite you to recognize that patterns imposed on or perceived as our landscapes have both reflected and shaped the relations of power among people throughout American history. Mapmaking, after all, creates space; it does not merely record it. In choosing the scale, borders, and symbols, the mapmaker—not unlike the historian—makes a statement. He/she imposes a scheme as a reality and attempts to persuade the audience that a certain pattern of cities, roads, neighborhoods, parks, and parking lots is as natural an element on the landscape as mountains, lakes, and trees.

We hope to show how space—like history—is a product of human imagination and more often than not serves as an arena of social competition and conflict. But when we talk about "space" in our text and illustrated pages, we're not only referring to the geometric attributes of the world—acres, square miles, latitude and longitude—but also to the physical and social spaces within which people interact. As James A. Delle points out on pages 18–21, cities, highways, nations, and continents are not only geometric forms recognized by us as subdivisions or routes across the natural landscape, they are culturally created phenomena that shape the ways in which people live, move, and understand the structure of their world.

Naturally those who have the ability to construct the forms of space—governments, city planners, and even mapmakers—have great influence over the patterns that the resulting human interaction will take. Many of the maps in this book illustrate such patterns of power: We will show, for example, how the placement of Spanish missions in the Southeast in the sixteenth century facilitated the disintegration of native cultures; how eighteenth-century formal landscapes attempted to celebrate the power of an emerging merchant elite; how subways and highways have shaped the circulation of labor and consumer goods; and how the floor plan of post–World War II suburban houses encouraged and even created a new kind of nuclear family.

James Delle also notes on pages 28–29 that the control exercised by city planners, road builders, and architects is, of course, not absolute. People often have some choice in the building in which they will work or live. They can change physical space by adding rooms onto houses, for example, or by choosing and arranging the furniture and decorations for their apartments. The use of space on any scale—from global to domestic—not only reflects the dominant concepts of culture that define it but can also become an active instrument in its eventual transformation. This recursive definition of space, which sees space as defining as well as defined, has a very significant implication: Those who can exert control over the creation of space can control the context of human interaction. Therefore, our maps and illustrated pages are not meant to be representations of nature; they are meant to offer illustrations of relations of power in American landscapes. They are meant to show the spaces that some Americans have made for themselves as well as some of the spaces other Americans have been forced to live in.

FOLK ART AND POPULAR CULTURE

We have filled this book with pictures of things, as well as maps and versions of history. Some might call many of these artifacts "folk art." But while folk arts and crafts in the United States are generally viewed today as quaint throwbacks to an older and allegedly more pleasant era, we see them as something different. John Michael Vlach, on pages 30–31, contests patronizing stereotypes of folk art, in which the traditions of folk groups are understood to be simple, amateurish, anonymous, and, by any common measure, moribund. We attempt to show that the traditional arts and crafts of the United States throughout all of its history have been and are complex; that the creators receive exacting training; that they are connected to specific social and cultural groups; and most importantly, that folk crafts are very much alive and well and, in some places, even thriving—as a response and resistance to the mass production of our industrial society.

HISTORICAL ARCHAEOLOGY

So far we have dealt with history, space, and folk art in isolation. Historical archaeology is the activity and method of analysis that, we believe, can bring these separate themes together in a meaningful way. Many of the contributors to this book are historical archaeologists; like classical archaeologists or prehistorians, they discover, record, and analyze artifacts and other remains of past societies by excavating them systematically. Yet there is an important difference. Classical archaeology, first developed in Italy in the 1400s, has long concentrated on the contributions of the cultures of

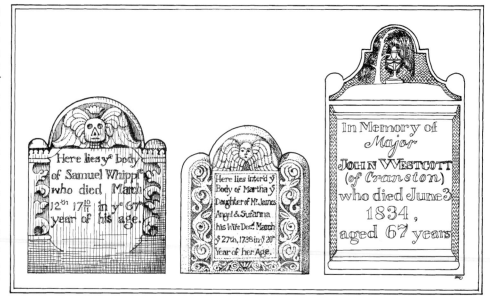

The creations of folk artists can sometimes bear evidence to major historical trends. James Deetz demonstrated this clearly in his pioneering study of early American gravestones in eastern New England. The three headstones pictured here, from North Burial Ground in Providence, Rhode Island, illustrate death's head, soul effigy, and urn-and-willow motifs that Deetz argues reflect shifting beliefs about death and the afterlife within New England Protestantism during the eighteenth and early nineteenth centuries.

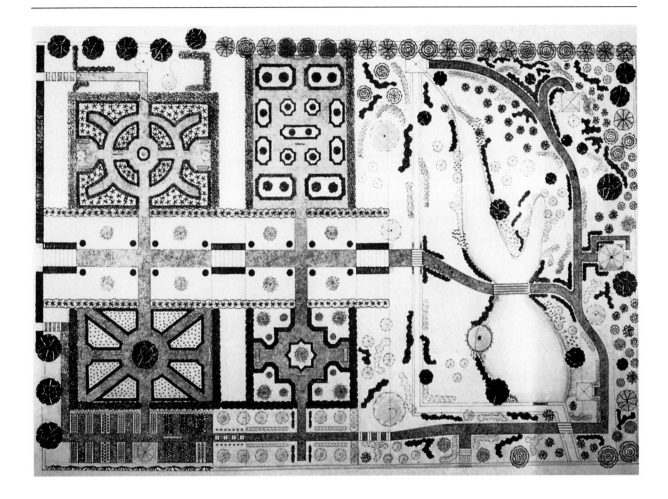

The formal garden behind the William Paca House in Annapolis, Maryland, is an example of the way in which space was arranged and ordered by eighteenth-century aristocrats as a demonstration of the power of Reason over Nature. Originally built in the early 1760s, and destroyed early in the twentieth century, the William Paca Garden was excavated and rebuilt in the 1960s and 1970s. Its outline, topography, major features, and pond have been archaeologically verified. The parterres and most plantings are conjectured.

Greece, Rome, and the Eastern Mediterranean to the development of European society. Prehistoric archaeology, founded in Scandinavia and Britain a hundred and fifty years ago, excavates all over the world for ruins, artifacts, and human remains from periods long before written records. Yet it too seeks to investigate developments that are understood as basic to European civilization: human evolution and migration, early agriculture, and the rise of the first cities and states.

Historical archaeology is concerned with a different problem, and looks at European society, in a way, from within. Its interest is in examining how a distinct kind of European society and culture spread so explosively throughout the world from the middle of the 1400s to today. Historical archaeology studies the evidence for and remains of European colonial expansion, trade, intensive agriculture, and industrialization. It excavates and studies the remains of the settlements and cities, plantations, factories, roads, and canals built by Europeans in North America and North Africa, South Africa, Australia, South Asia, and anywhere else that Europeans colonized.

In North America, historical archaeologists have discovered the Spanish missions in Florida, Georgia, Arizona, and California. They have uncovered the graves of converted Indians, the kitchens of the friars, the flimsy construction of the churches

Historical archaeologists investigate the remains of everyday life at sites that are not necessarily recognized as historical monuments. From the broken or discarded artifacts found in backyards, privies, and filled basements of workshops and private homes, excavators can reconstruct the material life of both the well-to-do and those Americans who left no written histories.

and forts, and the houses of the Spanish settlers of the 1560s, 1570s, and 1580s. Excavators have also been able to reconstruct daily life in nineteenth-century laboring neighborhoods, such as the Chinese in Sacramento and the Irish in Cleveland. Historical archaeology has shown how slaves lived on plantations all over the South and in slave-holding cities such as Annapolis, Maryland. It deals with forts, town plans, schools, houses, wells and toilets, prisons, factories, worker housing, backyards, mansions, and shacks. Unlike prehistoric archaeology or classical archaeology, historical archaeology rarely discovers things or events that were completely unknown or utterly forgotten; it does, however, engage people directly and con-

cretely with their past. The fifty-one Spanish missions built in the 1500s from Mobile, Alabama, to the Chesapeake Bay were not unknown. But only the most esoteric areas of historical scholarship were aware of them. And even then, their locations, organization, materials, activities, cemeteries, foods, and relations with Indians were all speculation. Historical archaeology has begun to reveal some of these things.

Why are these discoveries important? Historical archaeology does not aim simply to dig up artifacts from earlier periods in our history; it seeks to explain the larger political, social, and economic context in which those things were produced and the role they played in the shaping of colonial and industrial culture. Historical archaeology is in fact the archaeology of our own society's beginnings and recent practices. Thus, it can be a direct form of knowledge of ourselves. It attempts to understand the past of workers and slaves, women and children, who were marginalized by official histories. It does so by explaining the role they played in an intensifying world economy. It addresses the history of people who were anonymous. Native Americans, Chinese Americans, slaves, free African Americans, tenement dwellers, utopianists, teenagers, and suburban homemakers of the 1950s are only a few of the groups whose hidden histories and geographies are explored in this book.

Through the study of changing economic patterns and the distribution of artifacts, we can discover the significance of the difference between domestic and work space, and between rich, middle class, and poor people's areas in a site. We can contrast the lifestyles of slave and overseer, even though the overseer might be white or black; Chinese and Irish or Chicano; printer and physician. Indeed, the world interpreted by historical archaeology is the world that Europeans first called the "Other," or foreign, and which they settled, exploited, eliminated, or colonized in some form. Such contact areas have only recently become a zone of understandings. Previously, they were largely dismissed as "backward," "countryside," and "wilderness."

Historical archeology has begun to reveal how, over the course of European settlement, the North American landscape has come to reflect the historical patterns of inequality, resistance, and separation between social groups. Those defined as Others have been confined to reservations, plantations, ghettos, ethnic neighborhoods, factories, prisons, insane asylums, and schools. The land itself—often personified and considered sacred by Native American peoples—came to be objectified as a resource and dominated by technology. And while modern nostalgia for the days before industrial civilizations has led us to create "wilderness areas" as preserves for wildlife and living history museums for the recreation of simpler times, the very appeal of such places for entertainment and rejuvenation underlines how we have destroyed the integrity of these domains. We may even be able to see that the "New World" was not discovered but conceptually reconstructed by Europeans over five hundred years. They did so by erasing many of the landmarks and meanings of indigenous peoples, and by drawing distinctions and, often, boundaries between others and themselves.

Invisible America is an exploration, by means of material culture, of what we are as a society and what we have come to be. Our point is not simply to engage in a nostalgic display of antique settlements, primitive peoples, and old-fashioned things. We invite you to begin to look for hidden histories and landscapes wherever you live, work, and travel in the country. For in adding protesting voices, a knowledge of otherness, and the social and economic backgrounds to understand our national history, we may be able to recognize that American history is—to a degree that is not often appreciated—not an inevitable march of progress, but the result of continual struggle among those who would dominate and those who would resist.

THE IDEOLOGY OF SPACE

The intent of any map is the control of the physical world through a static two-dimensional representation of a dynamic three-dimensional complex of phenomena that we call space. The definition of the term *space* is itself complex. It refers not only to the geometric attributes of the world but also to the physical and social areas within which people interact. Physical and social spaces are created by people and they create the context for human interaction. Those who have the ability to construct the forms of space have the power over the forms human interaction will take.

Cartography is one such strategy of spatial construction; that is to say, the creation of any map is the creation of space. The creation of a map is wrapped in several levels of power relations. The cartographer must have access to the technical knowledge of map construction. The reader must have knowledge of the symbols used in the map. On one level, whoever controls the dissemination of this knowledge controls those who can create space and those who can understand this creation. On another level, whoever controls the distribution of maps can decide who has even the opportunity to try to understand that space.

Architecture, including landscape architecture, is another form of spatial construction that, like cartography, is based on particular relations of power. Architects and builders have access to knowledge and techniques that define the spaces in which people live and work. The floor plans of buildings will in large part define how people will interact within that building. The size and shape of rooms; the proximity of rooms to one another and to strategic areas such as bathrooms, elevators, and stairwells; the proportion of "natural" to "artificial" light in a room; the size, shape, and orientation of windows; and the location of the building itself all create the context of human relations. Architects and builders have more power in defining this context, this space, than do the occupants of the buildings themselves.

This is not to imply that ordinary folk are not active agents in the definition of space. Identical rooms in identical buildings can be used for a variety of purposes from office to bedroom to nursery to den, and will have distinctly different meanings. Two apparently similar physical spaces can therefore be two distinctly different social spaces.

Space on any scale is similarly constructed. Cities, highways, nations, and continents are culturally created phenomena that simultaneously create culture. This recursive or interactive definition of space has a very significant implication: Those who can exert the most control over the creation of space can control the context of human interaction and thus define the nature of social relations. Although the meanings of space are continuously produced by each individual who perceives and interacts within each space, access to that space is mediated by political and economic forces over which most individuals have very little control.

■ JAMES A. DELLE
University of Massachusetts, Amherst

Alexander Jackson Davis's rendering of Jay Gould's house Lyndhurst, near Tarrytown, New York. The construction of space can be used to legitimate social structure. Many of the newly wealthy American capitalists of the nineteenth century built monumental houses in a medieval style. Even though their money had been made recently from commerce or industry, construction of such spaces made their wealth feel "old."

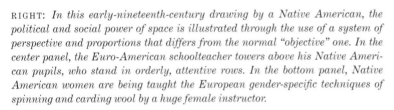

The political nature of space is illustrated in this view of Hartford, Connecticut, from a school atlas of the late nineteenth century. The state capitol building is most prominently displayed. In the background the most visible features on the landscape are factories, churches, and a railroad.

RIGHT: *In this early-nineteenth-century drawing by a Native American, the political and social power of space is illustrated through the use of a system of perspective and proportions that differs from the normal "objective" one. In the center panel, the Euro-American schoolteacher towers above his Native American pupils, who stand in orderly, attentive rows. In the bottom panel, Native American women are being taught the European gender-specific techniques of spinning and carding wool by a huge female instructor.*

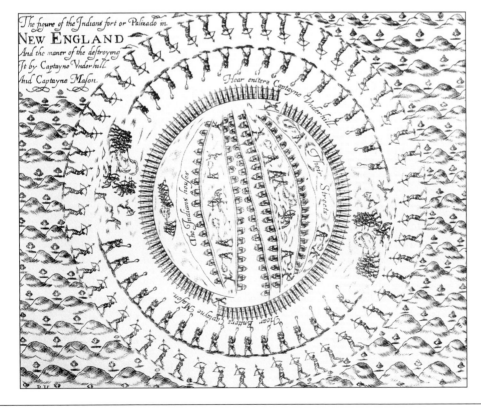

Both physical and cognitive space change over time. This seventeenth-century rendition of the English attack on the Pequot in Mystic, Connecticut, seems unusual to our eyes. The depiction of the encirclement of the village idealizes the English lines as perfect concentric circles.

tobacco

cotton

Sugar cane
Sugar beets

A key element of any atlas is the location of important resources, yet such geographical information has implications that are not always expressed. These three maps from an early-twentieth-century school atlas, identifying the regions of the United States in which important staple crops are grown, tell a larger, if hidden, story of social and economic realities. If you were to superimpose these maps, the southern United States would be a solid block of agricultural production in contrast to other areas. The same atlas defines the plantations of the South as being "large farms devoted mainly" to a single crop, thus casually avoiding mentioning anything about the planter-labor social divisions on such "farms."

WHAT ATLASES ARE

A tlases are material things produced for a specific purpose. Like dictionaries and encyclopedias, atlases are tools created by intellectual and political elites for defining, standardizing, and controlling knowledge. The knowledge atlases create is that of space. In the contemporary world it is often taken for granted that the maps in an atlas, like the definitions in a dictionary, present some kind of universal truth. But space, like language, is ever changing; the physical and political worlds that atlases represent are not static. Atlases can thus be seen as tools designed to control the ephemeral nature of the world—if not on the ground, then in the minds of people.

Pictorial representations of the world have existed in many cultures for hundreds of years. The forerunners of what we today call atlases first appeared in fifteenth-century Europe, contemporaneous with the first universal histories and during the earliest period of Europe's Atlantic expansion. Because of the great wealth that could be amassed in trade to distant lands, the knowledge contained in early atlases was jealously guarded. Powerful princes, like famous Henry (the so-called navigator) of Portugal, displayed great interest in the creation and control of maps and charts. In order to maintain control of trade, the basis of power, laws controlling information were severe. In fifteenth- and sixteenth-century Portugal, for example, a mariner giving or selling maps or charts to a foreigner could be put to death.

It is a modern assumption that atlases have been made more complete and accurate since those days. It is probably better to say that atlases have become more detailed and comprehensive, allowing more complex representations of space.

During the age of European expansion (formerly called the "Age of Discovery"), certain techniques were developed to allow the sphere of the earth to be rendered as a flat map. These included the creation of an imaginary grid on the world. The grid lines became known as lines of *latitude* and *longitude*. These imaginary lines are sometimes called *parallels* and *meridians*; the former circling the

Arctic Scene   Grizzly Bear & Indians   Commerce & Manufactures

globe east-west (like the equator), the latter north-south (like the prime meridian). The technique for interpreting and rendering the spherical earth on a flat page is called *projection.* Any projection will make some compromise on either the shape or the scale of a landmass.

For example, the famous *Mercator projection,* developed in the sixteenth century for making navigational charts, represents all the parallels of latitude as the same length. On a globe, the parallels grow increasingly smaller toward the North and South poles. As a result, the shape and size of northern land forms will be exaggerated. On a Mercator projection, Greenland will look to be the size of South America, while on a globe it will appear to be about one eighth the size. Such distortions are particularly significant when political or social entities struggle over possession of land. Our premise is that there is nothing true or absolute about any space or place; every building, city, sea, road, state, country, or continent is culturally constructed and makes a political statement.

■ JAMES A. DELLE
University of Massachusetts, Amherst

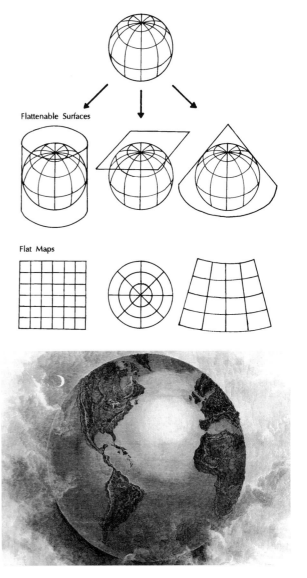

Flattenable Surfaces

Flat Maps

TRAVEL GUIDES AND PICTURE BOOKS

Travel accounts, past and present, are really an attempt to make sense of the foreign, the "Other," in terms that are familiar to the reader. While travel accounts have existed since antiquity, the literature that followed the European discovery of the New World was different. This travel literature served as both impetus to and consequence of the development of world economic ties, the expansion of European hegemony, and a new spatial perception of the world. The European preoccupation with travel—often called the "Age of Discovery"—has been explained in terms of Renaissance scholarship, whereby the pursuit of knowledge for its own sake was the most important goal of human endeavor. The quest for new lands and better sea routes, however, can also be seen as being driven by economic interests at a time when Europe commanded what came to be a global economy.

The real consequence of early travel literature was to fixate the popular imagination on issues of trade, particularly in the Far East, or colonization, as in the New World. Such accounts encouraged the authors' countrymen to pursue economic interests abroad, or enticed them to live in foreign enclaves.

The hazards of foreign travel were overwhelming, but the economic imperative was so dominant it acted to encourage a virtual state-sponsored travel industry. While we tend to think of travel today as primarily a private matter, states were active agents in promoting and directing the flow of travel in earlier periods. Indeed the rise of European nation-states, and their worldwide hegemony, should be seen as one of the results of exploration and discovery, which were themselves promoted by and through the help of travel literature.

Travel literature was a literary fashion, but it was also a kind of "esoteric knowledge" that was both passed around and managed as a source of information and propaganda between competing nations. The popularity of early travel accounts in their own times is difficult to assess today, but we do know that the most celebrated of narratives of exploration, adventure, and "discovery" of unknown lands and strange peoples were frequently duplicated and translated into a variety of European languages. Such accounts were written, like many modern adventure novels and films, using standard formulas. Each writer (only a few of whom had

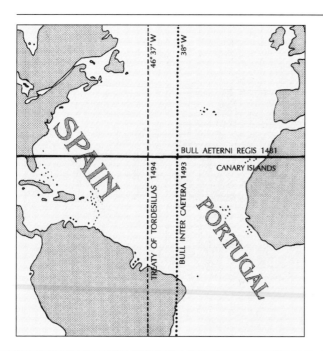

LEFT: *The "Age of Discovery" led to a new spatial perception and the division of the globe between competing European powers. In 1481, Pope Sixtus VI issued the bull* Aeterni regis, *granting Spain a colonizing monopoly on all territories north of the latitude of the Canary Islands; Portugal was granted rights to all lands lying to the south. In 1493, after Columbus's first voyage, the partition plan was revised with Pope Alexander VI's bull* Inter caetera, *expanding Spain's domain to include all territories lying west of 38° west longitude. Portugal's subsequent claims in the New World resulted in yet another change in colonizing boundaries. The 1494 Treaty of Tordesillas, endorsed by Pope Alexander VI, moved the north-south line about eight hundred miles westward, allowing Portugal to lay exclusive claim to Brazil.*

FACING PAGE, BOTTOM: *These woodcuts, from Hans Schedel's* Liber Chronicarum *(1493), depict the peoples of far-off lands as mutant, monstrous races. While some were known from European or Greco-Roman literature and given specific names (top left, Cyclops; top right, Blemmye; center left, Panotius; bottom left, Monopod), others were completely imaginative creations. The illustrations vividly conveyed the idea that the distant, newly discovered territories were not inhabited by normal human beings.*

Travel accounts also commented on the distinctive aspects of the "Other," such as this 1535 woodcut of Amerigo Vespucci's arrival in the New World. In it, a naked female personification of Native America reclines in a Caribbean hammock, a device that was soon adopted by European sailors. Travel writers often endowed the "Other" with qualities usually relating to their own social and sexual taboos.

ABOVE: *Despite some attempts at what can be termed early ethnography, the main topic of early travel accounts was trade, varying only in terms of geographic destination and variable commodities. The detail at the right-hand side of this woodcut illustrates the use of tobacco as witnessed by Columbus in the Caribbean. Through such means, tobacco became popular in Europe as an addictive fad and a major economic commodity for many European countries by the mid-1500s.*

actually ever been to the places described) knew what kinds of stories had been successful before and, for the most part, introduced new elements of specific geography and trade interests such as natural wonders, spices, jewels, strange animals, plants, and of course people.

For many writers, the line between reality and imagination was ill-defined. Authors unashamedly borrowed incidents from each other's books and publishers reproduced pictures freely from areas that originally depicted vastly different geographical regions. Their effect, if not conscious intention, was to make unfamiliar cultures seem alien and bizarre. While the literary intent of this was apparently to make sense of the unfamiliar in terms of the understood, the fact that myths and inaccuracies about the exotic peoples remained alive for centuries after the original publication of such guides suggests that such literature served primarily to justify European domination over the "strange" or "uncivilized" peoples of the world.

■ JANICE BAILEY-GOLDSCHMIDT
University of Pennsylvania

THE SEARCH FOR OTHERNESS

Enrico Causici's Landing of the Pilgrims *(1825) is carved above the east door of the Rotunda in the U.S. Capitol. Every schoolchild knows that Squanto brought corn to the starving Pilgrims and taught them how to cultivate it. But the story of Squanto is more than one of "Indian contributions to civilization." Six years before the Pilgrims arrived in his native Massachusetts, Squanto was kidnapped and taken to Europe, where he learned English (and perhaps how to fertilize grain with fish). Squanto returned to find his people annihilated by a European epidemic and offered his allegiance to the English.*

Capellano's Preservation of Captain Smith by Pocahontas *(1825) is carved above the west door of the Rotunda. The most famous of all Euro-American captives among Indians is Virginia's John Smith, and the most famous of all Indian women is Pocahontas, daughter of Powhatan, a powerful chief. John Smith credited the young Pocahontas with saving him from execution. She may have been taking a role in an adoption ritual designed to win Smith's allegiance to her father. Later Pocahontas was captured by the English to secure Powhatan's submission.*

Cultural identity is achieved, at least to some extent, through opposition to Others. Yet, there are many ways human groups have related to strangers or outsiders—in addition to hatred or domination—throughout history. In some cases (regrettably few to be sure), a respect and tolerance for cultural differences may be maintained or even venerated as superior and powerful, as, for example, the transcendent Others people worship as sacred, or the indigenous Others that some conquerors respect as spiritual guardians of the land. Most often, Others are viewed with ambivalence, with a mixture of envy, suspicion, curiosity, and fear. While savage Others are degraded as uncivilized for what they are said to lack—clothing, technology, reason, religion, laws, private property, government, restraint—they are also idealized for lacking the burdens of civilization. Savage Others are admired for possessing natural or original human qualities: strength, freedom, spontaneity, expressiveness, innocence, spiritual purity. Euro-Americans, therefore, have generally expressed a certain regret as they destroyed Native American cultures, and look back to a presumably innocent past with considerable nostalgia. Similarly, southern plantation life was idealized by referring to "happy darkies." However, neither the judgmental nor the nostalgic form of Otherness allows for the complexity, meaningfulness, and pathos characteristic of all human experience. And whether they are denigrated or idealized, those people who are considered "savage" are dehumanized.

The Euro-American Self and its Native American Other are represented profusely in public spaces in the United States. In the U.S. Capitol Building, paintings and sculptures portray two types of Indians—Noble Others, such as Squanto and Pocahontas, who embrace, protect, and further the cause of Euro-American civilization, and Savage Others, who oppose and threaten to destroy that civilization. In the Capitol and elsewhere, Savage Others are often portrayed as tomahawk-wielding captors of Euro-American women and children—captors who are ultimately overcome by the superior force, rationality, and authority of Euro-American males. Whether

ABOVE: *John G. Chapman's* Baptism of Pocahontas at Jamestown, Virginia *(1840) is one of eight large oil paintings in the Rotunda representing the European conquest of America. Like Squanto, Pocahontas served the English as a valuable ally. After converting to Christianity, Pocahontas married tobacco planter John Rolfe, bore his child, and accompanied him to England, where she became ill and died. Rolfe is shown to the right of Pocahontas; behind him are Pocahontas's brother, her sister (seated), and the leader Opechancanough, who later led two wars against the English.*

LEFT: *Enrico Causici's* Conflict of Daniel Boone and the Indians *(1826–1827) is carved above the south door of the Rotunda. Daniel Boone is the most famous of the frontiersmen who are glorified for "taming the wilderness"—for wresting it from the hand of its native inhabitants and making it available for Euro-American settlement. John Filson's narrative about Boone, who adopted Indian dress and skills while captive among the Shawnee, made Boone a national hero.*

RIGHT: *Horatio Greenough's sculpture* The Rescue *stood on the east front of the U.S. Capitol from 1853 to 1958. This sculpture celebrates the triumph of American "civilization" over Indian "savagery," portraying the Indians as brutal Others who must be restrained in order to protect women and children—civilization at its most vulnerable. The helmet and robe of the Rescuer associate the United States with classical civilization. The captivity of Euro-American women and children is used frequently in frontier literature and art as a justification for conquest, as also seen in the illustration on page 3.*

Noble or Savage, Indian Others are represented as actors in a drama that inevitably brings about their own destruction and affirms the superiority of patriarchal Euro-American civilization. Unlike Mexican national monuments, which present national identity as a mixture of Native and European civilizations, monuments in the United States recognize only one form of civilization. All else is savagery.

■ PAULINE TURNER STRONG
University of Texas at Austin

HORRID MASSACRE IN VIRGINIA·

African Americans found many ways to resist the oppression of slavery. Learning to read and preserving traditions went hand in hand with running away and open resistance. Nat Turner's Rebellion in 1831 terrified white America and led to restrictive laws on enslaved African Americans and abolitionists. This broadside spread news of the rebellion.

I. W. W.

ONE BIG UNION
OF ALL THE WORKERS

THE
GREATEST THING
ON EARTH

FOR INFORMATION ADDRESS I W W .1001 W MADISON ST CHICAGO. ILL., U S A

PROTESTING VOICES

History tends to be presented as the story of winners. Whether in books, on historical markers, or in museums, the public hears about an unfolding and unending series of success stories. Historical events appear to happen in smooth, natural sequences, suggesting that Americans in the past spoke with one voice and had one vision of the future. In reality, American history was rarely based on consensus. If we can, even briefly, take off our historical—and ideological—blinders, we may be able to construct a history based on a very different premise: American history is a history of diversity and conflict, a story of both success and protest, of roads not taken and opportunities lost. Our shared history, then, would be composed of many voices, the dominant and the resisting alike.

Yet in order to identify the protesting voices in the historical record, we have to know what forms resistance took in the past. Sometimes resistance has been expressed violently, like the slave revolt led by Nat Turner in 1831; the war waged by Native Americans against New England colonists in the seventeenth century, a conflict that the English called "King Philip's War"; or the uprising of Massachusetts farmers just after the American Revolution known as Shay's Rebellion. Other protests were organized political struggles like the civil rights movement of the 1960s, the marches of the suffragettes, or the hundreds of labor strikes organized by such unions as the AFL-CIO, Knights of Labor, and the Wobblies. Political cartoons, boycotts, and mass rallies are all forms of protest.

Resistance has also taken the form of alternative lifestyles. Early in our history groups such as the Shakers and the Owenites established utopian communities; in the late twentieth century, hippies started communes. People have always expressed dissenting views through posters, broadsides, and buttons; folk singers have always linked protesting voices to popular music.

Not all of the protests were successful, but all had their effects. Restrictive laws were passed in the wake of some protests, while dramatic positive changes were the result of others. However, to gain

ABOVE: *Contemporary debates over abortion and pay equity are only the latest of many struggles over women's rights. The 19th amendment, which established women's right to vote, was ratified in 1920, only after years of protest.*

RIGHT: *Divisions between rich and poor have been the driving force of many protests, as shown in this 1906 image (*From the Depths *by William Balfour Ker).*

FACING PAGE, BOTTOM: *The organized labor movement has been a major source of protest since the nineteenth century. Workers have often found themselves at odds with their employers and have joined together in such diverse unions as the Knights of Labor, AFL-CIO, and the I.W.W. to press their rights.*

a fuller reading of American history, that history must be seen as the product of conflicting interests. We cannot understand the Constitution without Shay's Rebellion or the end of the Vietnam War without anti-war demonstrations. The American tradition of political and cultural resistance is vibrant and diverse.

■ MARK BOGRAD
National Park Service,
Lowell National Historic Park

SPACE AS ACTION

The time to get up is determined by one thing, a commuting schedule, and is mediated by another thing, an alarm clock. After waking, we move from another thing, a bed, in a particularly defined space, a bedroom, to yet another thing, a shower, in yet another space, a bathroom. After returning to the bedroom to put on some things, the style and nature of which are at least partially determined by our job, we travel to another defined space, be it a parking lot, bus stop, or subway station. From here we are propelled through space in some thing, a car, bus, subway, or pair of walking shoes, on something else, a highway, a set of tracks, or a sidewalk. Perhaps we stop at a fast-food place to pick up a cup of coffee and maybe a doughnut. If we are driving, we delicately sip the coffee from a plastic travel mug, being careful not to stain our work clothes. If we are walking, we take special care to avoid dangerous neighborhoods and isolated alleyways. Once at the workplace, we might punch a time clock or inform our supervisor or colleagues that we have arrived on time. If we have been at the same job for a year or two, this is routine. What is not so conventionally understood is that our action—our thoughts and behaviors—is in turn defined and created by the things we create.

Now imagine that it is the first day of a new job in a new city. Not knowing the city well, a friendly coworker has given us a set of directions and a handwritten map. The trip to work this day is not a commute but a journey. We have to think about everything, from where the alarm clock is to the address of our workplace to the time the subway leaves the station. We gulp down last night's cold coffee, not knowing if there is a convenient place on the way. We get on the wrong train and wind up ten blocks from where we thought we would be. Not knowing a way to remedy the situation quickly, we jump on the next train back to where we started. We finally catch the right train and get to the proper building only to realize that the coworker neglected to note which floor the office was on. After stopping on every floor of the building, we

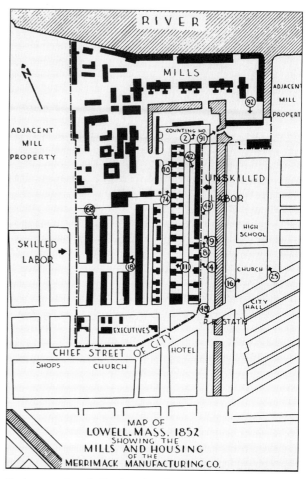

Perhaps nowhere in the American landscape is the relationship of manipulated space and a desired set of behaviors among workers more obvious than in such planned industrial cities as Lowell, Massachusetts. The plan for this city created ordered domestic and work space for laborers. Factory managers had houses of their own among the rows of factory-owned workers' tenements. Behavior was to be supervised and controlled by the same people both at work and at home.

finally find the office. The whole journey took nearly three hours.

When our morning actions have become routine, the things that we used and encountered will have been critical to this change and actually have combined to enforce what and how we think and act. The material things we use—space included—affect all of our thoughts and actions, often without our realizing it.

■ JAMES A. DELLE
University of Massachusetts, Amherst

ABOVE: *Thoughts, actions, ideas, and behaviors are in part created by space. From an early age, schoolchildren in North America are taught to be orderly, attentive, and obedient to authority. These appropriate behaviors are learned in spaces specific to such disciplining—schools.*

BELOW: *With the rise of industrial capitalism, behaviors taught in the space of the public classrooms were for the most part behaviors that would be appropriate for the regimen of factory work: to honor time, to sit doing rudimentary exercises in a small space for the better part of the day, and to obey a supervisor who was not a relative.*

Some social theorists tried to improve factory life by designing utopian factory towns on a socialist model. Robert Owen was among the most famous. His scheme at New Harmony was not nearly as successful as the capitalist schemes at places like Lowell.

FOLK ART AS CONSCIOUSNESS

ABOVE: *Burlon Craig of Henry, North Carolina, is a stoneware potter who uses a very old regional glaze formula utilizing wood ashes. He is particularly known for making large jugs sculpted with faces.*

Sidonka Lee of Lyons, Wisconsin, is a maker of Czechoslovakian wheat weavings, household decorations commonly used during celebrations of Easter and harvest festivals.

Over and over again, from coast to coast, in villages and in cities, close to home, within the network of family, kin, and neighbors, works of folk art and craft are as important as they have always been. While these communities may now depend on a flow of outsider-visitors to purchase their works in order to survive economically, the craftsmen use these transactions to allow themselves to stay put, to remain stable and rooted, even as they send their traditional objects to strange new homes. Objects made especially for export may be significantly different, even less well made than works that are retained in the community. But as long as the artisans control the means of production—their potters' wheels, looms, chisels, and expertise—they will feel empowered not only as creators but as bearers of tradition. In this sense the "folk" products of craftspeople, their mass popularity, and the livelihood they provide for their makers represents the refusal of many traditional artists/shapers of American culture to allow modern ways to destroy vital links between present and past.

Among the main assumptions made by urban-based art critics about folk art is that its practitioners are innocent naifs, lacking imagination, who turn out second-rate (if often charming) productions, which are primitive and basically unchanging. Therein, critics have often suggested, lies both folk art's conceptual weakness and its aesthetic appeal. Yet while there are still many traditional craftspeople working in the United States in the late twentieth century—just think of the millions of quilters currently at work and one begins to get a sense of their ubiquity—they no longer have the same concerns as their forebears, who inspired them. Now, as in earlier periods of history, "folk" artisans have often transformed tradition, adapting it to serve new goals and aspirations. Folk arts and crafts are, after all, responsive expressions closely tied to the dynamics of cultural experience.

The vitality of contemporary folk art and craft is best proved by meeting folk artists where they live and work; that is, on their home ground. The number of artists is as great as the number of folk

ABOVE AND TOP RIGHT: *Philip Simmons of Charleston, South Carolina, is an African American blacksmith who in the course of a sixty-year-long career has left more than two hundred examples of his decorative wrought-iron fences, gates, and window grilles throughout the city.*

CENTER RIGHT: *The Lopez family of Cordova, New Mexico, includes two active generations of wood-carvers, who carry on skills traceable in their lineage back to the middle of the nineteenth century. They focus their talents primarily on* santos, *holy images of saints used locally by fellow members of the Catholic church in domestic acts of veneration.*

groups in the United States. Some are identified by ethnicity (Irish, French), religion (Jewish, Amish), region (southerner, westerner), occupation (cowboy, logger), or some combination of these attributes (Italian Catholic fisherman from the West Coast). Specific traditions will also vary with genre and medium (wood-carvers vs. chairmakers). In sum, folk art is an important means of creativity and material production. It is neither a quaint survival nor an isolated backwater in our society.

■ JOHN MICHAEL VLACH
George Washington University

Raymond Sedotal of Pierra Part, Assumption Parish, Louisiana, is a Cajun boatbuilder, who is shown here seated in one of his plank pirogues, a modern version of an old type of boat that was formerly hewn from a single log.

2

COLLISION OF CULTURES

1492–1607

WITH CONTRIBUTIONS BY

David S. Brose

Patricia Galloway

Faith Harrington

Bonnie G. McEwan

David Hurst Thomas

Charles R. Ewen

Jeffrey L. Hantman

Alice B. Kehoe

Patricia E. Rubertone

Steadman Upham

At the moment in history we call the European Renaissance, the continent of North America was occupied by many peoples, cultures, and ways of life, no less complex than the patchwork of European city states, fiefdoms, farms, and villages that stretched from Scotland to the Black Sea. As in late medieval Europe, hundreds of languages and dozens of dialects were spoken throughout America. Population densities varied widely, across plains, forests, and tundra, in seasonal camps, isolated farmsteads, religious and political centers, and commercial entrepôts.

Native North America in the late 1400s was composed of dozens of distinct societies—many prospering, some rising in power, some in decline. It is important to keep in mind that our society's conventional picture of the American Indian—moccasin-shod, living in tepees, red and forever stable—is our myth, one with powerful influence. It masks precisely those elements of native cultures that give them their humanity. And if we can see the native peoples of North America on the eve of their first meetings with Europeans as intelligent historical actors—not as passive victims, savages, or harmless children of nature—we may be able to recognize the enormity of the changes that the European "discovery" of North America brought.

As in Europe, climate, terrain, and natural resources shaped the characteristics of regional cultures in North America. The inhabitants of the forests of the Northeast, the lakes and river valleys of the Midwest, the plains, mountains, and deserts of the West each raised distinctive food crops, hunted different game animals, and developed widely different architectural styles, social systems, and art forms. Yet when the first Europeans came to claim for themselves American lands and their resources—and to conquer or subdue the inhabitants—most rationalized that invasion simply by dismissing the various Native American cultures as variations of savagery. In their refusal to acknowledge the cultural history of the Americas, the European explorers and conquerors lumped the peoples of the "New World" together on a scale of intelligence and refinement far lower than that of Europe and gave us the stereotyped image of nomadic, stubborn, non-Christian hunters in impermanent homes that still burdens relationships between Native Americans and people of European descent.

Today, of course, we've been taught to reject the early Europeans' ethnocentrism, but so long as our understandings of Native American history and culture were based largely on the early Europeans'

Native peoples across the continent of North America developed a wide range of architectural styles and village types. Pictured here is a reconstructed single-family dwelling from Sunwatch Village in southwestern Ohio, reflecting the common house type of the thirteenth through fifteenth centuries.

written records and hostile impressions, it was difficult for any new image to emerge. Beginning in the late nineteenth century, however, with the development of archaeological analysis of the material remains of Native American cultures and with the development of anthropological study of living native cultures, the economic, political, and social integrity as well as the complexity of native societies began to be recognized by scholars. Through the study of settlement patterning—the distribution of isolated farmsteads, villages, medium-sized towns, and major ceremonial centers across the landscape—archaeologists have been able to reconstruct social and political relations within various native societies. Through the identification of distinctive artifacts and rare raw materials at sites throughout the continent, archaeologists have been able to recognize patterns of active long-distance trade. Though archaeological theories are far from definitive or final, and often reflect as much about the theory-makers as their subjects, it is now undeniable that the native peoples of North America were neither completely peaceful nor irrationally violent. And when we examine the archaeological and ethnohistoric evidence for the diversity of customs, gender roles, and patterns of leadership and language among Native American cultures, we may see that their destruction was not simply a regrettable side effect of the heroic European "Age of Discovery." It was a turning point in the history of the entire late medieval world.

Our narrative here is designed to challenge some of the schoolbook tales and popular conceptions long given and dearly held about the "Discovery of America." With this challenge comes our attempt to provide an alternative view. We claim this story is useful for today, for just as the traditional tales involve heroes and villains, luck and wisdom, tragedies and victories, the alternative focuses on instability, material culture, ideas and deceptions, struggle, and the continual difficulty of many groups in changing or even challenging the status quo. In fact, many people who have traditionally been squeezed out of the standard story are now speaking up. Native Americans, in particular, are reclaiming their story, their land, resources, history, and ways of telling it and keeping it. Our cure for an unsolvable problem—how to tell a story neutrally—is to be candid about what is usually hidden and unnoticed: that we are all narrators with intentions, and that our stories about the past both reflect and help shape how we see the world today.

A CONTINENT-WIDE NETWORK OF EXCHANGE

All the traditional Columbus-discovers-America stories notwithstanding, the significance of the first European contact with the peoples of the Western Hemisphere has little to do with royal treasure, a yen for exploration, religious freedom, or even commercial success. It has to do with the profound changes that occurred in the lifeways of two civilizations, the mixed messages presented by traded items of material culture, and the way in which each side used what it considered to be worthless commodities to deceive the other into making valuable exchanges. The familiar scenes of these early European–Native American contacts—stout, stolid European gentlemen opening chests of inexpensive trinkets to the gasps of incredulous Indians—are profoundly misleading. Both sides were actually quite familiar with each other before 1600—and both sides were experienced and skillful in trade.

As Columbus-doubters with a wide range of motivations have insisted for generations, the famous captain-for-hire from Genoa in the service of Queen Isabella was certainly not the first European navigator to anchor his vessel off American shores. Archaeological evidence now confirms longstanding historians' contentions that the first contacts of the peoples of North America with Europeans occurred around A.D. 1000. The sagas of Viking voyages and the famous hand-drawn map identifying a place called "Vinland" mesh neatly with Norse artifacts excavated at a site called L'Anse aux Meadows in Newfoundland. But apparently the voyages of exploration and colonization to the icy, granite shores we now call Labrador, Newfoundland, and perhaps even Nova Scotia were unsuccessful or met with resistance. It was not until the early sixteenth century, at a time when the Spaniards were conducting campaigns of con-

This sixteenth-century Venetian woodcut map depicts the North Atlantic region of Labrador, Newfoundland, Nova Scotia, and the land then known as Norumbega. It was here that the first sustained contact in North America between Europeans and Native Americans took place. From Giovanni Battista Ramusio's Terzo Volume delle Navigationi et Viaggi, *Venice, 1556.*

quest in Mexico and Central America, that a renewed and even more pervasive kind of contact between Europeans and Native Americans resumed along North Atlantic shores.

The historical context and motivations were, as in the South, European, though the initial attraction was fish, not the Indies' spices and gold. The rapid growth of population in Western Europe and the pressing need for more food resources brought an increasing number of enterprising Basque and Breton fishing captains to venture far into the North Atlantic, to the rich, cold shallows that came to be known as the Grand Banks. The native peoples of the nearby coasts had been taking advantage of this natural abundance for centuries, venturing far out to sea in dugout canoes. Yet as Faith Harrington shows on pages 50–51, by the mid-1500s dozens, perhaps hundreds, of Basque and French fishing boats could be found there every spring hauling in the bounty of codfish and flounder and pursuing right and bowhead whales. Eventually extending their fishing season into summer and autumn, the European seamen established shore stations to butcher the whales, render their blubber, and salt the freshly caught fish. And

at these shore stations a lucrative connection was made between European fishermen and native hunter/gatherers that was destined to change both their lives.

For the Europeans, the thick brown fur of the beaver was an almost irresistible attraction. Soft, warm, and water resistant, it was the perfect material to shield the body from the iciness of winter. As time went on, it was also appreciated as an ideal raw material for the manufacture of stylish felt hats. Unlike the pelts of the few fur-bearing animals left in the forests of Europe, the beavers and muskrats of the forests of America could be found in abundance—great abundance. And, as both David Brose and Patricia Rubertone describe later in this chapter, many native people soon discovered that beaver pelts, exchanged with the Europeans, could bring a treasure trove of valuable items: metal kettles, glass beads, lead-glazed pottery, and new kinds of tools. And these were not worthless trinkets. Rare or unusual goods had long been a source of status and power; the Europeans themselves had sacrificed a great deal to obtain exotica from China and India. Soon enough, the promise of trade fueled the single-minded hunt for beaver.

And long before the Europeans ventured more than a few miles inland, an active trade network—exchanging European goods for furs over thousands of square miles—was established by enterprising native middlemen.

The concept of trade was certainly nothing that Europeans had to teach to Native Americans. As several of our contributors suggest, the routines of specialized exchange over long distances—calculating what was valuable to others in return for something even more desirable—were well-honed. For example, on pages 52–53, Alice B. Kehoe points out that far to the West, on the High Plains, the Rockies, and along the Pacific Coast (a part of the historical stage that is usually left in darkness in the retelling of American history), trade, during prehistoric times, had for centuries been active and complex. In these relatively lightly populated regions, useful raw materials such as obsidian, flint, seashells, and food products, including grain, meat, and fish, were collected, processed, and traded at major market towns. Long before they obtained horses from the Spanish, the nomadic peoples of the Great Plains had developed sophisticated techniques for hunting bison—and not for subsistence alone. For centuries bison carcasses were skinned and butchered and huge quantities of dried bison meat, called pemmican, were traded by plains hunters to native farmers at the main towns along the Missouri River for corn and other agricultural products.

Dr. Kehoe shows that before the contact period an equally active network of cultural contact and exchange existed on the western side of the Rockies, down the Columbia River, and along the Pacific Coast. In fact, the sheer volume of travel and commerce between traders of many nations gave rise to a regionwide trade jargon known as Chinook. The yearly salmon runs provided a major source of tradable food commodities; other items exchanged in yearly trade fairs included rare seashells, feathers used for ornaments, and human slaves—most often captives taken in war. To the south, archaeological evidence of foreign goods indicates that the people of California were also active in trade, exchanging finished goods and raw materials with the peoples of the Rockies, the Southwest, and Mexico.

Ironically, at the very time that the first European fishermen-turned-traders were making contact with the native peoples of the North Atlantic, archaeological evidence suggests that the fishermen-turned-traders of the Northwest coast of North America were also making their first contact with the Old World's natives. They did this through their participation in the vast Russian trade fairs held in Siberia from the beginning of the seventeenth century.

THE VARIETY OF CHANGING NATIVE NORTH AMERICAN SOCIETIES

As we have seen, when Europeans first landed on American shores, they did not encounter "Indians" who lived and behaved the same everywhere. Despite their first impressions and preconceptions, they encountered people as varied as those they had left behind in the Old World, people who lived in dynamic and often sophisticated native societies with their own tensions and distinctive cultural norms. These societies shared some cultural features, but in other ways—including the size and scale of community organization—were as varied as the large towns, small fishing villages, and seasonal hunting camps they occupied. The people were farmers, hunters, and fishermen; their settlements clustered densely in the larger river valleys where corn could be grown, and around estuaries or bays where seafood was easily harvested. Women played a significant role in almost all areas of society, and the most prominent among them apparently received honors equal to those accorded to elite men. They participated in a community life that included seasonal gatherings for rituals, celebrations, and communal work projects such as the construction of mounds and earthworks that had religious significance.

We almost never think of Native Americans in the context of sophisticated urban life. Even though there were certainly cities in Mexico, we do not give them much heed. It has been fairly easy to overlook their complex organization and economic life in reaction to their ritual human sacrifice. In the

Despite the common image of primitive and largely nomadic cultures in North America before the arrival of Europeans, many native peoples participated in active long-distance commerce and constructed regional centers. In this artist's reconstruction of the great ceremonial and trade site of Cahokia (near modern St. Louis) around A.D. 1150, the central market and plaza are pictured in the foreground with the largest of the site's monuments, now called Monk's Mound, in the rear. During this period, Cahokia rivaled the largest cities of Europe in population size.

area that later became the United States, we have not usually considered that Native Americans built or lived in cities. Yet as Patricia Galloway shows on pages 56–57, the great Mississippi Valley, dominating the central third of North America, was for centuries a center of urban life, home to hundreds of thousands and possibly millions of people. In the thirteenth century A.D., its huge metropolitan center, Cahokia, in the rich bottomland opposite modern St. Louis, was larger than contemporary London or Paris, making it one of the most important urban concentrations in the contemporary world. Although Cahokia had declined and was almost deserted by 1500, many other large mound sites in the Mississippi and Ohio valleys served as central hubs for flourishing societies that produced surpluses of food, supported full-time specialists of many kinds, and had a religious and political class as well.

Another major cultural area with its own urban characteristics was the Southwest. Some of its major features are decribed by Steadman Upham on pages 54–55. There, the ancestors of today's Pueblo Indians occupied dozens of distinct geographic zones, each consisting of from five to more than a dozen towns. Each town was inhabited by a few hundred to a few thousand people, and was built in the characteristic multistory pueblo style. They were often planned architectural units that incorporated plaza areas and kivas, which were semisubterranean chambers for rituals. On page 54 Dr. Upham provides archaeological evidence indicating that the regional settlement systems of the late fifteenth and early sixteenth centuries in the Southwest were interdependent economically, giving rise to high levels of interregional trade. To overcome the arid climate, elaborate irrigation and water-preservation systems supported a population that numbered in the hundreds of thousands. Specialized production of foodstuffs, pottery, and a host of other commodities were exchanged and built the essential ties between diverse populations and communities.

Throughout the entire continent, distinct cultural groups existed in sometimes tense, sometimes peaceful relations. We are not at all sure of how well groups knew one another, aside from what we can infer from trade and exchange activities. Yet we want to present an overview of Native America that

Disease Epidemics in Florida, 1512–1672
(after Dobyns, 1983)

Date	Disease	Probability	Mortality Rate
1513–14	Malaria (?)	Likely	Unknown
1519–24	Smallpox	Nearly certain	50–75%
1528	Measles or typhoid	Nearly certain	About 50%
1535–39	Unidentified	Documented	High
1545–48	Bubonic plague	Nearly certain	About 12.5%
1549	Typhus	Very probably	Perhaps 10%
1550	Mumps	Possible	Unknown
1559	Influenza	Nearly certain	About 20%
1564–70	Unidentified and endemic syphilis	Documented	Severe
1585–86	Unidentified	Documented	Severe
1586	Vectored fever	Probable	15–20%
1596	Measles	Documented	About 25%
1613–17	Bubonic plague	Documented	50%
1649	Yellow fever	Documented	About 33%
1653–	Smallpox	Documented	Unknown
1659	Measles	Documented	Unknown
1672	Influenza (?)	Documented	Unknown

points out how varied it was and what a mistake it has been to see it as uniform. At the same time, we do not want to continue the mistake by presenting an overview that implies that just because we can now see a continent full of diversity, such was apparent to Native Americans in their own time.

It seems quite clear that differing languages, customs, histories, allegiances, and competition for farming land often gave rise to clashes between clans and villages. This warfare was generally carried out on a small scale, and conquest and occupation in the European sense were rarely the goals. Although there was no strife that was continent-wide—no Crusades, no Mongol invasion—there were chiefdoms powerful enough to coerce their neighbors by violence or threat of violence to offer tribute in the form of foodstuffs and high-prestige goods. The growing power of these regional leaders was bound to come into violent conflict with the ambitions of Europeans, who assumed that the coastlines, valleys, and forests of America were nothing more than a wilderness to which they could lay claim in the names of distant kings and patron saints.

Worse even than the arrogance that the Europeans brought with them were the diseases they carried that were unknown in the New World. These diseases, acute European crowd infections like smallpox, measles, and influenza, eventually ravaged native populations in virtually every region of the continent and were, we now realize, the biggest single cause of loss of life and social disintegration among Native Americans. Archaeologists now suspect that the population loss during the first seventy-five years of Spanish contact was catastrophic, causing severe disruptions in settlement, subsistence, economy, and polity. This biological onslaught apparently made it impossible for the peoples of the Southwest, for example, to maintain their complex irrigation systems, led to the collapse of their trade networks, and caused the progressive isolation of individual communities. Elsewhere, the ravages of disease had differing effects, but nowhere on the continent were native populations left unscathed. It seems likely that even the most prosperous and powerful societies of the Mississippi Valley had been seriously damaged or altered by the ravages of disease well before the

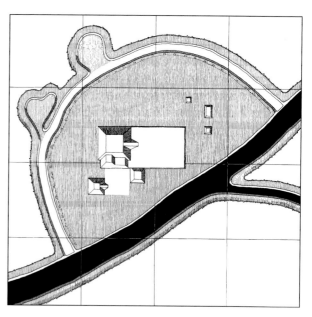

Surrounded by a dry moat and a palisade of wooden posts, Etowah, a site in northwestern Georgia, contains the remains of a town and a complex of truncated ceremonial platforms. Archaeologists suggest that the settlement here was founded around A.D. 950 and continued until shortly after European contact. It has been identified with the town of Itaba visited by the De Soto expedition.

actual arrival of the Europeans in their region. And in the forests of the Northeast, communicable diseases accompanied the kettles, beads, and blankets along the wide-ranging routes of European–Native American trade.

Native North America had been settled for at least twelve thousand years and maybe as much as twenty thousand before Europeans got to it. Cultures were distinct, and although there was little political unity, the continent was well known topographically, in terms of resources useful to hunters and farmers. Native America was not one society; there were many. They were not "Indians"; they had their own names. Theirs was not a New World; it was a world that was heterogenous, just as dynamic as Europe and similarly in a process of change, even if for different reasons. This dynamism and change was compounded by the arrival of Europeans who, depending on who they were and where they arrived, had their own issues, quests, and reasons for coming. And it was in the intersection—the collision—of these worlds that we can locate the point of departure for the subsequent developments of American history.

As the two worlds came into contact, both began to trade. Trade for one dealt in profit; for the other, in needed goods through barter, since there was neither money nor the accumulation of capital for Native Americans. Instability was produced because each society was changing anyway; when the two met, the exchange was based on different principles, and the things exchanged were themselves dynamic. The items carried included diseases, guns, pots that were unbreakable and fireproof, and beads that glistened permanently. The material culture of Europe covered the continent and remains a material expression of conflicting social purposes.

LA FLORIDA

More than a half century before the Pilgrims landed at Plymouth, and several decades before the establishment of Jamestown, a distinctive European society had already been established on American soil. The place was La Florida, a vast and

This engraving on a conch shell imported from the Caribbean, inscribed with the image of a man in a boat and other unidentified symbols, is characteristic of the constellation of Native American art and ritual that archaeologists have come to describe as the Southeast Ceremonial Complex.

(for the Spanish) almost entirely unexplored territory whose outer boundaries were limited only by the grandiose imagination of imperial Spain. The name of this territory was chosen by Juan Ponce de Leon, who arrived on the peninsula during the Easter season of 1513 and, in appreciation for its natural beauty, named the land Pascua Florida or "flowers of spring."

Flowers, though, were not its primary attraction, nor was a legendary Fountain of Youth. Rumors of gold in the interior drew Ponce de Leon and subsequent explorers, including Pánfilo de Narváez in 1528 and Hernando de Soto in 1539. These early *entradas* did not result in permanent Spanish settlements, but in episodic, violent encounters with native peoples that left a residue of bad feelings and the first victims of contagious European diseases. It was not until 1565 that the first permanent settlement in Spanish Florida was established by Pedro Menéndez de Avilés at a place he called St. Augustine. This settlement was intended by the royal authorities to defend the Spanish treasure fleets as they made their way back home. It was also intended as a territorial buffer against French and British incursions into the area. But as Bonnie McEwan shows on pages 62–63, St. Augustine's most long-lasting significance was as the main seat of power of an imported aristocratic elite.

In La Florida, as in the rest of their New World dominions, the Spanish had problems of control. On pages 66–67, David Hurst Thomas relates how once the initial flush of exploration and conquest was over, the royal colonizers sought to pacify and utilize the labor of native peoples by royal and papal command. In some areas of the New World, the *encomienda* system was established to keep indigenous peoples as unfree laborers in plantations where both the resources and inhabitants of a specific area were apportioned as a feudal fiefdom. In La Florida, a network of self-supporting frontier missions was established in which the native peoples of the region would be given religious instruction and trained in a new, productive way of life.

These architecturally uniform missions rank with pots, beads, guns, furs, and other homogenizing items introduced or sought out by Europeans. They were the material manifestation of dominance. Not only were they used to dominate, like guns, but they also were themselves dominating social factors once Indians began to use them systematically—like kettles, which made potting less relevant. Thus, the material culture, now widely known through archaeology, became a means of conquest when used as Europeans intended.

In the course of archaeological excavations at the site of Santa Elena, one of the early capitals of Spanish Florida (located on what is known today as Parris Island), an abundance of Spanish pottery and luxury goods has been uncovered. Shown here is a Spanish majolica bowl being excavated from a refuse pit.

CHRISTIAN IDEOLOGY

The Jesuits began mission work among the Indians of South Florida in 1567, but, encountering considerable resistance and the murders of several of their members, they abandoned their activities in Florida after only six years. The first Franciscans arrived in 1573, and they fared better in making the missions work. By 1587, they had succeeded in establishing missions among the eastern Timucuan Indians in the vicinity of St. Augustine and northward into the territory of the Guale people. The outbreak of the Guale Rebellion of 1597 halted the Franciscans' progress only temporarily. Native outrage at the friars' insistence on monogamy and increasingly strident opposition to traditional native ceremonies and healing methods led to the destruction of missions over a wide area. Yet when order was restored—by means of a campaign of violent Spanish reprisal—the Franciscans resumed what they confidently believed was God's work. They rebuilt burned churches and dormitories and, as Dr. Thomas explains, eventually expanded their activities across much of northern Florida and far up the Atlantic coast.

In the missions, Native American neophytes were required to exchange their traditional farming methods, perfected over centuries, for the techniques needed to grow the wheat fields and vegetable gardens of Andalusia and Castile. European Christian concepts of good and evil, of the Holy Trinity and Satan, were at first overlaid on native spirits, with the latter identified as demons. Familiar customs like meetings in the council house, communal dances, and even ball games were banned. By the end of the seventeenth century, the mission system of La Florida had more than proved its effectiveness. The native peoples of this region who had not fallen prey to disease, or been killed in raids or uprisings, or been uprooted from their traditional lands, had almost entirely lost their cultural integrity.

Christianity was central to the worldview of contemporary Europeans because it was both a reason to colonize and a mask to conceal what colonizing did. The missions of La Florida, through their attempt to transform people into followers of Christ by using Scripture and the lives of missionaries and saints as models for the new behavior of

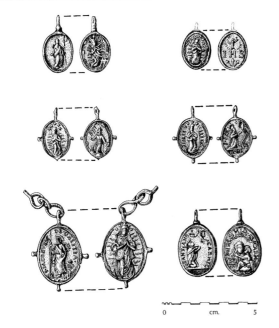

These religious medals, excavated at the site of the Mission Santa Catalina de Guale, provide material evidence for the proselytizing that went on among the native peoples of the region.

the recently saved, Europeanized their adherents and converts. And because Christianity was so powerful—and remains so powerful—an ideology, the painfulness of the destruction of native cultures by missions is often denied, or is even celebrated. We see Christianity here as acting frequently as an arm of Western colonialism, and when used as intensively as it was by Europeans from the sixteenth to the nineteenth centuries, it aided the virtually complete transformation of Native American cultures. This was achieved through both its penetrating ideology and its use of many forms of material culture: church compounds, ritual objects, and illustrated books.

IMPERIAL RIVALRIES

The European scramble for possessions, peoples, and resources in the New World—usually described in our schoolbooks as the Age of Discovery—was an extension of the great power conflict going on in Europe itself. Too often the Spanish

colonial experience in the Americas is described with a constellation of stereotyped cultural symbols: Castilian knights, devout friars, and flaming Latin passions. But it is worth remembering that in the sixteenth century, Spain was only a part of the vast Hapsburg Empire that stretched northward to the shores of the Baltic, eastward to Poland, and southward to Sicily. The Spanish Crown's allocation of resources and manpower in the New World was thus in large measure determined by its imperial strategy in Europe, and developments in Europe had their impact in the New World as well.

On pages 60–61, Dr. Thomas describes the American manifestations of European power struggles. At mid-sixteenth century, Spanish King Charles V (and later, his son Philip II) made northern Europe increasingly central to Spanish interests. Dynastic aspirations also led the then Prince Philip to marry Henry VIII's daughter, Mary Tudor, heir to the English throne. But this use of dynastic ties to solidify Hapsburg power and territory did not come cheaply. The massive quantities of gold and silver Spain extracted from its American colonies were spent to administer its far-flung European territories and pay for inconclusive, exhausting wars with France. Eventually even New World riches were not enough to support Hapsburg ambitions. The increased taxes imposed in Spain provoked a domestic revolt that badly damaged the Spanish economy. And as Spain faltered, North America became increasingly attractive to the European rivals as the basis for their own ambitions—a source of raw materials, a place to off-load surplus population, and a territory in which to build outposts, plantations, and strongpoints to contest Spanish mastery.

As Dr. Thomas discusses, France seemed to be the only power with the potential for competing with Spain in North America. Colonial promoter Jean Ribault and his lieutenant René de Laudonnière attempted to further French interests in the New World in the 1560s by establishing Huguenot refugee colonies along the Atlantic coast of North America. Yet these colonies of French Protestant pilgrims proved no match for civil servants and soldiers of Spain, and Ribault's colonies were ultimately destroyed by Spanish attacks. To make matters worse, France's warfare with the Haps-

After raiding Spanish colonial possessions throughout the West Indies, Sir Francis Drake attacked St. Augustine on June 6, 1586. Since their large ships could not cross the treacherous bar, Drake's forces landed on Anastasia Island and crossed Matanzas Bay to the mainland in smaller boats. Drake and his men remained in the area for more than two weeks. After sacking and burning the town, they reportedly cut down the surrounding orange groves and destroyed the crops in the fields.

burgs and other European powers proved ruinous—as it had already done in Spain. And within France itself religious unrest and officially sanctioned violence against Protestants persuaded the French government to abandon its direct competition with the Spanish in La Florida by means of Huguenot colonies. Instead they focused on the north and more strictly commercial interests, exploiting the absence of other European powers in the rich fur-hunting grounds of the St. Lawrence River Valley, and secured a permanent foothold at Quebec in 1608.

The English were relative latecomers to the imperial enterprise. Although English navigators were almost completely absent from the New World between the voyages of the Cabots in the 1490s and Martin Frobisher in 1576, explorers and colonial investors grew increasingly enthusiastic about America's economic potential in the late sixteenth century. After the destruction of the Spanish Armada in 1588, and the elimination of the direct threat Spain posed to England, commercial schemes and domestic political developments soon thrust England into the forefront of New World colonialism. Entrepreneurs such as Francis Drake and Walter Raleigh, displaying contempt for Spanish claims to North America, ranged widely along the Atlantic Coast, raiding Spanish ships and outposts and establishing several colonies. The ultimate success of the English colonies was due in large part to the extraordinary civil and religious unrest at home. In contrast to the case in France, English dissidents were granted charters. And political fragmentation and economic tensions brought about by the growing Puritan movement, when added to the effects of overpopulation in the early seventeenth century, persuaded some sixty thousand English subjects to migrate to colonies in the New World.

That part of the story is of course familiar, but we would like to direct your attention southward, for it was at this time that pirates arose in the Caribbean—not in the storybook images of our childhood, but against a background of imperial rivalry, overpopulation, social upheaval, and cutthroat economic competition. In the quiet inlets and bays of the Caribbean isles, ragtag bands of adventurers of many nations, flying the skull and crossbones, took advantage of the larger exploitations under way to grab some wealth for themselves. As

Charles Ewen points out on pages 64–65, Spain's determination to maintain rigid control over the resources and trade of the New World was the kind of policy of economic exclusion that could not succeed for long. The merchants, adventurers, and entrepreneurs of other nations simply could not ignore the wealth of the New World, especially since the once-flourishing trade of the Mediterranean had been significantly curtailed with the expansion of the Ottoman Empire. The islands of the Caribbean and the Atlantic Coast of America therefore became magnets to all who would dare challenge Spain's New World monopoly.

The boundaries between criminal, terrorist, and military actions became exceedingly blurry as the interests of individuals clashed with the power of states. The Portuguese trade in slaves and the French trade in foodstuffs, though officially prohibited by Spanish law, were in many cases facilitated by corruptible or enterprising administrators and officials of the Spanish colonies. And the freebooting attacks of English noblemen such as Francis Drake and Walter Raleigh against the centers of Spanish power can be seen as a part of a larger, unfolding drama that would culminate in Spain having to yield most of the Atlantic Coast and important parts of the Caribbean to other European empires.

Although the impressive fortifications of the ports of the Caribbean are still intact and the romance of the pirates continues to entrance us, the larger context is not often revealed. The expensive measures Spain was forced to underwrite to restore order, or at least provide protection, sheared its profit margin substantially. In this effort, as in the European campaigns, Spain was badly weakened, paving the way for the ascendancy of other European nations in their struggle for hegemony on the continent. In the atmosphere of intensifying imperial rivalry, acts of piracy became, in many cases, international politics by other means. And since one might say that the basis of all the initial European activities in the New World was the extraction of wealth through violence, one-sided edict, or threat of violence, it is hard to ascribe piracy to the pirates alone.

So we conclude that the European exploitation of America's wealth helped to change relations of power in Europe and, far more thoroughly, transformed economic, social, and political life in America. The greatest material transformation was from a system in which resources were held in common and people were related to each other through kinship to one in which all things, including many human relations, were seen as private property. This different vision of the material world allowed for the possession and occupation of a whole continent, including all native labor, imported African laborers, and even poorer European migrants. And while neither Europeans nor Native Americans would ever be the same again, neither side benefited as much as the mythmakers and traditional historians would have us believe.

While material items like potatoes and choco-

The now-picturesque Spanish fortifications at Puerto Plata, Hispaniola, and throughout the Caribbean are the archaeological remains of a desperate and costly attempt by the royal authorities to maintain their monopoly of exploitation in the New World.

late, horses and iron plows, and vast amounts of gold and huge numbers of humans were exchanged and stolen between societies, and while this exchange sometimes improved living conditions, other results were tragic and ruinous. The cost of being "discovered" was paid by Native American peoples in epidemics, the breakdown of traditional societies, and the loss of social integrity. And for Europeans, the transformation of America into a vast field of ideology and plunder served to bankrupt absolute monarchies, impoverish the lower classes, dump surplus populations in distant colonies, and cultivate an attitude of contempt for the rest of the world that masked a profound internal vulnerability.

RESISTANCE TO EUROPEAN COLONIZATION

Once we see conflict and struggle, instead of "Discovery" or "Encounter," we can also see how and why some people tried to push European colonizers back.

The New World was neither an easy nor an inevitable catch for European powers. There is substantial evidence that in many cases Native American peoples had the will—and the ability—to resist. This story is told by Jeffrey L. Hantman and David S. Brose on pages 68–69 and 70–71. It is important to record such resistance in order to appreciate that European culture merited opposition from many Native Americans. And it was not just that some Europeans were cruel, it was that the European powers intended to treat the whole land as their property, for their good. The arrogance of this assumption was actively resisted, reminding us that some people were not willing to submit to an idea that other people took for granted. In fact, the 1597 Guale Rebellion along the Atlantic coasts of modern Florida, Georgia, and South Carolina against the Franciscan missionaries sent to convert them was just an opening shot in a struggle that would continue with intensifying violence to the end of the nineteenth century, and by other means, until today.

This native rebellion, according to contemporary Spanish sources, resulted from growing resistance

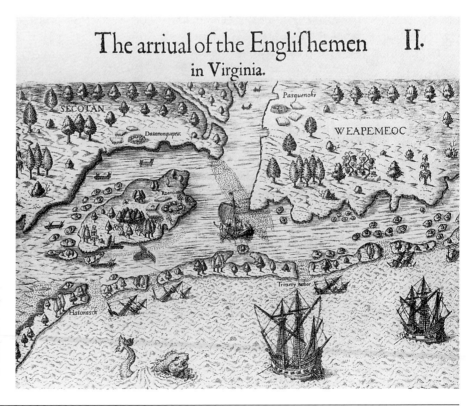

This sixteenth-century engraving depicts the arrival of the English in Virginia in 1584. The English ships are a powerful cultural force in this image; the Indians so small as to be nearly invisible, a part of the natural landscape.

to the missionaries' interference with traditional Guale practices. It may also have had a purely political aspect, with the intervention of the Spanish on the side of an unpopular candidate in a native leadership dispute. Whatever its motivations, however, the rebellion was ultimately suppressed by a Spanish "pacification" program, which included the burning of the ringleaders' village to the ground. No conciliation or compromise with Native autonomy or lifeways was possible when the Europeans were so thoroughly convinced that they were instruments of God's will. Nevertheless, Native Americans continued to seek methods of resistance. Along the Atlantic Coast, they even temporarily joined forces with the English (who were themselves claiming and naming territory) and helped push the Spanish forces southward to the area around St. Augustine.

In other parts of the continent, native policies were strong and vital, and they could successfully resist the establishment of foreign colonies. Such was the case along the Middle Atlantic Coast, where an Algonquian people, known as Powhatan, were rising in power and gaining influence over their neighbors, as Jeffrey L. Hantman relates on pages 68–69. Resistance, however, was often undermined by accompanying trade, which led to changes in both partners.

TRADE AND THE BIRTH OF NEW SOCIETIES

In the St. Lawrence Valley, and into the Great Lakes region, the first contact between Europeans and Native American peoples can be seen as a continuation of the economic and political histories of both. As we have seen, obtaining exotic or rare merchandise from trading partners was not a new experience for either side.

In the Northeast, and especially along the Atlantic Coast and on both sides of the St. Lawrence River, native middlemen traveled among scattered villages and hunting camps, collecting furs and other commodities prized by the Europeans and bartering for them with their own secondarily acquired stock of European trade goods. The travels of these native middlemen were far-reaching, and with every transaction, they expanded the boundaries of native–European cultural exchange.

Superficially, this was no different from the trading networks that had developed and expanded across the continent over the course of centuries. But this one proved to be different. Earlier partners had shared a basic worldview and parallel, if not shared, objectives. But in the 1500s and 1600s, native peoples came into contact with trading nations that were intent on claiming the entire continent, all its resources and people, for their own.

The initial trading connections were made easily enough. Yet along the exchange routes came merchandise that proved deadly: manufactured metal goods that discouraged the patterns of local pottery production and flint knapping; blankets and clothing bearing microorganisms that would in time depopulate entire villages; and, no less destructive, European firearms that would make possible the rapid extermination of fur-bearing animals of the forests—these would prove equally fatal when turned by Europeans on Native Americans and by the native peoples on each other, as David S. Brose points out on pages 70–71.

The sudden rise of the Dutch in southern New England, as Patricia E. Rubertone explains on pages 72–73, must have seemed both surprising and threatening to the other European powers. On one level, the Dutch explorations and trading expeditions to North America could be seen as part of the ongoing rebellion of the Netherlands against the rule of the Hapsburg Empire. Yet the Dutch overseas empire was one in which permanent agricultural colonies and military outposts were of less vital importance. Rather it was their active commerce and contact with Native peoples like the Iroquois that were crucial—and in which handsome profits could be made at little cost. No massive waves of Dutch migration followed reports of discoveries or fortunes made, as among the English or the Spanish. And even after the establishment of small settlers' colonies in 1624 at Fort Nassau (modern Albany) and in 1631 on Manhattan Island, eventual return to the comforts of Holland was the goal of most of those who ventured across the Atlantic.

For the Dutch, business in North America was something to be conducted with partners—not enemies. No less important, they came to grasp the importance of wampum, also known to them as sewan. These small shell beads figured prominently in native social and ritual life, but now, transformed by the Dutch into money, wampum became the central medium of negotiation in trade. And Dutch control of wampum, like their regulation of kettles, blankets, and firearms, became critical to their commercial success in this region and heralded an ever-tighter intertwining of European and Native American affairs.

WHERE HISTORY BEGINS: THE TRIUMPH OF UNIFORM INTERPRETATION

Despite all the history, conflict, and social transformations that occurred in the century following the first voyage of Columbus, it is a curious tradition in American schoolbooks to assert that the real history of our nation began with the establishment of the first permanent English settlement at Jamestown, Virginia, in 1607. Traditional presentations of American history still insist on seeing that British settlement as initial and the Indians whom they encountered as previously untouched. Acted out by stereotyped, cartoon figures, the Jamestown story is little more than a melodramatic morality play. There's the brave and noble Indian chief Powhatan (bearing the same name as his people) and his beautiful daughter Pocahontas. There are the brave and noble colonists John Smith and John Rolfe. And in Pocahontas's heroic act of mercy toward the English leader about to be executed by her father, we have the same sort of mythic image of goodwill and miraculous salvation that we later find in the early history of the Plymouth colony.

Yet English success at Jamestown—or at Plymouth—was not inevitable. Jeffrey L. Hantman relates on pages 74–75 that at the time of the establishment of the former, the powerful Algonquian leader Powhatan claimed the allegiance of tributary villages and peoples over a wide stretch of the Middle Atlantic Coast. The small band of

Kidnapped by colonists while she was living on the Potomac River, Powhatan's daughter Pocahontas married English colonist John Rolfe in 1614. Two years later she left Virginia for England where she was given the name Lady Rebecca, displayed at court, and painted in this portrait, a symbol in London of the potential civility of the Virginia Indians. Her time of celebrity was short; she died and was buried in England in 1617.

English refugees, speculators, and soldiers who landed on the river they named the "James," after their own monarch, were certainly no match for Powhatan in status, power, or wealth. Yet in their promises of friendship and unexpected abundance of copper trade goods, they appeared to Powhatan to be a potentially controllable and useful presence in his territory. Those colonists were ready, after all, to exchange their copper for corn and seal their alliance with Powhatan with a marriage between one of their number and a native woman of noble birth. How could Powhatan have possibly predicted that the Englishmen would begin planting tobacco for profit—or that the sudden, addictive popularity of Virginia tobacco in Europe would quickly lead to the exhaustion of the soil and spark a violent land hunger among the English colonists?

The quaint and romantic image of Jamestown—engraved in our minds and now reconstructed on the banks of the James River in modern Virginia—masks the enormity of the changes wrought by that first permanent English colony in North America. Indeed, in microcosm, this charming story disguises the larger processes by which the representatives of the imperial powers of Europe did their best to overcome and dismantle the native cultures of North America. Of course, we must add the biological factor. Without the decimation wrought by the sudden, terrifying spread of European diseases, it is unlikely that the conquest of the land could have been so complete. The image of civilized (though perhaps brutal or insensitive) Europeans overwhelming naive and primitive children of nature is simply not in accord with the facts as we know them today. Deceptive and, as we have seen, inaccurate myths have sustained the idea of the inevitability of the European conquest of America.

Was there another possible outcome? Could the European attempt at conquering North America have ended like the short-lived Jesuit mission in Virginia or the "Lost Colony" on Roanoke Island? Even at Jamestown, we might now see that it was Powhatan, not John Smith, who determined the course of events. If Powhatan had rejected the lure of copper and demonstrated to the English that any attempt to establish colonies in his territory would be costly and unpleasant—as earlier Algonquian leaders had done—it is likely that the course of American history would have unfolded quite differ-

ently. But because we are rarely made aware of the political or economic background, we are encouraged to see the rebellions of Powhatan's brother and successor Opechancanough—and indeed all Indian resistance in the Caribbean, North Atlantic, Southeast, and across the continent—not as a desperate attempt to restore a balance of power but as the personal work of sullen savages or villains who shattered the peace.

In the history of an era so neatly bracketed between Columbus's first voyage and the establishment of the first permanent English colony at Jamestown, there is for us a great void, a cultural silence our society has made and sustained. Yet, as we've tried to show, within this silence are the complex economic, political, and social interactions between Europeans and Native American peoples, not some inevitable march of progress leading to the "founding" of America at Plymouth and Jamestown. Between 1492 and 1607 there was a continual and mutually influential interaction between Native Americans and Europeans. Neither group was homogeneous, nor were the results everywhere the same. But we tend to ignore the whole era and see only the triumphs of Europeans and the extermination of Native Americans. The categories of conquered and conqueror, European and Native, never existed in forms as sharply defined as they do in the myth. The myth of the discovery of America is not a lie but a powerful modern reality. The myth prevents us from seeing the roots or history of the forces—private property, profit, individualism, and the commodification of products and people—that still drive our own particular society.

THE NORTH ATLANTIC: *Fishermen and Traders*

An imaginary boat trip in the North Atlantic is the best way to experience this region from the viewpoint of the first Europeans here. We can begin our journey at the southeastern corner of Labrador, at Red Bay, once a huge whaling port. The cold waters surrounding this region attracted Basque whalemen from the 1530s until the early 1600s. Archaeologists from Memorial University of Newfoundland and Parks Canada have begun excavating the Red Bay shore station. Their finds of whalebones, barrel parts, navigational instruments, Spanish coins, iron knives, and ceramic vessels testify to the intensity of activity here—long before the founding of permanent European farming settlements in New England and Canada.

Crossing the Gulf of St. Lawrence and heading south to the north shore of New Brunswick, we can sight the Gaspé Peninsula on the starboard side of the vessel. This is the region where early Basque fishermen and later traders exchanged large amounts of European brass kettles, knives, axes, paternostri (beads), jewelry, hats, and cloth for hides of beaver, otter, and even caribou. Prince Edward Island, Cape Breton Island, and Nova Scotia were a seasonal home to many French, English, and Spanish fishermen from the sixteenth century onward as dry cod fisheries were established for the exploitation of the vast resources of the nearby Grand Banks.

Entering the Gulf of Maine, we pass the site of the short-lived and ill-fated Popham Colony (1607–1608) at the mouth of the Kennebec River. We might end our voyage at the ruggedly beautiful Isles of Shoals, a group of nine islands off the coast of Maine and New Hampshire. Archaeological research being conducted here by the University of Southern Maine has shown that the earliest English settlers (including, by the 1650s, women and children) supported themselves by a combination of fishing, farming, and trade. At first the Euro-American trade in this region may have been conducted primarily by Native American middlemen, sailing throughout the region and trading European copper and brass ornaments, kettles,

Earthenware ceramic vessels from the Iberian Peninsula excavated from the Red Bay whaling station in Newfoundland provide evidence of intensive European occupation during the late sixteenth century.

Another detail from the 1556 Gastaldi map presents a highly stylized depiction of a native of the region. The costume and headdress are fanciful and show how inexperienced Europeans were at depicting foreign worlds.

iron axes, and clothing to more geographically isolated Native groups. However, English, French, and Dutch expansion into the Gulf of Maine during the seventeenth century—and their insistence on dealing directly with the local populations—brought on a series of devastating epidemics which, by about 1640, decimated vast numbers of the Native peoples of the Northeast.

■ FAITH HARRINGTON
University of Southern Maine

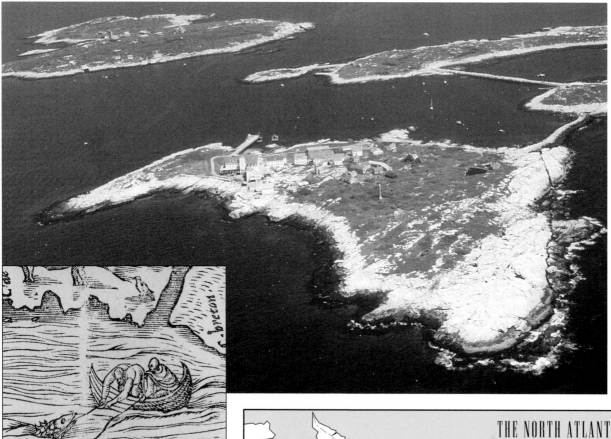

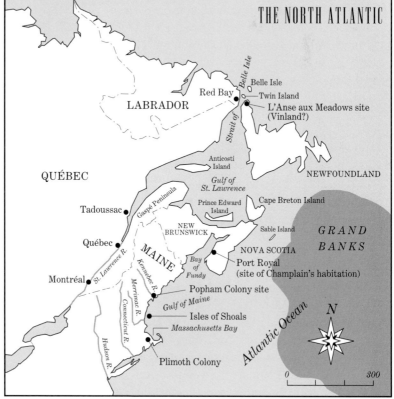

ABOVE: *Detail from a 1556 Venetian map of La Nuova Francia by Giacomo Gastaldi. The square and horizontal stripe at the bottom are meant to depict the barren, sandy landscape of Sable Island, south of Nova Scotia. To the north, two European fishermen hook a large cod on a handline, graphically illustrating the richness of these waters.*

TOP RIGHT: *Aerial view of several of the Isles of Shoals, site of an early seventeenth-century English dry cod fishery.*

THE GREAT PLAINS AND THE NORTHWEST
Hunters and Markets

For two thousand years, Native Americans carried on a regular trade in bulk food products as well as high-quality raw materials and ornaments along the Missouri River. Dried bison meat (pemmican) and hides were produced in commercial quantities on the High Plains of the Northwest by driving herds over cliffs into specially built corrals to be slaughtered. The nomadic hunters exchanged these for corn produced in the fields of the Missouri River towns. With the arrival of European traders in the eighteenth century, the Northern Plains hunters expanded their market, supplying tons of pemmican to feed the European posts and the canoe brigades ferrying pelts to the ports on Hudson's Bay or to Montreal.

Westward, trade passed over the Rockies, through the pleasant valleys and along the rivers feeding the Columbia. Trade and visiting were so common in this Northwest region that most people were either bilingual or trilingual, with the Chinook jargon serving as a lingua franca for traders and travelers. The head of the Columbia Gorge, the Dalles, was both an extraordinary salmon fishing station and a major market. Wishram and Wasco peoples living on the riverbanks produced tons of dried, pounded salmon to trade to travelers on the Columbia and hosted an annual fair, featuring gambling, that drew thousands of visitors.

Once down to the Columbia Mouth, Native American trade fanned north to the Salish and, beyond, to the Northwest coast of British Columbia and Alaska, eventually reaching the Russian trade fairs in Siberia beginning in the seventeenth century. Native trade also went south from the mouth of the Columbia and into California. San Francisco Bay welcomed both sea trade and overland travelers from the Southwest. Northern Californians traded inland across the southern plateau to the Columbia; slaves were one item in demand there as in Northwest Coast societies. The nobility among the Northwest Indians managed the work of laborers, commoners, and slaves, eschewing manual

Habitants de Californie

work themselves. California Indians struck European visitors as relaxed, not bothering much with clothes, enjoying what seemed a natural abundance of native grains, nuts, and aquatic animals. Earth lodges, thatched houses, or, in the north, plank houses, blended into hillsides and valleys that supported, prehistorically as now, a major segment of the population of North America.

■ ALICE B. KEHOE
Marquette University

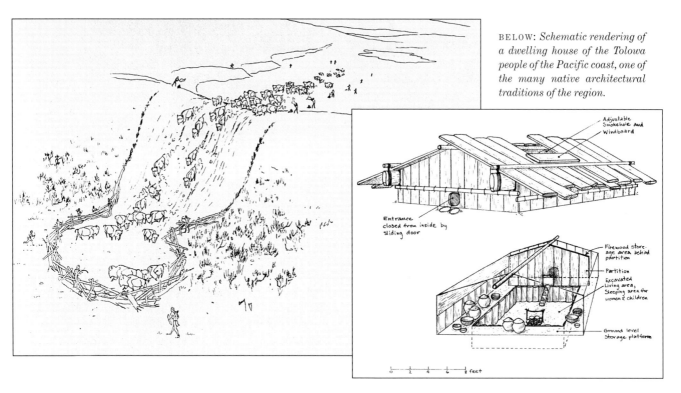

BELOW: *Schematic rendering of a dwelling house of the Tolowa people of the Pacific coast, one of the many native architectural traditions of the region.*

ABOVE: *Archaeological reconstruction of "buffalo jump" excavated at the Boarding School Site near Browning, Montana. It was in use as late as the sixteenth century.*

FACING PAGE, TOP: *Rock art depiction of Tsagaglalal, "She-who-watches," carved in the basalt cliffs along the Columbia River, in Washington's Horsethief Lake State Park. The river was once an active route of Native American cultural and commercial exchange.*

FACING PAGE, BOTTOM: *The Coastal Miwok people, who inhabited the area just north of modern San Francisco, were part of the diverse cultural landscape of the Pacific coast before contact with Europeans.*

THE NORTHERN PLAINS AND PACIFIC COAST

THE SOUTHWEST: *Pueblo Towns*

The collapsed walls of Tsiping, a fourteenth- and fifteenth-century Pueblo town, cascade across Pueblo Mesa. This and dozens of other ruins were once thriving population centers.

Motorists traveling today across New Mexico and Arizona on Interstates 25 and 40 pass directly through the heart of Pueblo territory. Eighteen-wheelers grinding up Glorieta Mesa toward Santa Fe on I-25 growl past the ruins of Pecos Pueblo, where five hundred years ago an impressive Towa town was part of an interregional web of interdependent Pueblo communities. Far to the west near Flagstaff, the ruins of Nuvakwewtaqa, an ancestral Hopi town, cling to the jagged scarps of Anderson Mesa, where they stand silent guard over Chavez Pass. During the fourteenth and fifteenth centuries, the pass was a gateway between north and south and Nuvakwewtaqa functioned as an interregional port of trade, sustaining a large population with its economic primacy and intensive agriculture.

Today, much of the vast territory between Pecos and Nuvakwewtaqa is empty. Between 1275 and 1500, however, large Pueblo towns such as Hawikuh, Mats'a:ka, Kiatsukwa, Tonque, Paa'ko, Sapawe, Poshuingue, and Tsiping were home to many and were destinations to travelers and traders. These towns and others were linked by elaborate trading relationships, often based on exchanges of specialized goods. The characteristic yellow Jeddito ware pottery of the Hopi, for example, was produced in large quantities at only a few locations, but was traded extensively over the entire Southwest and beyond.

With climate and rainfall patterns similar to the modern arid conditions of the region, Pueblo populations developed intensive agricultural systems that used methods of field preparation and cropping to maximize scarce rainfall. In addition to terraced hillside fields, Pueblo farmers used other types of intensive agricultural systems, including canal irrigation along the Rio Grande and Little Colorado rivers and seasonal drainages like Silver Creek and Cottonwood Wash. The labor investment in these intensive field systems was substantial, requiring community cooperation and the use of communal labor for construction and maintenance.

The distribution of Pueblo settlements during the fourteenth and fifteenth centuries consisted of more than twenty distinct groups of towns or settlement clusters regularly spaced at intervals of thirty to fifty miles apart. The archaeological record suggests that there was a high level of interaction and exchange between them; indeed, the view of Pueblo society at 1500 provided by the archaeological research record shows an extensive and expanding settlement system with links across the central and northern Southwest. The coming of the Spanish to Pueblo territory crippled this political and economic network and began a process of demographic collapse among the Pueblo that has only recently been reversed.

■ STEADMAN UPHAM
University of Oregon

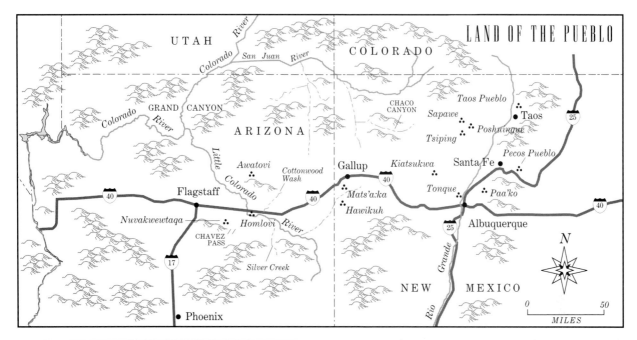

LAND OF THE PUEBLO

Two Jeddito black on yellow pottery bowls from the site of Nuvakwewtaqa bear characteristic fourteenth- and fifteenth-century geometric and zoomorphic decoration.

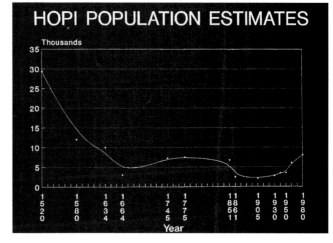

ABOVE: *This graph of Hopi population levels shows the unintended consequence of Spanish colonization among all Pueblo groups—the catastrophic spread of fatal epidemic diseases.*

LEFT: *The Pueblo of Taos retained its traditional architectural style throughout the nineteenth century, when this photograph was taken. Characteristic are the multistory construction, plaza areas, and kivas or ceremonial areas.*

THE SOUTHEAST: *Farmers of the Mississippi Valley*

During the years from A.D. 800 to 1100, as Native American populations grew in the Mississippi Valley and the eastern woodlands, a more sedentary lifestyle developed, at first on the basis of cultivated wild seed-bearing plants and varieties that produced small ears of corn. At some time during this period, Northern Flint corn, which could be harvested as far north as southern New England, was introduced and became the staple crop of settled agricultural communities. In the alluvial valleys of southeastern North America, and especially in the greatest of them, the Mississippi, the mound-building culture known as the Mississippian became the most visible evidence of a demographic and cultural florescence.

When Europeans first saw these mounds, they wove amazing fantasies ascribing the monuments to a race of giant "Mound Builders," probably fair-skinned, who had been driven away or killed by the "savage" Indians who currently occupied the land. This view held sway until the turn of the century, when an intensive archaeological study of the mounds concluded that they had in fact been built by the ancestors of the Native American peoples. Yet the first attempt at constructing an archaeological history of the Mississippi Valley wrapped maize and mound building into a very neat package: It was imagined that both maize and a sun cult were imported from Mexico and points south. The evidence for this cult was seen in the objects and symbols of the so-called Southern Cult (now known as the "Southern Ceremonial Complex"), which were found distributed across southeastern North America from the Atlantic to the eastern border of the Great Plains.

The current view of this phenomenon is not nearly so neat. We now know that the ceremonial platform mounds were built very early in the southern end of the Mississippi Valley and that corn cultivation spread long before the first appearance of the "Southern Cult." Most of the major Mississippian cultural developments grew gradually from the societies that already existed in the region. Archaeologists tend to concentrate these days on the larger questions of how complexity developed in the societies of the region during the late prehistoric

period and why, after nearly seven hundred years and with an extraordinarily rich environment, no native polity was ever able to "achieve" the character of a European-style state—and perhaps be able to have resisted more effectively the sixteenth- and seventeenth-century European military, political, and economic onslaught.

■ PATRICIA GALLOWAY
Mississippi Department of Archives and History

FRVMENTVM INDICVM.

Where the growing season was long, and fertile land abundant, corn cultivation could produce enough surplus to spur significant population growth and support a class of elite rulers capable of controlling the now-valuable farmlands.

By 1500, the great metropolitan center of Cahokia, which in its heyday in the thirteenth century had been larger than contemporary London or Paris, had been superseded by many smaller mound sites that served as regional hubs.

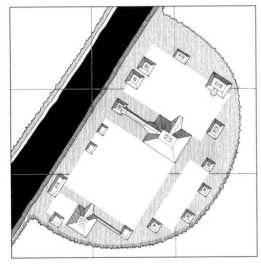

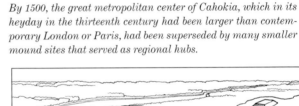

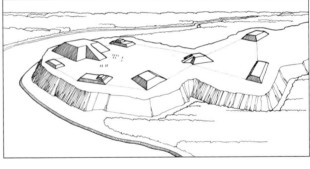

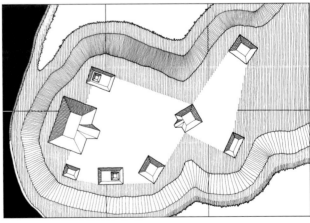

ABOVE: *The Winterville ceremonial complex, near modern Greenville, Mississippi. Like Anna, it is one of dozens of ancient religious, political, and economic centers established in the major river valleys of the Southeast.*

FACING PAGE, TOP: *An effigy pot from the important Mississippian ceremonial center at present-day Moundsville, Alabama.*

FACING PAGE, BOTTOM: *Fine slate obtained from the Ozarks provided the raw material for this disk engraved with a rattlesnake and hand-and-eye design—symbols of what archaeologists have come to describe as the "Southern Ceremonial Complex."*

ABOVE: *An artist's view of the Anna mound group, constructed between A.D. 1200 and 1500, at a site about twelve miles north of modern Natchez, Mississippi.*

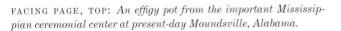

DE SOTO: *Memories of the Invaders*

In the spring of 1539, Hernando De Soto and a crowd of some six hundred mostly Spanish expeditionaries made their way in five ships from Cuba to the western coast of Florida. In 1543, a rather smaller crowd of three hundred expeditionaries, minus De Soto, made their way in two makeshift boats to the port of Panuco on the northwestern coast of Mexico, having failed to find gold, convert natives, or establish a settlement. Although the expedition was a failure, no less than three narrative histories claiming to contain the reports of eyewitnesses were written to recount it. Their popularity has helped build the image in school history

Tubular blue Nueva Cadiz beads and faceted chevron beads are archaeological discoveries that can be closely dated to the De Soto expedition period. The so-called Clarksdale bells are less closely datable but still appropriate to the period.

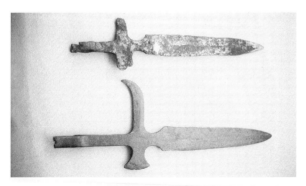

Several halberds found in regions De Soto is thought to have passed through may be authentic—there were halberdiers among the expeditionaries—but these artifacts may also date to as late as the Civil War.

texts of the daring conquistadors "discovering" the Mississippi River (although more than a million people were living along its banks).

Beginning in the eighteenth century, huge amounts of effort have been expended to determine where De Soto and his men went and what they did, but the answers are still far from clear. We know that the expedition landed on the western coast of Florida, wintered on the northwest Florida coast, went north into and through the southern spur of the Appalachians in search of gold, took a westward route to the Mississippi, and examined the rich agricultural lands of the Mississippi Valley. When De Soto died and was buried in the Mississippi, his men abandoned the colonization project, and attempted to get back to Spanish-controlled lands, first traveling far west of the Mississippi and then taking the river route to flee increasingly hostile Indians. Although archaeological evidence has been amassed in support of various routes, neither the narratives nor the archaeology are precise enough to choose a definitive one.

Plans to create a national historic trail to commemorate the four hundred fiftieth anniversary of the De Soto Expedition have revived a wave of local sentiment across a region that is still largely underdeveloped and that would prefer to identify with the shining Castilian knight rather than the inscrutable "savage." Only one site, the 1540 winter camp at Appalachee Province (within the city limits of modern Tallahassee), has been certainly identified, and Arkansas, Tennessee, and Mississippi are still battling to claim the site of the first crossing of the Mississippi, although the actual site is almost certainly long since washed away.

While the De Soto expedition continues to be a continuing source of fascination and speculation for many southerners, the few remaining reservation Indians of the region find the whole "celebration" offensive and the "discoveries" of the early explorers laughable.

■ PATRICIA GALLOWAY
Mississippi Department of Archives and History

An early face of De Soto, from Historia de los hechos de los Castellanos *(1601–1615).*

A heroic face of De Soto: Discovery of the Mississippi by De Soto, *painted by William H. Powell in 1855. The many errors in this romanticized picture include Plains Indians with tepees rather than the settled, farming Indians of the Mississippi Valley and well-dressed Spaniards rather than the desperate, ragtag band that actually reached the river. This painting is now displayed in the U.S. Capitol.*

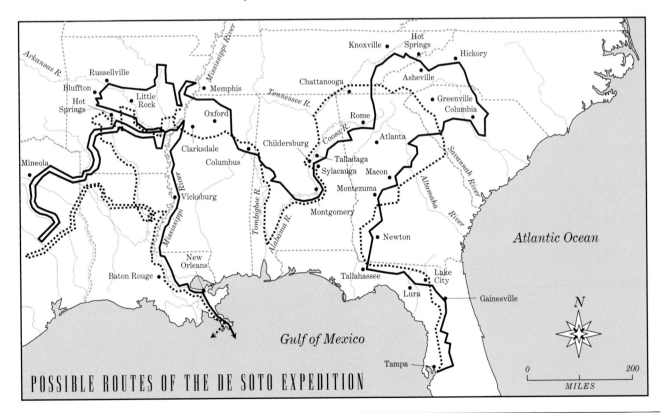

POSSIBLE ROUTES OF THE DE SOTO EXPEDITION

IMPERIAL RIVALRIES
Spanish-French-British Competition Along the Atlantic Coast

Fort Caroline (shown in this reconstruction), near the mouth of the St. John's River, was one of the first French footholds in the New World.

Along the three-hundred-mile-long coastal strip from St. Augustine north to Charleston, South Carolina, travelers can find traces of a three-cornered European conflict that raged during the sixteenth and seventeenth centuries. This was a direct extension of the unrest that swept through Europe during the same period, as imperial rivalry, religious reformation, and mercantile competition fueled a scramble for colonies in North America—increasingly attractive as a source of raw materials, a place to off-load surplus population, and key to mastery of the seas.

The first blow in this international competition was struck by the Spanish nobleman Vásquez de Ayllón who, in 1526, established a colony named San Miguel de Gualdape with six hundred persons, including women and African slaves. Recent research suggests it was located near Sapelo Sound, Georgia. Yet within two months of the colony's founding, the death of Ayllón and internal dissension brought the enterprise to a sudden end.

For the next three decades—the failure of the San Miguel colony notwithstanding—Spain's predominance in the New World was largely uncontested. Yet the gold and silver Spain reaped from its American colonies was squandered, and by 1557, the Spanish Crown was bankrupt. This brought Spain's traditional rivals into action: In 1562 a group of French Huguenots under Jean Ribault established the Charlesfort colony on what is now Parris Island, South Carolina. A second French colony, Fort Caroline, was founded in 1564 by René de Laudonnière on St. John's River in Florida.

The Spanish saw this colony as a serious danger. At the behest of King Philip II, Pedro Menéndez de Avilés was assigned the task of eradicating it. After establishing St. Augustine in September 1565, Menéndez moved decisively against the French, capturing nearby Fort Caroline, renaming it San Mateo, and killing most of the French. In the fol-

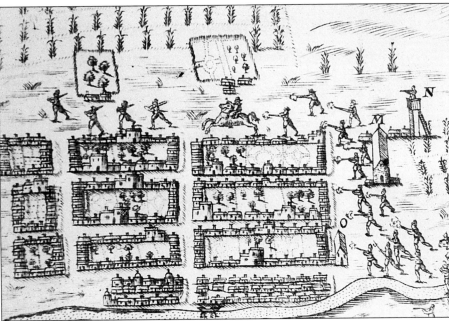

In the career of Sir Francis Drake (1543?–1596), one can see the intertwined elements of geographical exploration, international conflict, and private interest in the European involvement in the "New World" in the sixteenth century. Knighted by Queen Elizabeth in 1581, Drake was one of England's foremost explorers, a leader of the naval attacks against the Spanish Empire, and one of England's wealthiest privateers.

In 1586, Sir Francis Drake devastated St. Augustine with a fleet of forty-two vessels carrying two thousand men. A stylized contemporary engraving depicts the attack.

lowing year, Menéndez established a garrison farther north on the Georgia coast, where the head of the Guale chiefdom resided. He later founded the city of Santa Elena on Parris Island. More than four hundred settlers were sent there, and by 1569 Santa Elena—recently rediscovered by archaeologists—had become capital of Spanish Florida.

The English role in the New World was limited at first. Walter Raleigh's Roanoke Colony was a failure, but in 1587, Sir Francis Drake led a lightning raid against Spanish power at St. Augustine. After the destruction of the Spanish Armada in 1588, rapid commercial and political growth thrust England into the forefront of New World colonial efforts. And its ultimate success in North America would be due in no small part to the depth of civil unrest and religious unease at home.

■ DAVID HURST THOMAS
American Museum of Natural History

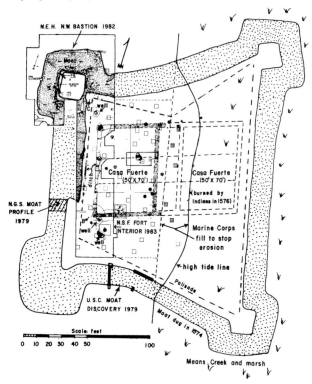

A reconstruction (stippled area) based on archaeology of the moat around one of the forts—called Casa Fuerte—excavated at the site of Santa Elena (1566–1587) on Parris Island, South Carolina, under the direction of Stanley South of the University of South Carolina.

SPANISH FLORIDA: *Governors, Priests, and Entrepreneurs*

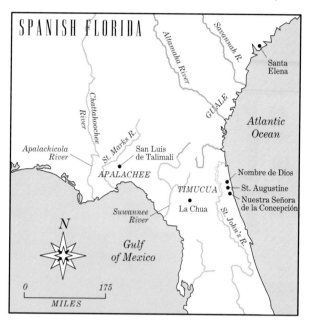

SPANISH FLORIDA

Altamaha River
Savannah R.
Santa Elena
Chattahoochee River
GUALE
Atlantic Ocean
Apalachicola River
St. Marks R.
San Luis de Talimali
APALACHEE
Nombre de Dios
TIMUCUA
St. Augustine
Nuestra Señora de la Concepción
La Chua
St. John's R.
Suwannee River
N
Gulf of Mexico
0   175
MILES

This eighteenth-century engraving from a formal Titian portrait of La Florida's first governor, Pedro Menéndez de Avilés, shows him in the characteristic dress and demeanor of a Spanish aristocrat, a way of life he and his extensive entourage brought to Spanish Florida.

When most people think of Florida, they have visions of sandy beaches, palm trees, theme parks, and alligator-infested swamps. Yet hidden beneath Florida's modern highways, housing developments, and resort areas are traces of a very different cultural landscape, which included over thirty Spanish missions, cattle ranches, and this country's oldest continuously inhabited city. The far-reaching transformation of the region began in 1565, when the Spanish nobleman Pedro Menéndez de Avilés established St. Augustine, hoping that it might become a self-sufficient colony to provide defense for the treasure fleets as they sailed through the Straits of Florida on the way back to Spain. As military governor of La Florida, Menéndez parceled out positions of authority to a close-knit group of kinsmen and followers from his native province of Asturias. In time, Menéndez's entourage became the nucleus of a Spanish-born elite who directed the cultural and economic transformation of La Florida.

With the arrival of an increasing number of Franciscan missionaries in the late 1580s, another important element was added to the Spanish colonial population of La Florida. Missions were established among the eastern Timucuan Indians around St. Augustine and northward into Guale Province. The church of Nuestra Señora de la Concepción in St. Augustine served as the headquarters of Franciscan activity in Florida from 1588 until 1763. This was the site where incoming friars were trained, provisions were stored and distributed, and ill friars were cared for.

Intermarriage between Spaniards and natives had long been encouraged by the Crown as a means of cementing Spanish-Indian relations. The marriage of Doña Maria Melendez, chieftain of the village of Nombre de Dios, north of St. Augustine, to a Spanish soldier and her conversion to Catholicism were instrumental in extending European influence among the Timucuan Indians.

By the first decades of the seventeenth century, a *criollo* (American-born Spaniard) class had emerged with quite different aspirations from that

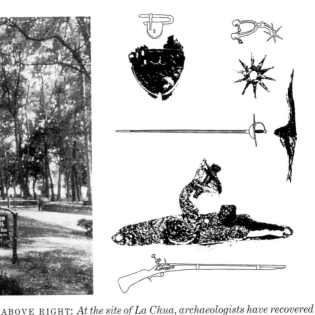

Located just north of St. Augustine, the village of Nombre de Dios was one of the many eastern Timucuan settlements transformed by the missionizing activity of the Franciscans. Their efforts are not entirely forgotten. This Spanish-style chapel was erected by a local congregation in 1915 to commemorate the three hundred and fiftieth anniversary of the landing of Pedro Menéndez de Avilés.

ABOVE RIGHT: At the site of La Chua, archaeologists have recovered some characteristic artifacts of seventeenth-century cattle ranching: a padlock, spur, sword cross guard, and lock assembly from a flintlock. Granted to the well-connected Menéndez-Marquez family, La Chua was one of the most important cattle ranches in North Florida. Its name is preserved in the modern city and county of Alachua.

RIGHT, CENTER AND BOTTOM: Though archaeological research at the site of San Luis de Talimali in the Appalachee Province has shown that the outward appearance of criollo farmsteads contrasted sharply with those of aristocratic landowners in Spain. Remains of luxury goods such as jet amulets, cut-glass pendants, silver sequins, and silk embroidery thread indicate a desire for high-status European styles.

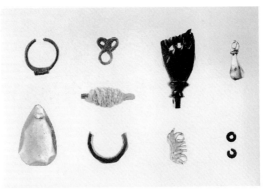

of the original Spanish community. They wanted to be part of a landed aristocracy, not government officials—to enjoy a more "noble" way of life. Influential Hispanic families therefore secured land grants, and by the mid-seventeenth century much of north Florida had been parceled off to influential *criollos* as cattle ranches and farms. Direct trade contacts with Caribbean suppliers along the Suwanee and St. Mark's rivers provided the colonists in prosperous areas of Florida with access to a range of luxury goods and enabled them to create a unique composite society that imposed medieval Spanish traditions on the human and natural landscape of La Florida.

■ BONNIE G. McEWAN
Florida Bureau of Archaeological Research

THE CARIBBEAN: *Pirates and Trade*

The word *pirate* conjures up vivid images in the modern psyche, and many of the popular stereotypes do have a basis in fact. The pirates of the Caribbean did fight with cutlasses, drink rum, and fly the "Jolly Roger." But the story goes much deeper than the ones depicted in *Captain Blood* or *Treasure Island.* European pirates played an important role as smugglers and mercenaries during the sixteenth and seventeenth centuries.

Spain's restrictive commercial policy was one of the causes. Merchants of other nations, excluded by decree from Spanish possessions, were forced to pursue illegal alternatives if they were to obtain any of the New World's wealth. At the same time, many Spanish colonists, denied access to scarce trade goods, were eager to engage in *rescate*, illegal trade, with smugglers known as buccaneers. The name of these smugglers was derived from the French word *boucan*, a grill used for smoking meat. Apparently the earliest European freebooters in the Caribbean hunted wild cattle and pigs on the northern coast of Hispaniola and began trading cooked meat and hides to passing ships. The level of smuggling by the *boucaniers* steadily expanded during the sixteenth century, involving Por-

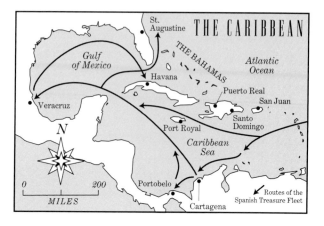

tuguese, French, English, and Dutch mariners. Eventually, the buccaneers began to prey on Spanish ships and settlements rather than trade with them.

The response of the Spanish Crown was predictable. In 1542, Spain started shipping its goods to and from the New World in large convoys of merchant vessels accompanied by heavily armed galleons. Key points such as Santo Domingo, Cartagena, Havana, San Juan, and St. Augustine were fortified against pirate attack. Yet this system of defenses was expensive to maintain and was not

LEFT: *Isolated inlets and deserted stretches of coastline like this one at Coquina Beach, Florida—just south of St. Augustine—provided convenient bases for smuggling and attacks against Spanish shipping by sixteenth- and seventeenth-century buccaneers.*

FACING PAGE, BOTTOM LEFT: *Spanish bullion, mined by native slave labor and minted in the New World, was the lure for attacks on Spanish treasure fleets.*

completely effective. Denied the opportunity to trade peacefully, the French corsair Jean Bontemps (aka Johnny Good Times) seized twelve vessels and burned the town of Puerto Real in 1566. In fact, under the pressure of pirates, Spain eventually abandoned its most vulnerable settlements in western Hispaniola in 1605.

As the struggle for control of the New World intensified, Spain's imperial rivals, France and England, began to sanction the activities of seagoing interlopers in the Caribbean. In 1585, Sir Francis Drake, supported by two thousand troops, sacked the heavily fortified ports of Santo Domingo and Cartagena before moving to attack St. Augustine. The loss in both commerce and prestige threatened Spain's New World dominion and its position in the European community. Thus, the pirates of the Caribbean—whether viewed as entrepreneurs in a global economy or as pawns of imperial ambitions—played a pivotal role in the colonial history of the New World during the sixteenth century.

■ CHARLES R. EWEN
East Carolina University

The most notorious of the Caribbean pirates terrorized civilian populations throughout the region. The threat they posed continued well into the eighteenth century. This engraving depicts the hanging of the notorious pirate Stede Bonnet in Charleston, South Carolina, in 1718.

RIGHT: *Many small Spanish colonial settlements in the Caribbean—as vulnerable points in a vast trade and extraction network—proved tempting targets to pirates of many other nations. This seventeenth-century woodcut depicts the sack of Puerto Real on Hispaniola.*

SPANISH MISSIONS: *Ideology and Space at Santa Catalina*

It has been said that since the fall of the Roman Empire no world power has been faced with so great a need to conquer, populate, and hold a vast new territory as the Spanish in the New World. Spain's intrusion into the Americas was a highly regimented endeavor, conditioned by social and economic policy ingrained deeply in the Spanish consciousness. The earliest Spanish conquests in the Caribbean and Mexico relied on an *encomienda* strategy—a system by which indigenous peoples were allocated as vassals to colonial officials to work on plantations or in mines. Spanish Florida, however, lacked the concentrated populations necessary to make the *encomienda* work. As a result, the mission outpost became the main instrument of territorial conquest and control throughout the Spanish borderlands of North America.

A mission comprised an entire settlement, not just religious edifices. Years of New World experience enabled Spanish friars to perfect their techniques of wholesale religious conversion, which also had far-reaching cultural and economic objectives: to raise native populations from their perceived "primitive state" to that of civilized and responsible subjects of the Spanish Crown. Scattered Native American groups were gathered in these new settlements and encouraged to lead a regimented life through religious instruction. No less important, they were made aware of new crops and farm animals and taught European methods of cultivation.

The mission of Santa Catalina de Guale, one of many founded in the sixteenth century, consisted of a central group of structures, including a church (*iglesia*), a residence (*convento*), and a communal kitchen (*cocina*), laid out along a rigid grid pattern. Recent archaeological excavations at the site have begun to delineate the layout of the sacred compound, consisting of a rectangular plaza flanked by the mission church and by the friary. Inside the *convento* were the refectory, cells, offices, and workshops. The kitchen and granary were separate buildings. Less is known about the *pueblo*, or native village, adjacent to the mission. It seems

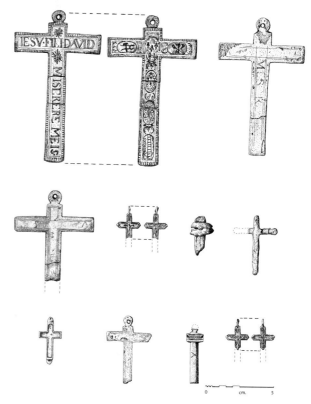

Among the artifacts found in the graves dug beneath the floor of the mission church at Santa Catalina are these small crosses, possibly belonging to members of the early Guale Christian community.

likely, however, that housing in the *pueblo* at Santa Catalina consisted of rectangular buildings, perhaps separated by streets.

The Spanish friars dispatched to frontier missions like Santa Catalina de Guale profoundly influenced religious and social conduct within the colony of La Florida, and also acted as primary agents in the establishment of new settlements, determining the nature of defensive installations and formulating agrarian policy. The missions of La Florida, though largely invisible today, had a lasting effect on the cultures of its native peoples—and on the course of its early colonial history.

■ DAVID HURST THOMAS
American Museum of Natural History

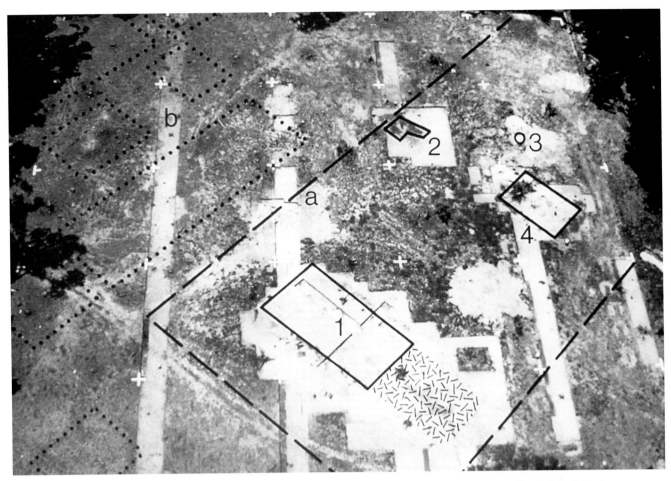

ABOVE: *Aerial view of the excavations at Santa Catalina de Guale. The main features shown are 1) mission church (iglesia) and associated cemetery; 2) kitchen (cocina); 3) mission well; and 4) priest's residence (convento). Traces of a possible fortification wall (a) surround the mission. The remains of the Guale pueblo are at the upper left (b).*

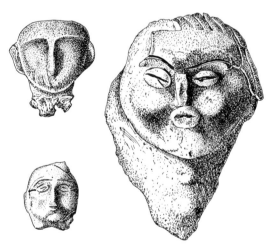

The native pottery figurines found at Santa Catalina testify to the continuation of Guale traditions—at least initially.

RIGHT: *A religious medal depicting Our Lady of Guadelupe, with the inscription* CONCEBIDA SIN PECADO ORIGINAL *("conceived without original sin"), is one of the many religious items discovered at the site of Santa Catalina by the excavations of the American Museum of Natural History.*

THE MIDDLE ATLANTIC: *Resistance to Foreign Colonies*

For generations, American schoolchildren have learned that their nation's history began with the successful settlement of North America by European colonists. But focusing only on the establishment of European colonies obscures two other important histories of the continent: the political history of Native Americans in the sixteenth century and the *unsuccessful* European attempts to colonize the Middle Atlantic Coast.

As the imperial powers of Europe were fighting among themselves to carve up the New World, several distinct Native American cultures were living in the area we now call the Middle Atlantic/Chesapeake region. Algonquian-speaking people occupied the coastal areas of modern Virginia and the Carolinas; Iroquoian groups lived inland in what is now southeastern Virginia; to the west, in the Piedmont and Blue Ridge Mountain area, were Siouan groups who were traditional enemies of the coastal Algonquians. All these groups were engaged in active and often-changing political relationships— sometimes trading, sometimes in alliance, and sometimes at war.

The Spanish were the first to try to stake a claim in the territory known to them as "Ajacan," apparently today's Virginia. In 1570, a small group of Spanish Jesuits established a mission about ten

A cheiff Lorde of Roanoac.   VII.

According to the account of Governor John White, who returned to the abandoned Roanoke Colony in 1590 with a relief convoy, the only evidence of the vanished English colonists were some buried chests and the tribal name CROATOAN *carved on a tree. While some early commentators suspected that a massacre had taken place, some historians have speculated that the colonists joined a nearby native people.*

miles above the mouth of the York River, across the peninsula from the site where Jamestown would eventually be built. Their guide was a young Powhatan man, kidnapped some years before and christened Don Luis de Velasco in Spain. Once back in his native land, he returned to live with his people. After only five months, in February 1571, the Powhatan—having apparently learned from Don Luis more about the Spaniards and their intentions—destroyed the Spanish mission and killed its inhabitants. The European intrusion was clearly an unwelcome one, to which the Powhatan people reacted swiftly, decisively, and successfully.

The "Lost Colony" of Roanoke in the Outer Banks of North Carolina—planned by Sir Walter Raleigh and established in 1585—is best seen as another example of the rejection of a European colonial effort. Here, too, it appears that the Algonquian chiefdoms of the Carolinas responded decisively. The Indian executioners—reflected by the enigmatic word CROATOAN carved into the bark of a tree at the site of the abandoned colony—are depicted as the unwitting, savage agents of moral retribution, not as representatives of a polity fully as jealous of its own power as were the courts of the Spanish and English queens.

The colony was found abandoned in 1590 by a returning English supply flotilla. Yet today, Roanoke has a place in American mythology—many ponder the "mysterious" disappearance of the "lost colonists." Like the Columbus story, the Roanoke myth features a visionary explorer, the dashing Raleigh, who gains the confidence of a powerful queen, Elizabeth.

This mythology makes the events of the colony appear almost mystical, outside the hands of human actors and the political events of the colonial encounter. But in the struggle for control of the Middle Atlantic coast, native groups were active players. Although ultimately unsuccessful in preserving their cultural and territorial sovereignty, the peoples of this region never passively accepted the direct challenges that confronted them.

■ JEFFREY L. HANTMAN
University of Virginia

THE GREAT LAKES: *Trade Goods, Warfare, and Expansion*

Few regions of the North American continent before 1492 had a more diverse human and natural landscape than those of the Great Lakes and the major rivers of the Midwest. Amid glacially scoured granite outcrops, isolated moose stood knee-deep in the boggy spruce and birch forests of the northern lake country. Vast herds of bison trampled the cane and pecan trees in shallow riverbottoms that crossed the more southern and western prairies. Farther east, deer peered across openings in the oaks along deep streams spilling from dark Appalachian forests of hickory and chestnut, beech and maple. In no other region of the country did Native cultures differ as much, nor did the conflicts with Euro-American cultures last longer.

Prior to European contact, the people of the ceremonial mound centers of the Mississippi and Ohio River valleys traded raw materials and ritual objects with the hundreds of fortified but agriculturally self-sufficient villages scattered in loose tribal confederations along the lakes and rivers between the Canadian tundra and the Carolinian

hardwood forests. And everywhere within this culturally diverse Great Lakes region were the beaver, muskrats, and other small mammals whose thick fur provided the attraction to European traders, and which, within centuries, would lead to the creation of an image of a homogenized pan-Indian culture in thrall to the Euro-American political economy.

By the late 1550s, the native trading partners of the French post at Tadousac, two hundred miles up the St. Lawrence, were providing neighboring tribes not only with glass beads and pewter rings but with copper kettles, iron knives, axes, needles, fishhooks, and even firearms, on which they would shortly come to depend. In the summer of 1609, the ultimate stakes of the fur trade—and the power of a certain class of European trade goods—suddenly became clear to the Iroquois. The Frenchman Samuel Champlain and two compatriots accompanied a band of Algonquian-speaking allies across eastern Lake Ontario to attack a fortified Mohawk village near Nichols Pond, New York. Such raids had been conducted for generations along formal-

ized, agreed-upon lines: ritualized taunts, lightning attacks, and the counting of coup. Native warfare was almost a ceremony. But now, with the deadly fire of these Frenchmen's muskets trained on an Iroquois village, the conflict between Algonquians and Iroquois was no longer like either ritual or sport.

Seldom have three inaccurate muskets had greater effect. What began as a routine intertribal skirmish convinced the Iroquoians that the French were deadly enemies and that muskets were needed at once. Soon enough, the Dutch—bitter trade rivals of the French—were happy to provide them for enormous profit. And for the next two centuries, the cultural landscape of the Great Lakes was changed forever as the League of the Iroquois, well armed with muskets, expanded their control over vast fur-trading territories and remained implacable foes of the French.

■ DAVID S. BROSE
Royal Ontario Museum

ABOVE RIGHT, TOP: European kettles discovered by archaeologists at Native American burial sites. Though still out of direct contact with European explorers, hundreds of the Iroquoian-speaking Seneca buried between 1540 and 1580 in western New York had acquired such trade goods.

ABOVE RIGHT, CENTER: An imaginative European engraving portraying an attack against an Iroquoian longhouse village by Champlain and his Algonquian allies. The musket fire was a sign of things to come.

FACING PAGE: The reconstructed multifamily longhouses and palisade of the Lawson Site in southwest Ontario are typical of a fourteenth- to sixteenth-century Iroquoian village whose economy included farming, fishing, and hunting.

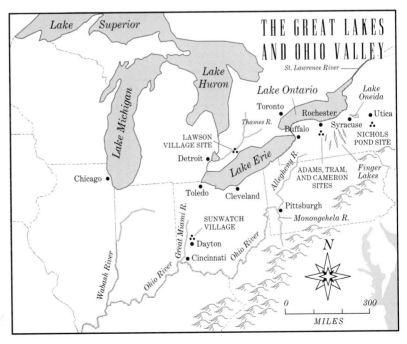

THE GREAT LAKES
AND OHIO VALLEY

Lake Superior

Lake Michigan

Lake Huron

Lake Erie

Lake Ontario

St. Lawrence River

Lake Oneida

Toronto

Rochester

Utica

Thames R.

Buffalo

Syracuse

NICHOLS POND SITE

LAWSON VILLAGE SITE

Detroit

Allegheny R.

ADAMS, TRAM, AND CAMERON SITES

Finger Lakes

Chicago

Toledo

Cleveland

Pittsburgh

Monongehela R.

Great Miami R.

SUNWATCH VILLAGE

Dayton

Cincinnati

Ohio River

Wabash River

Ohio River

N

0   300

MILES

SOUTHERN NEW ENGLAND: *Beaver, Wampum, and Profit*

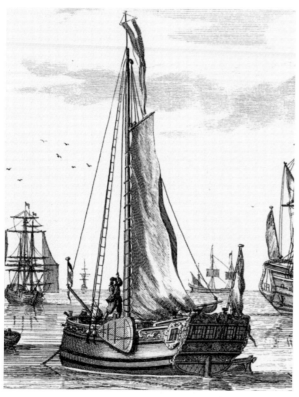

Block's vessel Onrust *was probably similar to the yacht shown at center here. Built after his ship* Tyiger *("Tiger") burned in New York Harbor, this small craft must have been quite seaworthy, for Block sailed it through Hell Gate and out into the uncharted waters off the coast of New England.*

The trading voyages of the Dutch along New England's southern coast in the early seventeenth century have much in common with the long processions of caravans that crossed the Sahara and Arabian deserts at the same time. Both served merchant capital: But in place of natural oases to temper their journeys and replenish their spirits, Dutch fur traders developed a network of rendezvous points, based on their intimate knowledge of the southern New England coastline and of the Hudson and Connecticut rivers, and on their close relationships with native people. Like merchant caravaneers of the desert, the Dutch understood that commercial success depended as much on the consent and cooperation of their hosts as it did on the vicissitudes of nature.

Following a route taken by the navigator Adriaen Block on his yacht *Onrust* ("Restless") in the spring of 1614, we leave Manhattan through the treacherous channel the Dutch called *Hellegat* (Hell Gate) and enter Long Island Sound. Sailing eastward, we can stop at some of the sheltered coves and small islands that served as places of rendezvous where Native Americans and Dutch initiated the protocol of trade, exchanging European cloth and manufactured goods for the thick pelts of the American beaver, so useful in the production of the stylish felt hats worn in Europe. This trade resulted in the virtual extinction of the beaver in southern New England and in a far-reaching change in the relationship of Native Americans and Europeans. Yet all that remains of those commercial interactions (about which conventional history has been conspicuously silent) is a lingering attachment to "Dutch-named" places along the coast.

Just beyond Old Dutch Neck on the Rhode Island coast is Fort Ninigret, a small earthwork, whose rectangular plan with five-sided bastions suggests a European design—and perhaps an association with Dutch traders. Yet this "fort" was apparently meant to protect goods rather than territorial claims. Archaeological evidence, including debris from wampum-making, has pointed to Native American occupation at the site. From Fort Ninigret, we enter Narragansett Bay through its western passage—what early navigators called "Sloop Bay"—to make landfall on "Dutch Island." This place, too, served as a rendezvous for Dutch traders in their dealings with native people. Yet there are no historic placards to recall the identities of those who participated in the trade. Only fragments of wampum beads, Dutch pottery, glass, and metal objects scattered along sites on the shores of Long Island Sound testify to the profitable trade that flourished here long before the first English plantations were established.

■ PATRICIA E. RUBERTONE
Brown University

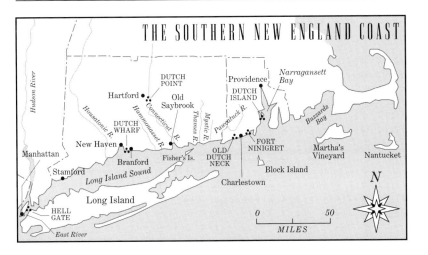

THE SOUTHERN NEW ENGLAND COAST

The object of the trade. A beaver from Conrad Gesner's Historia Animalium, published in Zurich in 1558.

ABOVE: *Ninigret II, son of the powerful sachem who forged close contacts with the Dutch traders.*

LEFT: *An aerial view of Fort Ninigret. The very name suggests an association with the native peoples of coastal New England. Ninigret was an important Niantic sachem who controlled this rich wampum-producing area in the seventeenth century. Some believe that he built the fort to protect his interests in trade.*

VIRGINIA: *Jamestown*

The site of the Jamestown colony is a prominent landmark on the Virginia landscape. For tourists, the emphasis in the public interpretation of this first permanent English colony in North America has traditionally been placed on peaceful coexistence between the Powhatan and the colonists. Yet too often the accommodation has been idealized or exaggerated, and the story of the native resistance to the expansion of the English colony ignored.

By the early seventeenth century, the Powhatan were a powerful network of small chiefdoms, held together by a paramount leader named Wahunsonacock, known to outsiders as Powhatan. There is little doubt that had he chosen to, Powhatan could easily have eliminated the tiny English colony, as had already occurred at Roanoke Island and at the ill-fated Spanish mission of Ajacan. Powhatan nevertheless entered into an alliance with the English.

One possible reason for this is that the English settlers brought with them a stock of copper trade items. These, the English had learned, could gain enormous goodwill from the local Algonquian chief, who depended on such prestige goods for his power and authority. The sudden inflow of English copper did, in fact, enhance Powhatan's power, and enabled him to expand his chiefdom. Relatively peaceful relations ensued, and Powhatan's alliance with the Jamestown colonists was further cemented by the marriage of his daughter, Pocahontas, to the Englishman John Rolfe.

Yet the requirements of the newly created English tobacco market soon created tension and imbalance in the relations between the English and Powhatan. As the Jamestown colony became more entrenched, more capable of seizing and controlling land for tobacco cultivation, Powhatan's ability to counter English demands diminished. After Powhatan's death in 1618, his brother Opechancanough succeeded him and led the Powhatan in futile armed rebellions against the English until his death in 1644. By 1677, the Powhatan of Virginia were no longer sovereign in their own land.

Land hunger for the cultivation of tobacco fueled conflict between the English and the Powhatan. This late-sixteenth-century engraving depicts one of the main strains of tobacco cultivated by the Jamestown colonists.

Opechancanough is rarely included in the Jamestown story. When he is mentioned, he is seen as an anomaly, a violent opponent of accommodation and peacefulness. Yet in a history that begins before 1607 and encompasses *both* Native and European viewpoints, such resistance to foreign colonization is not unusual. Both the Roanoke Colony and the Spanish mission in Ajacan—in the vicinity of Jamestown—were destroyed by native leaders before they could become a threat. Ironically, some historians have suggested that Opechancanough was none other than the young Native American man who accompanied the Jesuits to the ill-fated colony of Ajacan (thus theorizing that he was the mysterious "Don Luis," whose story is told on pages 68–69). Yet whether or not this is true, the two names Don Luis and Opechancanough are an important part of the rarely told history of native resistance to European colonization along the Middle Atlantic coast.

■ JEFFREY L. HANTMAN
University of Virginia

LEFT: *Visitors to Jamestown today can walk through a reconstructed Indian village. The emphasis in interpretation has long concentrated on the Powhatan technology and use of natural resources. Descriptions of their political and military conflicts with the English are usually avoided.*

BELOW: *This shell-embroidered deerskin robe is thought by many scholars to depict a paramount chief at the center of a network of smaller chiefdoms, that is, Powhatan's domain in 1607. The robe, in the possession of the Ashmolean Museum in Oxford, England, since the mid-seventeenth century, may have been part of a royal exchange between Powhatan and the governor of the English colony of Jamestown.*

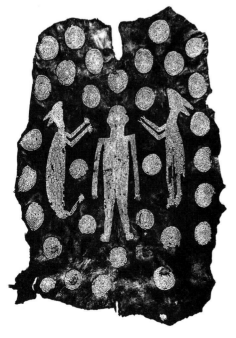

Captain John Smith of Jamestown threatens Opechancanough with a pistol, an illustration from Smith's Generall Historie of Virginia. *In the background are stylized scenes of massed native warriors and small groups of Englishmen driving them off with firearms. Incidents like these are largely forgotten in the popular version of Jamestown's history.*

3

COLONIAL AMERICA

1607–1780

WITH CONTRIBUTIONS BY

James A. Delle

Patricia Galloway

Russell G. Handsman

Randall H. McGuire

Patricia E. Rubertone

Terrance W. Epperson

Amy Elizabeth Grey

Elizabeth Kryder-Reid

Paul R. Mullins

John Seidel

We have been taught to think of the Colonial Period in American history as a time of exceptional freedom and unlimited opportunity for those Europeans who chose to come to the New World. From the founding of Jamestown in 1607, to the landing of the Pilgrims at Plymouth in 1620, to the settling of Massachusetts Bay by the Puritans a decade later, through the colonization of dozens of groups in major waves throughout the seventeenth and early eighteenth centuries, our schoolbooks extol the American wilderness as a place where congregations could choose their own form of worship and, hardly less important, where fortunes could be made. There is certainly a historical basis for this perception. Most of the non-enslaved poor people of the first generations of colonial immigrants to America nurtured the hope, largely justified, that with hard work and some luck, they too could achieve a measure of comfort and prosperity unattainable in their European homelands. But as this chapter will show, there were other realities, too.

A CRISIS OF OPPORTUNITY

Despite all the talk and speculation about the freedom of the "New World," those in positions of power in the colonial administrations of most colonies strove to create or re-create forms of hierarchy and exploitation such as feudalism, tenancy, and chattel slavery. No matter what individual colonists thought, the ruling elite of every European power saw North America primarily as a place where valuable natural or human resources could be utilized so as to sustain those in power at home. In the case of Spain, the Crown needed continual infusions of wealth in order to maintain its hold on a shrinking kingdom—now more a nation than a continental empire.

The increasingly disenfranchised Spanish nobility sought to bolster or re-create their power by establishing medieval-style fiefdoms in the New World. Other colonizing powers, like England and France, were anxious to make profits by importing raw material and exporting finished products; they

As part of its living history program, Plimoth Plantation in Plymouth, Massachusetts, attempts to re-create the original Pilgrim Colony seven years after its initial settlement in 1620. In marked contrast to later periods of New England colonial history, the first decades of the Plymouth Colony were characterized by a lack of class distinctions or overt conflict. Its transformation from religious community to commercial and agricultural colony created clearer social and economic hierarchies.

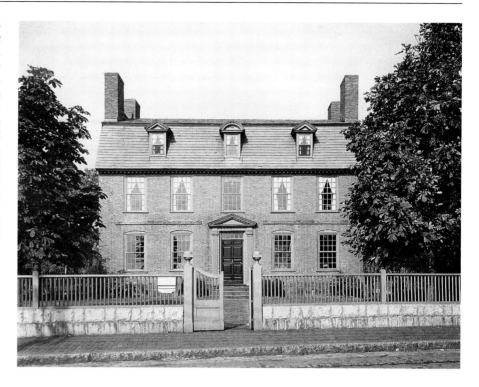

The Derby House in Salem Maritime National Historic Site, Salem, Massachusetts, constructed in 1761, represents Salem's heyday as a commercial port. Salem's waterfront embodies the outcome of transformations begun during the late seventeenth century, and the widespread adoption of the Georgian style reflected the shared class interests of local merchant capitalists. In the southern colonies, other architectural styles were used both to express and reinforce social hierarchy.

also sought to rid themselves of surplus population and religious dissenters. The Dutch began by concentrating almost entirely on trade. It's important to remember, therefore, that whatever hopes some colonists may have harbored, the transatlantic connections of every European colony were far stronger and persuasive than the possibility of escape from them.

Two factors initially limited efforts of the administrators and rulers of the American colonies to re-create the economic structures of European society, based as these had to be on the unequal distribution of wealth. First, high mortality rates of the European settlers and colonial officials delayed the formation of American-born elites and fostered a higher degree of social mobility than was common in any European homeland. The high death rates also caused a continuing shortage of wage laborers, despite the continuous importation of indentured workers and slaves. This shortage of labor made slaves a particularly profitable commodity. And with the profit motive never far from the minds of colonial merchants and traders, the commerce in captured, enslaved Africans became a major industry.

Second, some of the poorer European colonists were able to evade authority by migrating to the margins of the settled areas. Because the colonial authorities could closely control only relatively restricted areas immediately surrounding administrative centers, missions, and forts, those European settlers who established scattered farmsteads in remote areas were able to evade surveillance and control. More important, those who chose to opt out of European-controlled cash-crop economies could at least temporarily attain some measure of economic independence by growing or hunting most of their own food.

By the mid- to late-seventeenth century, however, dominant groups in most of the European colonies of North America were able to solidify their hold on people and resources. In New England, the Middle Atlantic, and the lower colonies, these groups created an artificial scarcity of land by declaring huge tracts of territory to be property of the colony; by requiring all settlers to possess formal, legal title to the fields they farmed; and by heightening tensions along a hostile "Indian frontier." The military activities of many colonial governments, meant to effect the expropriation of land from neighboring Native American peoples, often sparked a cycle of intensifying violence that effectively discouraged extensive westward movement of settlers.

Eventually, an awareness of the painful outcomes of colonization began to dawn on many of the European settlers as well. Although the timing and circumstances vary widely, we find expressions of bitter disappointment arising among many groups of European colonists within two or three generations after the initial settlement. As landholders, merchants, and credit and capital holders solidified their control over vital economic resources, less-wealthy colonists—particularly in the English colonies from New England to the Tidewater areas of the Chesapeake and even farther south—began to understand that their economic position was limited and that perhaps America was not the land of equal opportunity and unlimited freedom that many had imagined it to be. And as Terrance W. Epperson explains on pages 94–95, the restrictive policies of the colonial government of Virginia eventually provoked violent unrest among the poorer classes and growing population of slaves.

For Native Americans, the suggestion that the European colonization of North America offered "freedom" or that it was a harmless or beneficial extension of Western, Christian civilization was false. By the end of the seventeenth century, the gamble of trading natural resources for prestige goods, begun with the first contacts with the Europeans, caused the profound transformation of traditional ways of life. As Patricia Galloway explains on pages 96–97, the origins of many of the Native American tribes encountered by the first European explorers and settlers did not lie in the remote past, but were directly connected with the pressure of European trading and colonizing activities.

In the Southwest, the Spanish instituted a system of sweeping colonial discipline. While colonial history (and the trade and exploitation accompanying it) is often described from the view of the American Northeast—Virginia, New Amsterdam, and New England—in the Southwest, the process was the same. In the Sierra Madre of northern Mexico, rich deposits of silver were located by the first Spanish explorers and extracted by native slave labor under the supervision of subsequent generations of Spanish administrators, only to fill the holds of seventeenth- and eighteenth-century treasure galleons returning to Spain. As noted in the last chapter, this cash was spent in futile European wars designed to extend Spanish hegemony over Western Europe, suppress the rebellious Netherlands, and maintain the British Isles as an undeveloped peripheral region. Though none of these plans succeeded, the region we now call the "Southwest," which was actually considered the "Far North" to the Spanish administrators of Mexico, was colonized primarily to facilitate the extraction of newly discovered natural resources with poorly paid or slave labor—all for the benefit of the Spanish Crown.

In order to maintain a productive Native work force in the silver mines, the Spanish Crown used the cooperative Jesuit and Franciscan orders to gather the region's indigenous peoples into missions and to instruct them in Christianity. As in the Southeast, the priests forbade the practice of native religion, prohibited the observance of many native customs, and demanded regular church attendance and prayer. And as was already the case in the missions established in La Florida, one of the main objectives of this conversion process was the incorporation of the neophytes into the European economy as miners, laborers, or farm workers through ideological reeducation and the enforcement of a strict daily work routine. Yet the colonial exploitation was not established without opposition. On pages 98–99, Randall H. McGuire deals with violent resistance of the O'Odham people, the northernmost group to be missionized in western Mexico who rose in revolt against Jesuit missionaries and Spanish colonial administrators in 1695 and again in 1751.

The threat of rebellion, real or imagined, became a dominating image to the leaders of many American colonies. Patricia Rubertone describes on pages 100–101 the brutal campaign waged by the English colonists of New England to root out what they perceived to be a dangerous Native American conspiracy. The result was the near-complete destruction of native autonomy.

The adobe mission at Tumacacori, located in southeastern Arizona only eighteen miles from the Mexican border, was built in the 1730s by Jesuit missionaries and native workers. It was established at a site visited by Father Eusebio Kino, the founder of the region's mission system in 1691. Missions like this—and the system of domination they represented—were the focus of hostility during the O'Odham Revolt of 1695 and the Pima Revolt of 1731.

Eventually, the colonial authorities were able to reassert control over their territorial possessions and subject peoples, instituting laws that prohibited colonization without government sanction and, through strict economic control, forcing all but the most isolated colonists and native peoples into at least limited commodity production for the market. As Dr. Epperson stresses on pages 102–103, some of the ways in which aristocratic power was reasserted were symbolic—in public ceremonies and in architectural styles. Yet the control of the few over the many was real. In areas oriented toward the production of cash crops, particularly the tobacco-growing Chesapeake region, the wealthier planters who controlled not only land but also access to transatlantic shipping were able to control the availability of credit and the size of the labor pool.

That is an important part of the process that this chapter seeks to describe. In the English colonies along the Atlantic Coast, and in a quite different way in the Spanish domains at the western and southwestern ends of the future United States, there was a deeply felt crisis of opportunity during the colonial period. Although it is true that European colonization held out a promise of opportunity and enrichment for all involved (both Native American and colonist), it resulted in extremely unequal distribution of power and wealth. Yet the hard realities of extermination, exploitation, and disappointment of the colonial period have been almost totally masked by the nostalgic and idyllic images of Pilgrims, Thanksgiving, and Colonial Williamsburg that still dominate our current popular understanding.

THE IDEOLOGY OF THE GARDEN IN THE WILDERNESS

The metaphor of turning the wilderness into a garden was a powerful image in the American colonies and, later, in the newly established United States. Timothy Dwight, author, traveler, and president of Yale College in 1798, described the surroundings of Boston in this way:

A person who has extensively seen the efforts of the New England people in colonizing new countries, cannot fail of being forcibly struck by their enterprise, industry and perseverance. . . . I have passed the dwellings of several hundred thousand of these people, erected on ground which in 1760, was an absolute wilderness. A large part of these tracts they have already converted into fruitful fields; covered it with productive farms; surrounded it with comfortable and in many cases with handsome houses. Considerable tracts I have traced through their whole progress from a desert to a garden; and have literally beheld the wilderness blossom as the rose.

This turn of speech, so poetic and appealing to many, concealed a process of inexorable destruction. For the "desert" transformed into the "garden" was not an untamed wilderness crying out for the pruning hand of the gardener, but the homeland of many native peoples whose use of the land was disregarded by the arriving Europeans and whose physical presence was progressively constricted—and in many cases wiped out. On pages 112–113, Russell G. Handsman describes the particularly instructive case of the colony of Connecticut. Although the English colonists lived at first primarily along the coast and in the broad valley of the

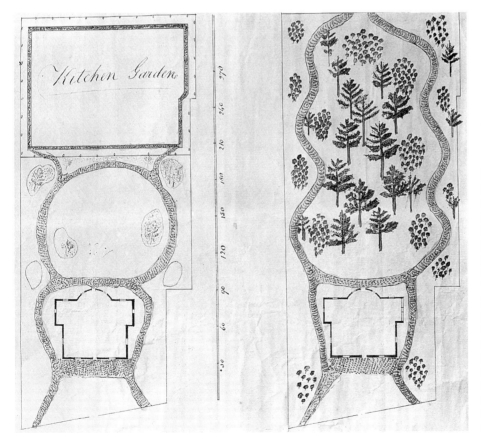

Elias Hasket Derby estate. Shown here are two late-eighteenth-century plans for the layout of grounds for the Elias Hasket Derby estate in Salem, Massachusetts. One plan utilizes geometrically regular lines while the more "naturalistic" style uses serpentine lines and irregular plantings. The contemporaneity of the two drawings suggests that there was a great deal of latitude in the supposedly sequential development of garden styles from regular to irregular. For examples of other formal gardens, see pages 104–105.

Thomas Jefferson's estate at Monticello, constructed in the late eighteenth century in the Palladian style, was designed by the President to be a ferme ornee, *or ornamented farm, where the useful parts of the working plantation were integrated with ornamental elements. Areas of work and leisure, production and consumption, were integrated so that the useful was beautiful and the beautiful useful. Like the residences of many other eighteenth-century planters, Monticello was meant to express the power and rationality of its owner.*

Connecticut River, by 1700, affordable land was becoming scarce. Thus was created another example of the "crisis of opportunity" already seen in other parts of colonial North America—this one resolved at the expense of the area's Native American population.

Native American fields, as far as Englishmen were concerned, were not "gardens." A garden, in the consciousness of the colonial settlers of North America, referred to the pastoral ideal of the European, and more specifically English, countryside. It alluded to the Edenlike possibili-

ties of a virginal "New World." There, the imposition of order on nature was the hallmark of civilization and the power over nature was often expressed in the art and science of garden construction. On pages 104–105, Elizabeth Kryder-Reid explores the significance of the elaborate formal gardens that became important status symbols for the emerging merchant aristocracy of the English colonies.

The idea of an ordered landscape, whether it was a carefully manicured garden, the regular grid of the streets in a newly established town, the rectangular plots of divided fields, maps of clear-cut colonial frontiers, or even carefully drawn charts of the heavens, all worked to reinforce the idea that nature and daily social life were inherently ordered and, through the extension of European civilization to America, that order could be discovered and applied to improving society. This ideology meant land could be an adjunct to social and economic position and could be seen as an outward sign of social prominence. Land defined this

way could be bought, sold, or changed because it was like any other part of nature; it was an object and could be possessed. From the moment of European settlement, land became either state property or personal property. Europeans saw land in terms of value and profit, often short-term profit, with no regard for the regeneration or replenishment of resources. In other words, land became a commodity.

No Native American group treated land like this. For most, the people belonged to the land, not the reverse. As Dr. Handsman stresses, in the case of the native peoples of southern New England, the human landscape was a mosaic of small wigwam settlements, sacred spaces including cemeteries, fishing sites used for generations, and meeting places where respected clan leaders lived. Networks of paths linked native peoples to their kin who lived throughout this homeland and to nearby territories. Scattered across the land were ancestral cornfields. Then more than five hundred years old, these fields, dozens of acres in extent, were worked communally by local communities and clans. For Europeans, land was never consid-

ered to be communal property, except in very rare circumstances like New England commons or some later American utopias. The differences between European and Native American ways of seeing land could not have been more profound. Yet the difference is still taught in our museums and texts as a childlike mistake on the part of the American Indians, not as a profoundly different concept.

Space, time, and person are cultural definitions, that is, they are coined and taught by society, and vary from one group to another. When land and resources are regarded as improvable, God's gift subject to "man's" domain, or as spaces and conditions to be civilized or to be made part of Christendom, land comes to be seen as exploitable. The invention of ideologies, of images of Eden, wilderness and frontier makes it difficult to recognize the conflict between deed and excuse and the dynamic—not accidental—relationships between the two. It also prevents an understanding of what happened as Europeans made a commodity of American space, an understanding that is explored by James Delle on pages 106–107.

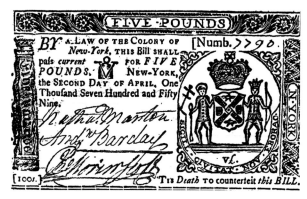

By the eighteenth century, the American colonial economy was becoming increasingly monetized. The earlier practice of paying taxes and repaying loans with agricultural produce had given way to the use of coins and banknotes. This was part of a larger economic transformation: the expansion of mercantile capitalism. Seen here is mid-eighteenth-century five-pound note from the New York colony.

THE CULTURE OF MERCANTILE CAPITALISM

In Colonial America, the concepts of wilderness and gardens, parks, commons, land speculation, ground rents, mortgages, and appreciation of property all were enshrined in the sacred idea of private property, which frequently meant land. As we have seen, the buying and selling of land, people, and things was at the core of the social order that Europeans introduced into North America. There is an even larger context: This social and economic order was something relatively new in Europe as well. It emerged between the fifteenth and eighteenth centuries, as the old feudal order—characterized by static hierarchies of lay nobility and clerics and faith in the immutability of God's Creation—gradually began to give way to faith in human reason and our ability (even responsibility) to change the world.

Since social, political, and economic interactions between "civilized" people became the center point of this new mode of thinking and acting, important parts of both the "New" and "Old" worlds began to be organized in a radically different way. Mercantile Capitalism, a culture full of sets of ideas, behaviors, and definitions of society's most basic mechanisms, was accepted and learned, became the root ideology of modern social norms, and remains the basis for the unwritten rules by which our society continues to be regulated.

In essence, the basic rule that Europe began to apply both to itself and to its colonial possessions was that everything had a value, if exchanged. Potentially, that value could be realized, or collected, as profit. Products and human labor could be bought and sold and the value derived from those transactions could be separated from those who made the item or performed the labor. Once products began to be made for a market—as opposed to home use—and people began to work for hire, they did not produce solely for their own use or good. What they produced as employees also created a profit for somebody else.

The idea of the market and commodities for sale in it was not fully expressed until the eighteenth century, but it was already in operation by the time of European expansion. One of its principles was the law of supply and demand. This meant that little could be said to be of ultimate or, alternatively, no value—because all goods were subject to the market, where supply met demand. That also applied, beginning to a significant

Spoons show two processes: mass production of tableware and mass distribution of the rules for their use. They could be purchased cheaply and in sets, and they were tied to rules such as "do not drip from your spoon," "do not make a sucking noise when using your spoon," and "push your spoon away from you, not toward you." Pictured here is a nineteenth-century spoon from excavations directed by Anne E. Yentsch at Reynold's Tavern in Annapolis, Maryland.

By the late eighteenth century, all kinds of dishes—like this Wedgwood cup and saucer and salt-glazed stoneware plate—were made to be collected over time as sets. The pathbreaking innovation here was the production of the kind of person who would use them correctly at home and thus learn to be correct everyplace else.

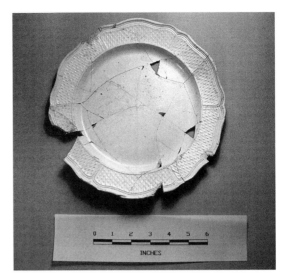

degree in the Colonial period, to the value of people's skills.

While people today rarely think of their labor as subject to the market (since we tend to see our worth as established by our own earned individual merit), our specific traits like strength, age, experience and so forth are, in fact, the commodities that we have for sale, which others buy and sell. And since the profits made by many manufacturers and employers in the expanding urban centers of Colonial America depended in large measure on the cheapness of the labor they employed, wealth was almost always unevenly distributed. The social and economic differentiation between employers and employees inevitably created groups of rich and poor.

The market—a search for products bought and sold for profit—knew no limits, because the search for profit knew none. Nor was it is supposed to, because it was argued to be beneficial. A whole continent was for sale, even though its original peoples never saw it that way. And, in addition, millions of people in Africa were bought and sold explicitly to be turned into slaves in the New World.

The developing capitalist market in Colonial America sold products to consumers, but these people were not necessarily distinct from the people who worked to produce the very same goods. The material transformation of people's lives within the capitalist economy often happened and

still happens through the use of products—maps, clocks, fast food—that ease old burdens but that also require new behaviors. A good example is the dramatic transformation of mealtime behavior in Colonial America. When people adopted the use of individual place settings instead of sharing common plates, bowls, and utensils and when they began to sit in chairs rather than share benches, they implicitly defined themselves more as individuals and less as members of families or communities. New houses of the late seventeenth and eighteenth centuries were also compartmentalized, both in reflection and reinforcement of the varying uses and separate domestic tasks inside the home that were distinguished clearly for the first time. Bedrooms, dining rooms, kitchens, sitting rooms, and workrooms were defined, where in an earlier era there were only large common spaces for the entire family.

Even though this is a book about material culture and archaeology, things—in themselves—are not its object. We want to see how in the economic system brought to America by Europeans, people were meant to produce profit. Their labor was crucial, even more than the products that they made. And as Paul R. Mullins discusses on pages 108–109, their skills and work habits were sold and bought as though they *were* things. Through the discipline of the body by using material culture and disciplines of the mind that went with the new things, colonizing Europeans redefined reality for themselves and everyone whose lives, land, or resources they touched.

Another important innovation in this period was a new understanding of childhood and the role of children, a theme that Amy Grey explores on pages 110–111. From an earlier conception of children as full-fledged members of their families and communities, childhood in the eighteenth century and thereafter was transformed into a period of preparation—a stage of growth and maturation that was distinct from "adult life," yet which prepared one for adulthood by teaching the rules and behaviors appropriate and necessary to full participation in the world of capitalism.

This book features children and women and Native Americans and African Americans because they were deeply and irretrievably affected by the market and by the transformation of land and labor into commodities. African Americans were themselves seen as actual commodities, bought and sold as slaves. Native Americans stood in the way of capitalism's need to make land into a resource for the market because they occupied it and because they had no notion of selling it. Since they were out-

side the capitalist system and usually could not comprehend it or would not participate in its processes, they were excoriated, exterminated, or pushed into reservations. People who were unwilling to participate in the market could not be left alone.

Thus, these influential elements—a market, a view of objects and labor as commodities, and social classes—were thought by its defenders to produce great wealth for all of the many people influenced by mercantile capitalism. Yet the assertion that capitalism produced widespread wealth and that the wealth (and consequent harmony) trickled down to everybody is ideology. Even today there is a tense contradiction, as in the Colonial period, between the harmony such a system claims to produce and the social instability that a society based on profit inevitably creates.

RESISTANCE

As pervasive as these new structures of life may have seemed to some Europeans, they were not passively accepted by all peoples on whom they

The image of Native Americans in the colonial period as a threatening, aggressive presence is expressed in this mid-nineteenth-century illustration. Despite the one-sided portrayal, threats and aggressiveness were more often characteristic of the behavior of the European colonists—as amply demonstrated in the Pequot War of 1637 and King Philip's War of 1675–1676.

Violent rebellion was the last and most desperate means of resistance available to American slaves. More common—and more subtle—strategies for personal survival and independence were developed in the course of everyday life and work. Pictured here is a scene of late-eighteenth-century slave life entitled Overseer Doing His Duty, *by Benjamin Henry Latrobe.*

were imposed. Serfdom, slavery, and killing working conditions are similar in all colonial circumstances and, indeed, exist wherever the cruder forms of profit-making appear. Sometimes expressions of resistance to these conditions had to be hidden; sometimes they were overt. Most discussions of slave opposition to captivity in the American colonial and antebellum periods focus on armed insurrections, large-scale revolts, and overt violence. The point we want to stress here is that when such slave or colonial revolts are included in our traditional histories, they are inevitably depicted as savage attacks on the public good and always without benefit for the rebels. Yet armed insurrections like the one at the Stono River in

South Carolina in 1739 (and the later ones at Pointe Coupee, Louisiana, in 1795 and 1811, and the rebellion led by Nat Turner in Southampton County, Virginia, in 1831) are unmistakable expressions of resistances to a system that exploited people as private property. Efforts of this sort proved to be disastrous failures in which the rebels and their leaders were captured and killed. And while plantation owners and slave traders certainly became more paranoid in the wake of these rebellions, their power, position, and profits were never seriously threatened.

In fact, the flash points of anger and frustration signaled by overt slave hostility deflect our attention away from a more persistent and successful type of slave protest: the day-to-day resistance carried out during the conduct of their work. Within the context of daily routines, slaves developed an elaborate strategy that allowed them to continually oppose their masters' authority. Their repertoire of tactics included feigned sickness, shrinking from assigned tasks, foot-dragging, feigned ignorance, stealing, lying, deception, sabotage, arson, and running away. A slave could select from among these so-called "weapons of the weak" the response that best suited a particular situation, and over time these individual acts of resistance would crystallize into a system of consistent and effective opposition.

Indirect, yet powerful resistance can also be seen by "invisible" populations like the Native American peoples of New England—supposedly wiped out or forced out by disease and the military confrontations of the early colonial period. As we've seen, the westward territorial expansion of the European colonies along the Atlantic Coast was relentless, but it was never complete. Though successive generations of European colonists, driven by their own crisis of land speculation and population growth, appropriated parts of ancestral homelands and planting fields along the numerous "frontiers" of North America, Russell G. Handsman describes on pages 112–113 how many native peoples adopted subtle strategies of resistance to retain a living connection to their lands.

That is not to say that the resistance of indigenous peoples never took overtly violent forms. It did. We have already mentioned O'Odham revolts in the Southwest, slave revolts in the South, and Native American resistance in New England. Resistance also arose among the Pueblos of New Mexico—yet it has been almost entirely ignored in the roster of official historical monuments and in the textbook versions of New Mexico's history. On pages 114–115, Randall H. McGuire chronicles the grim early history of the New Mexico colony, an island of Spanish settlement about five hundred miles from the northern border of New Spain, established in 1598 by Juan de Onate.

Accompanied by a few hundred Spanish soldiers and supported by Indian allies, he conquered a population of sixty thousand or more Pueblo Indians and executed a centralized plan of colonization that sought submission and tribute from the Pueblo tribes. Here too, the familiar story of ideological discipline—as well as physical discipline—unfolded. The Franciscan friars who arrived with Onate set up churches in the pueblos and tried to prohibit native beliefs and religious practices.

They whipped or executed religious leaders publicly and burned their kivas (sacred rooms). The Pueblo Indians suffered; their population was decimated by European diseases, declining to about twenty thousand in forty-six villages by 1680.

In that year, the Pueblos revolted. As Dr. McGuire relates in his account of the suppression of that revolt, the aftermath reactions of the survivors varied widely. Some welcomed the Spanish back, while others mounted stiff resistance or fled west. Yet even within the newly reestablished colony of New Mexico, conditions were changed. After 1694 the Spanish set up a new system of relations with the Pueblos—moderating the exploitation of Pueblo labor and allowing the Indians to practice their own religion as long as they also observed Christian rites.

We bring up these largely forgotten instances of resistance because their common causes, expressions, and outcomes help us to understand the fabric of a society based on making money. Profit making makes classes, and those classes of rich and poor, often separated along ethnic lines, do not always get along. And some of them resist and refuse to accommodate. These instances thus provide us with a way of seeing our lifestyles, economy, and culture from the outside.

Thus, we may question the deeply held belief that the structure of American society as Euro-

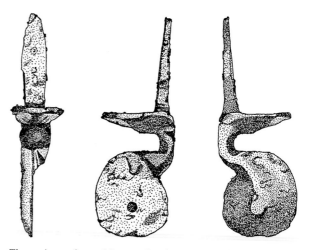

Three views of a cocking mechanism excavated at Pluckemin, from an American-made, mass-produced flintlock musket.

peans founded it was more or less inevitable and more or less good and harmonious. We are certainly surrounded by examples of its success and productivity. These are neither lies nor illusions but they are only part of the story. The single-minded search for profit by some people routinely generates resistance to it by others. And in the actions and expressions of its critics lie piercing descriptions of the reality in which we live every day.

THE LIBERTY-LOVING INDIVIDUAL

At the center of our images of the American Revolution is the image of the citizen-soldier, exemplified by the militia and personified by the figure of the Minuteman. This image has had a long and deep hold on American perceptions, yet as John Seidel emphasizes on pages 116–117, the image does not do justice to the historical reality. In many important ways, Seidel stresses, the American colonial militia system was designed to protect the power and property of the wealthy and powerful, not merely the "public good." In fact, the military successes of the Continental Army may have been due less to the fighting spirit of the hastily mobilized militia forces than to a program of industrialization that took place on a scale rarely understood before recent archaeological excavations at Revolutionary War sites.

On pages 118–119, Dr. Seidel describes how the industrial capacity built up before and during the Revolution was very large and sophisticated and clearly was an important precursor to the ensuing Industrial Revolution. With the outbreak of the war, industrial capacity—based on the principles of capitalist enterprise—became increasingly critical to the American military. Its logistical and even strategic importance is underlined by the fact that industrial installations along the Atlantic seaboard were targets for continual attacks by the British. Farther inland, Hopewell Furnace in eastern Pennsylvania is representative of the many ironworking plantations that supplied material to the Continental Army and served as models for the postwar industrialization of the country. As Dr. Seidel

The statue entitled The Minute Man of Concord *by Daniel Chester French, placed at the site of the North Bridge at Concord, Massachusetts, in 1875, became one of the most familiar icons of the American Revolution for generations of schoolchildren. The romantic image of the citizen-soldier, however, obscures some important facets of America's revolutionary reality.*

describes, archaeology at the "Artillery Park" at Pluckemin, New Jersey, has shown how Americans developed logistical expertise and organized industrial production to meet wartime needs. And there were naturally some important social and cultural implications to this development.

One of those implications was the triumph of the ideology of individualism. Since around 1680 in New England or around 1720 in the Chesapeake region, some people began to see themselves as individuals endowed naturally with rights, including freedom, willpower, the ability to control circumstances and the obligation to do so, and the capacity to better one's self. If one could learn the order of the natural world, so the ideology ran, apply it to farming, shipping, or to oneself, natural betterment would occur. One could express one's own merit this way and earn a more secure place in society through the possession of skills, knowledge, or virtues—which all represented acquisitions, just like land, profit, or power. In this world view, individuals are "liberty loving" in the sense that they aspire to control their lives through the free exercise of their powers of choice.

In the material domain, this means an endless quest to acquire more and better possessions; in the mental, but no less real, domain, the individual must never stop growing, learning, seeking to develop himself or herself to satisfy the ever-changing personal ideals and goals trumpeted in the marketplace. The result is that "liberty-loving individuals" find it difficult to enjoy themselves as they are because they are always in pursuit of more and better, which they firmly believe they can, someday, obtain.

Despite this ideology of free individuals, a very different dynamic came to permeate social, economic, and political relations on the North American continent. Between all colonizing groups, and within them as well, fierce competition existed for sought-after resources, and especially over the means to get them. Dramatic differences quickly developed in wealth, work possibilities, and profit potential for the European colonists.

The fact is that all people were *not* considered to be individuals endowed with natural rights. Indians were seen as savage, uncivilized, cursed, lost, and inhuman. Africans were characterized as lazy, beastlike, and submissive. Women were weak, emotional, and irresponsible. The only major distinction between the various European attitudes toward such groups was between those who believed that they could be trained to act as "individuals" through intensive missionization, discipline, training—and those who were convinced that they were fundamentally incapable of improvement.

The ideology of the liberty-loving individual was manifested in many ways in Colonial America: in personal habits, economic life, educational patterns, and social rituals. Of course, only a small proportion of the population—white, male landowners and property owners—could fully enjoy the privileges of being an "individual." Pictured here is an eighteenth-century portrait of William Paca of Annapolis, Maryland, by Charles Willson Peale. The portrait shows Paca's most prized possessions: a formal garden, classical education, and taste.

Although the ideal of the liberty-loving individual has come to be a central value in American culture, it is important to keep in mind that its centrality is by no means universal. Human beings are everywhere sustained by dense webs of social relationships, and many other cultures value ties of kinship and community far more than individual autonomy. From the perspective of such cultures, therefore, the values of liberty and autonomy that we so highly prize might seem unusual, if not downright dangerous to family ties and religious and cultural traditions.

Individuals in American culture are thought to be naturally motivated to "pursue" property and happiness, and an individual's sense of self-worth is often closely related to his or her material success. Americans often define their "true" selves in terms of the consumer goods and experiences that they have come to possess. Yet it is important to remember that there are other cultures which, though individualistic in the sense of placing value on human liberty and autonomy, do not tie individualism to material possession as we do.

As critics of modern American society, beginning with Alexis de Tocqueville, have repeatedly pointed out, there is a contradiction between the liberty that we value and the conformity that materialistic individualism ironically seems to generate. It is the source of the familiar spectacle of American consumers ceaselessly attempting to validate their individuality by purchasing products and experiences that differentiate them slightly from their neighbors. It is also because of this ingrained conflict between conformity and the mask of individualism that we routinely engage in democratic elections in which viable candidates resemble one another more than they differ, and that the only choices that citizens routinely face begin and end with homogenized consumer products.

That is an important part of our inheritance from early American history, which must be seen as the ultimately successful expansion of a distinctive set of economic, social, and political behaviors across North America. All—or virtually all—of the peoples and groups who sought to resist this development have been either wiped out, segregated in inner cities and reservations, or gradually assimilated into the comfortable mainstream. Indeed, the shared ideology of the "liberty-loving individual," who willingly and skillfully participates in the market economy of buying and selling and profit and loss—not the Minuteman Statue on Lexington Green, or the supreme individual of Mount Vernon, or the unifying cry of "Liberty!"—might be considered the most significant, pervasive, and triumphant monument of the Colonial Period.

A CRISIS OF OPPORTUNITY
Economic Change and Popular Unrest in Virginia

From almost the moment of their founding, the Chesapeake colonies were overwhelmingly oriented toward the production and transatlantic export of tobacco. Most Europeans who came to the Chesapeake during the seventeenth century arrived as indentured servants who were obliged to toil in the fields for four to five years on behalf of whomever owned their contract. Before about 1670, those who were fortunate enough to survive the term of their indenture stood a fairly good chance of becoming freeholders in their own right. After that date, however, the "shortage" of land, often artificially produced by the government's restriction of settlement, in combination with sagging tobacco prices, severely limited social and economic opportunities.

Bacon's Rebellion (1676–1677) is often described as the most important social conflict in prerevolutionary America. It was waged in Virginia by an unlikely coalition of well-to-do frontier planters, small freeholders, indentured and recently freed servants, and slaves. Nathaniel Bacon (himself a fairly wealthy western planter) and his followers realized that Gov. William Berkeley's restrictive policy about settlement in the inland regions was designed in part to monopolize trade with Native Americans and to maintain high land prices in the tidewater region. In order to open the west for colonization, Bacon's initial hostilities were directed at the Native Americans living on Virginia's frontier. Yet what began as a genocidal colonial war soon assumed the character of internal class struggle. In Bacon's words, "The poverty of the country is such that all power & Sway is got into the hands of the rich." Before they were subdued by English naval power, the "rebels" plundered and burned Jamestown (Virginia's first capital); Bacon declared himself General of Virginia and actually controlled the government for a short period. The response of the authorities was swift and violent. Governor

LEFT: *Built in 1655 by Arthur Allen, Bacon's Castle is the only surviving high Jacobean Manor house in North America. It is also the oldest extant house in Virginia. The Surry County property was occupied briefly by followers of Nathaniel Bacon during their 1676–1677 rebellion against the colonial government of Virginia and the ruling tidewater aristocracy.*

FACING PAGE, LEFT: *This 1718 plan of Annapolis shows the Maryland capital as it was designed in 1694 by Sir Francis Nicholson. Streets radiate from State and Church Circles (locations of the statehouse and the Anglican Church), orienting all eyes to the twin centers of state authority. When Nicholson later designed Williamsburg, he used a cruciform pattern to achieve the same ends by placing the capital, governor's palace, and public hospital at the ends of the arms, connected not just by streets designed for walking but for looking at powerful places as well.*

Berkeley executed fourteen Virginians for participation in the rebellion. Bacon himself died a fugitive.

This was only the beginning of a reassertion of imperial rule. During the late seventeenth and early eighteenth centuries the English monarchy made a conscious effort to solidify its control throughout the empire. One of the key players in this process was Francis Nicholson (1655–1728), whose tour of duty included North Africa, New York, Virginia, Maryland, Nova Scotia, and South Carolina. As governor of Maryland, Nicholson directed the transfer of the capital from St. Mary's City to Annapolis in 1694. Similarly, as governor of Virginia, Nicholson designed the new capital city at Williamsburg in 1699. The street plans and names of both were deliberately designed so as to reinforce the strong royal authority that the government desired.

■ TERRANCE W. EPPERSON
*Cultural Heritage Research Services, Inc.,
North Wales, Pennsylvania*

This reconstruction of a one-room tenant farmer's house at the "Godiah Spray" Plantation in Maryland—with its dirt floor and its chimney constructed of sticks and mud—was typical of the living conditions of most Marylanders and Virginians during the seventeenth and eighteenth centuries. In court documents of this period, the name "Godiah Spray" was the equivalent of the modern term "John Doe"; he was everyman, yet no one in particular. The site of which this house is a part is a composite reconstruction of a prosperous tobacco plantation of the 1670s, complete with owners' mansion, the tenant house, and two tobacco barns.

**ANNAPOLIS - 1718
J. STODDERT SURVEY**

HISTORIC ANNAPOLIS, INC.
194 PRINCE GEORGE STREET
ANNAPOLIS, MARYLAND 21401

FEBRUARY 2, 1983
BARBARA PACA

ABOVE: *As modern visitors approach the eighteenth-century Georgian mansion of Carter's Grove near Williamsburg, Virginia, they pass a reconstructed slave quarter where historical interpreters provide insight into the lives of the enslaved laborers who made the plantation economy possible. The willingness to provide visitors with a glimpse at the poverty and injustice of slave life represents at least the beginning of a new awareness of the social tensions of the colonial period.*

TRIBES, TRADE, AND COLONIAL WARFARE
The Rise of the Choctaw Confederacy

The origin of the many native peoples encountered by the early European explorers of North America—and the precise relationship of these peoples to the prehistoric populations of the continent—was long a matter of considerable historical debate. Yet it is now clear through archaeology and ethnology that the emergence of the historic tribes was closely connected to the spread of epidemics of European-borne diseases that decimated native populations throughout the continent. The case of the Choctaw, who appeared for the first time in Spanish documents of the late sixteenth century as inhabitants of the area west of Mobile Bay, is an example of this process of the creation of ethnic identity.

Though the prehistoric peoples of the Southeast had developed a complex culture known as the Mississippian, based on intensive agriculture and regulated through large ceremonial centers, the drastic population losses caused by the epidemics destroyed this way of life. Scattered groups of survivors gradually coalesced into new peoples in order to maintain their way of life. Thus, by around 1700, the Choctaw were settled in present-day Mississippi and Alabama and were functioning as a single entity in order to defend themselves from the slave-hunting raids by native allies of the English settlers of South Carolina. Their disparate origins were still evident in dialect variations in the Choctaw language.

The competition of the Europeans helped cement the solidarity of the emerging Choctaw confederacy. The French in Louisiana were anxious to gain native allies for themselves and they provided the Choctaw with firearms to fight off the English allies. And once they had armed the Choctaw, the French encouraged the Choctaw to expand the volume of deerskin trade. Though the French attempted to control the flow of this trade through diplomatic relations with a single paramount chief, they eventually found that they had to deal with the divisional chiefs who represented the real power in the confederacy. In exchange for the

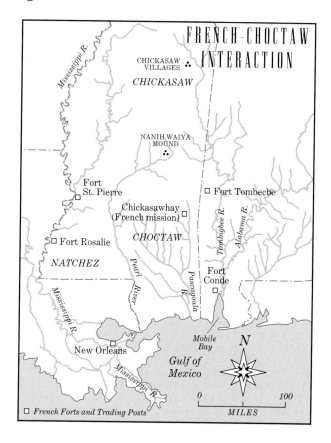

valuable deerskins, French traders presented these men with silver medals and gorgets and handsome uniforms of red cloth. The divisional chiefs, in turn, used the European trade items to build power and alliances for themselves and to maintain the autonomy of their divisions and villages within the confederacy.

Eventually, the Choctaw were drawn into the European colonial wars of the mid-eighteenth century. In 1736 and 1740, they joined with the French in an unsuccessful attempt to gain free passage for French traders through Chickasaw territory in present-day northern Mississippi and western Tennessee. After 1744, when a British naval blockade of Louisiana made it impossible for the French settlers to obtain trade goods for the Choctaw, a pro-British faction arose under the Choctaw war chief

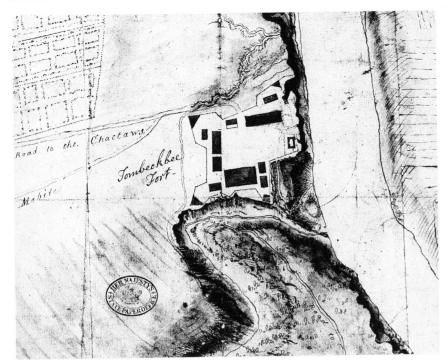

ABOVE: *Plan of Fort de Tombecbé, located southwest of present-day Tuscaloosa, Alabama, built by the French to support the 1736 Chickasaw War and maintained as a trading post for the Choctaw. After a 1737 drawing by Ignace François Broutin.*

TOP RIGHT: *Eighteenth-century French exchange goods like these were traded to Choctaw regional chiefs. Their status value among the Choctaw cemented ties both to the French and among the regional divisions of the Choctaw Confederacy.*

RIGHT: *A watercolor of a Choctaw warrior and two children, painted by the French artist Alexandre de Batz in the 1730s. The warrior's face is painted and he holds a staff with dried scalps. Though native dress and costumes were long thought to be of great antiquity, they were no less subject to change than those of the Europeans.*

Red Shoe. Still later, the Choctaw remained neutral during the American Revolution and their right to their territory was confirmed in a treaty with the United States in 1783. That treaty was rendered meaningless with the subsequent forced removal of most of the Choctaw Confederacy to the Oklahoma Territory in 1830. Yet even though scattered, the Choctaw people continued to maintain the ethnic identity that they had created for themselves in the earliest colonial period.

■ PATRICIA GALLOWAY
Mississippi Department of Archives and History

THE MISSION AS LABOR CAMP
Father Kino and the O'Odham Revolts

At the Spanish mission San Xavier del Bac, just a few miles south of Tucson, Arizona, tourists are told the story of how Jesuit Father Eusebio Kino missionized the O'Odham (consisting of the Pima and Papago peoples) from his arrival in the region in 1686 to his death in 1711. In this romantic tale, Native Americans welcomed the missionaries as agents of civilization bringing Christianity, domestic animals, and wheat. What the story does not tell is a less altruistic history of the missions depopulating the Southwest to make room for Spanish settlement and creating labor for Spanish enterprises—and how the O'Odham attempted to resist.

As in the earlier missions of Florida, the acceptance of Christianity by the native peoples came at a high price. In the case of the O'Odham, the Jesuits would build a church at a large native village and gather people from the surrounding countryside to support the mission with their labor. Each mission was self-contained, with its own blacksmith, weavers, masons, and carpenters. The Jesuits forbade the practice of native religion and many native customs and demanded regular church attendance and prayer. They expected the O'Odham converts to grow food for themselves and to labor three days a week for the mission. Discipline, often administered in the form of whippings, eventually caused the O'Odham to rebel.

In 1695 some O'Odham killed their overseers at the missions in Tubatama and Caborca. Despite attempts to calm the situation, open rebellion soon broke out. When Father Kino called the O'Odham to a reconciliation parley at the village of El Tupo, nervous Spanish soldiers fired on the crowd, sparking a widespread revolt that was suppressed with difficulty only after several months of bloodshed. And even then, the traditions of resistance among the O'Odham did not die. After Father Kino's death in 1711, the abuses against the native peoples continued. In 1751, the Pima, under the leadership of Luis Oacpicagigua, rose in rebellion, killing Spanish

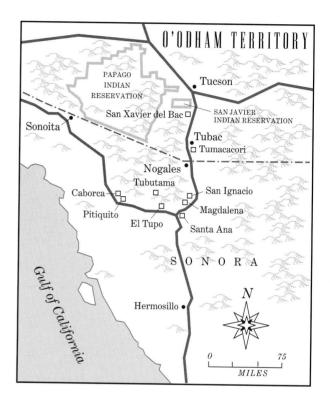

troops and attacking the mission at Tubutama in an attempt to eradicate Spanish and Jesuit influence in the area.

The 1751 rebellion failed and Oacpicagigua was captured and executed. The Spanish authorities acted quickly to reassert control over the native population, building a new presidio at Tubac, Arizona, to quell the sporadic O'Odham attacks that continued until 1760. Soon thereafter, the Jesuits clashed with secular authorities who coveted the mission lands and wanted mission Indians to work the mines and on the haciendas. In 1767, the Spanish Crown expelled the Jesuits from the empire. The Franciscans took over the O'Odham missions, which slowly declined until the Mexican government finally abolished them in the 1840s.

■ RANDALL H. McGUIRE
State University of New York at Binghamton

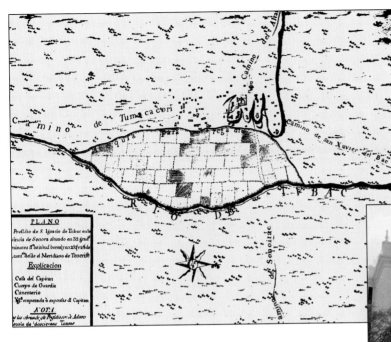

LEFT: *The Tubac presidio, as shown in this 1766 map, was never a walled fort, but instead a barracks with a cluster of buildings around it. It was established in 1752 to restore Spanish control over the native population. Today the fort is a state park and the surrounding town an artists' community. Archaeological excavations are now under way there.*

RIGHT: *At Magdalena, the faithful purchase small medals called* milagros, *such as this one, from the church and place them by Kino's grave to seek relief from physical, spiritual, and emotional afflictions. Periodically, the church gathers up the* milagros *for resale.*

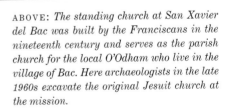

ABOVE: *The standing church at San Xavier del Bac was built by the Franciscans in the nineteenth century and serves as the parish church for the local O'Odham who live in the village of Bac. Here archaeologists in the late 1960s excavate the original Jesuit church at the mission.*

LEFT: *This nineteenth-century Franciscan church now stands in Tubatama, where in 1695 O'Odham rebels killed several Opata overseers who had been too zealous in whipping the mission Indians.*

THE SEARCH FOR PHILIP
King Philip's War in New England

King Philip's War began with Metacom, the Pokanoket sachem of all the Wampanoags whom the English called Philip. Like his name-sakes—Philip of Macedonia and the kings of Spain—Philip is an enigmatic figure described as wise and resourceful by some, and impetuous and foolhardy by those commenting on his role in seventeenth-century political affairs. In 1675, the English held him responsible for instigating a conspiracy aimed at destroying them. With their fears fueled by rumor and innuendo, King Philip (as he wished to be addressed by the English) became the scapegoat for the war that has come to bear his name.

We can trace the search for Philip from southeastern Massachusetts west and northward as far as the Hudson. Ironically, the trail ended in August 1676 in a swamp near Mount Hope, not far from where it had begun fourteen months earlier. En route there are recognized historic sites commemorating events of this often-forgotten American war. There are also places where there is something far more permanent than a historic marker to recall this struggle between Native Americans and the English. These are sites where neither tour guides nor illustrated texts describe the war and its heroes, yet which evoke indelible images of the hardships and injustices endured by New England's native people and serve as vivid reminders that for them the war never really ended.

There are wooded swamplands through which Philip moved undetected by the English. Here, where he found temporary sanctuary, are the remains of invisible campsites and fortifications long obscured. Occasionally there is the outline of an earthwork or the ruins of ancient defenses through the foliage and underbrush. Similar to the fortified garrison houses of the English, these served as places of refuge for native people during this time of siege. These murky enclaves became, like Philip himself, a symbol of resistance. It was

Smith's Castle at Cocumscussoc. As the military headquarters for the English forces during the winter campaign of 1675, this fortified garrison was later burned by Native American forces in retaliation for the attack at Great Swamp. Transformed over subsequent decades, the house and grounds of the postwar reconstruction seen here mask any traces of these early struggles between Native Americans and colonists.

King Philip. Portraits of King Philip are as varied as perceptions about his abilities and motivations. Ranging from grotesque caricatures to romanticized views, these images perpetuate the legends surrounding this historical figure.

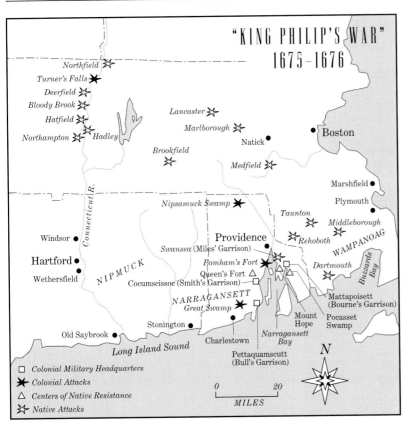

"KING PHILIP'S WAR"
1675-1676

Northfield
Turner's Falls
Deerfield
Bloody Brook
Hatfield
Northampton Hadley
Lancaster
Marlborough
Brookfield
Medfield
Natick
Boston
Marshfield
Plymouth
Nipsamuck Swamp
Taunton
Providence
Middleborough
Swansea (Miles' Garrison)
Rehoboth
WAMPANOAG
Pomham's Fort
Dartmouth
Buzzards Bay
Queen's Fort
Cocumscissoc (Smith's Garrison)
Mattapoisett (Bourne's Garrison)
NARRAGANSETT
Great Swamp
Mount Hope
Pocasset Swamp
Stonington
Old Saybrook
Charlestown
Narragansett Bay
Pettaquamscutt (Bull's Garrison)
N

Windsor
Hartford
Wethersfield
NIPMUCK
Connecticut R.

Long Island Sound

☐ Colonial Military Headquarters
✸ Colonial Attacks
△ Centers of Native Resistance
✸ Native Attacks

0   20
MILES

FACING PAGE, TOP: *Attack on Great Swamp, December 19, 1675. Some say that King Philip was among those who defended the Narragansett fort at the Great Swamp during the attack by the English. Many innocent civilians perished as the English forces in their retreat set fire to the wigwams located within the palisade. The precise site of this massacre remains a mystery to archaeologists.*

King Philip's Throne. This rock formation at Mount Hope is one of the many relics linked to King Philip. Like the objects and furnishings of royalty, it embodies beliefs about his kingly authority both for those who revere him as an ancestor and those who ridicule his power and influence.

from here that he steadfastly pursued the war against the English.

When he could run no more, Philip returned to Mount Hope. In his retreat, he continued to evade the English forces. Apprised of his tactics after months of relentless chase, they eventually tracked him down and assassinated him in the very environs that had sheltered and sustained him during the war. With his movements veiled in mystery, allusions to him, even posthumously, spread. Like other historic figures, his exile and his martyrdom transformed him into a legend that even today is kept alive through objects and places linked to his memory.

The fate of Philip's survivors was no less tragic than his own. War captives, including his wife and son, were sold into slavery; others were assigned to periods of indentured service in English households as part of their postwar rehabilitation. Small bands of starving and homeless natives embarked on an exodus that would last for decades. Some were quietly absorbed by villages that had remained neutral during the war and began to make the arduous adjustment to life as refugees in new homelands. But, like Philip before them, many scattered into the swamps where they attempted to escape the vengeance of their enemies. Living on the fringes of English settlements, they, too, resisted cultural annihilation. Their struggles for survival continued long after Philip's death.

■ PATRICIA E. RUBERTONE
Brown University

THE ARCHITECTURE OF POWER: *Class Identity and Class Conflict*

By the beginning of the eighteenth century, the tensions between rich and poor, slave and free, in many of the British colonies of America had erupted into open violence. In South Carolina, where enslaved Africans comprised the majority of the population in many districts, the dangers of open rebellion became frighteningly clear to the planter aristocracy with the bloody Stono Rebellion of 1739. This slave uprising west of Charleston was put down by the colonial militia, but fears of renewed revolts brought widespread panic and summary executions of suspected rebels in Charleston in 1740 and in New York and New Jersey, with the "Negro Plot" of 1741.

The need to reestablish order and reassert domination over the slave population and lower classes by the emerging American aristocracy also began to be expressed symbolically. Public respect for insti-

tutions such as the church and county courts was enforced through new laws and civil ceremonies. In many of the southern colonies, the Anglican Church, the established religion, was supported by a mandatory tax. Free whites who failed to attend public services were subject to fines. The county courts also became a place where the civil order was reinforced. In addition to being the scene of monthly court sessions where crimes were punished and civil disputes settled, the county courthouse was also the mustering place of the local militia, organized to protect the populace from threats both external and internal. Wealthier gentlemen served as officers—regardless of their military experience or prowess—and all other non-indentured white males were expected to serve.

The dominance of the wealthy planters in the South was also expressed by the architecture of

FACING PAGE: *Gunston Hall, the plantation home of George Mason (1725–1792), a delegate to the Constitutional Convention in 1787 and hailed today as the "Father of the Bill of Rights," was constructed in 1755 overlooking the Potomac River near the site of Mount Vernon. John Mason, son of George Mason, wrote a description of the plantation's formal landscape as well as the siting of domestic buildings and slave quarters, noting that "the Negro Quarters" were "masked by rows of large cherry and mulberry trees." Today, Gunston Hall is open to visitors. The plantation kitchen has been reconstructed, but other buildings have not been located.*

LEFT: *Drayton Hall, constructed in the Palladian style in 1738–1742 by the wealthy planter John Drayton near Charleston, South Carolina, now stands in splendid isolation, in contrast to its earlier appearance with flanker buildings, fences, and surrounding pastures for farm animals. An ongoing archaeological program is attempting to locate slave dwellings and other domestic structures that were part of the eighteenth-century plantation.*

ABOVE: *Christ Church, in Lancaster County, Virginia, was completed in 1734, with funds provided by Robert "King" Carter, one of the wealthiest and most powerful men in the colony. Though the establishment of Anglicanism as the colony's official religion presupposed a spiritual equality and commonality of interest among all worshipers, the seating arrangement within the church expressed an elaborate hierarchy of power and wealth.*

their homes, many of which began to be built in the Palladian style in the early eighteenth century. This architectural fashion, derived from the plans of the Italian Renaissance architect Andrea Palladio (1508–1580), had become extremely popular among the English upper classes; in its appropriation of the majesty of ancient Rome for modern homes and public buildings, it attempted to legitimize the social and political position of those who commissioned the architecture.

No less significant than the emphasis on certain structures and institutions was the conscious concealment of others. On many plantations, the slave quarters and outbuildings were positioned so as not to spoil the visitor's first view of the main residence. At the same time, when viewed from behind the facade of power, the grandeur of the residence in comparison to the poverty of the slave cabins was a symbolic way of expressing class hierarchy in the physical landscape and thereby discouraging rebellion against the "natural" order of things.

■ TERRANCE W. EPPERSON
Cultural Heritage Research Services, Inc., North Wales, Pennsylvania

The classical columns and pediment of the Gloucester County Courthouse, built in the mid-eighteenth century in Gloucester, Virginia, provides a visual similarity to the design of plantation mansions of the period. In addition to the dispensation of justice, monthly meetings of the Virginia courts provided an opportunity for white males of all classes to socialize and conduct business. The courthouse was also the mustering place of the county militia, though after 1757, nonenslaved "mulattoes, negroes and Indians" could no longer bear arms in the county militia. They were thus declared to be outside proper colonial society.

LIVING LANDSCAPES
Formal Gardens and the Ideology of Order

The ideology of opposition between "wilderness" and "civilization" was subtly yet powerfully expressed in the design and construction of the elaborate formal gardens that became popular among the aristocracy of gentlemen planters in the English colonies along the eastern seaboard in the 1700s. Many of these extensive gardens are known from contemporary paintings and plans, and many others have been lovingly preserved or re-created by local historical associations. They were geometrically regular, often terraced, and designed with a sophisticated control of lines of sight, both in and out of the garden. Their overall character—with green lawns punctuated by angled slopes, bordering trees, and planting beds—offered visitors who wandered through them, or peered toward them from the outside, a vision of nature that was productive, harmonious, and controlled.

The florescence of this type of planned garden construction took place in the 1750s to 1790s, precisely when the colonial gentry began to challenge the authority of royal rule and were in turn being challenged by the underclasses' increasing clamor for prosperity. The gardens that upper-class families built for themselves along the eastern coast of North America can be seen not only as ornaments but as advertisements of their wealth, their taste, and, most important, authority. In highly visible manner, the gentry's mastery of (or ability to hire professionals who were masters of) geometry, optics, botany, and astronomy, demonstrated in the elaborate plan and layout of these gardens, underlined their right to rule. By making themselves and their residences centerpieces in a formal display of natural and seemingly inevitable forces, the American colonial elite attempted to make their positions of power appear natural, inevitable, and therefore incontestable. Their gardens, like their use of the metaphor of civilizing the wilderness, presented a vision of elites in positions of authority, positions they sought to hold "naturally." The gardens were a claim by their builders or patrons that since they so

understood the natural basis for society, they could lead both the poor and themselves into a new naturally legitimate realm.

Landscape gardens surviving from the eighteenth and early nineteenth centuries dot the eastern seaboard. Most of the gardens remain in private hands, but a number are open to the public. Of these, the highest concentration is in the Chesapeake area, particularly along Virginia's James and Potomac rivers. Estates such as Carter's Grove, Middleton, Monticello, Montpelier, Mount Vernon, and the Paca House have used archaeology, documents, paintings, and photographs to reconstruct their original garden designs, plantings, and architectural elements. Some gardens have been transformed for other purposes: For instance, William Penn's estate Solitude is now the site of the Philadelphia Zoo. Other gardens, such as Morven, Mount Clare, and the Carroll Garden, have been studied extensively, but rather than being restored to a single period, they are today examples of the continuous evolution of living landscapes.

■ ELIZABETH KRYDER-REID
National Gallery of Art

This view of the Baltimore estate known as Bolton is interesting in part because it shows not only the beds and walks and plantings but also people walking through and working in the space. It also depicts the importance of three-dimensionality in these falling gardens, particularly for enhancing the view of the house and emphasizing its prominence atop the highest terrace.

Arc. Campbell

LEFT: *This detail of the Warner and Hanna plan of Baltimore shows a "four square" garden at the Campbell estate, Belmont, with an obelisk nearby. Such gardens and associated monuments came to be local landmarks and enhanced the social status of their owners.*

BELOW: *House and estate portraits were often commissioned by their owners for display within their new "country seats." This view painted on a chairback shows the falling garden at Mount Deposit, Baltimore. The slopes and terraces created a series of viewing platforms directing the gaze outward toward distant vistas and inward to focal points within the garden or to the house itself.*

FACING PAGE: *Box Grove. This vernacular garden of the late eighteenth century, whose precise location is unknown, was smaller in scale than the elite estates, but contained many of the same elements for turning "nature into art": a walled forecourt with a potted boxwood "grove," a pond, and, to the right, vines trained on an arbor.*

THE CONTROL OF SPACE: *Maps, Images, and Patterns*

Every map is created as an instrument of control. When a map is drawn and distributed, it creates in the mind of its readers a conception of space. During the period from 1607 to 1780, the definition of North America—the shape, size, and relationship of places—was created by Europeans as they laid claim to possession of those places. Even today, in some schoolbooks and historical atlases, the partition of the North American continent among competing European powers is taken as a historical fact, without serious consideration of the claims of Native American peoples, or of the fact that the European "control" of much of the continent was a political fiction until the nineteenth century.

The early maps drawn by Europeans often included illustrations of people and places as well as renditions of physical space. Part of the European strategy of domination was—as it had been in the earliest travel books about the "New World" in the sixteenth century—to draw native peoples as barbaric, cannibalistic beings, unworthy of the possession of the continent and needing to be "civilized" or else exterminated by Europeans. Maps were used to control not only conceptions of space and posses-

sion but through illustrations, the conception of indigenous peoples. European colonizers also used a second kind of map: the printed word on the page. Printed words organize thoughts in a directed linear fashion. When used in newspapers and broadsides, which at this time were read aloud in public as well as privately, they produce a mental (cognitive) map of things, thoughts, and ideas. The ability to print and distribute newspapers was thus the ability to direct people's thoughts in a specific direction. In the late seventeenth and eighteenth centuries, printers, publishers, and merchants created and distributed ideas about the newly developing mode of production known as mercantile capitalism. Ideas about this mode of production, when printed and read in newspapers, became part of the cognitive landscape. By the end of the colonial period, mercantile capitalism seemed as natural a part of the cognitive landscape as trees, rivers, churches, or barns were to the visual landscape.

This naturalization of the Euro-American social order was dependent on the segregation of social space. The dimensions and social space of the continents had to be controlled. As a result, space was

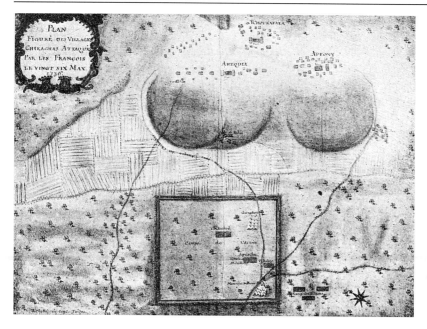

When the French marched against the Chickasaw in 1736 they camped with their Choctaw allies in a special precinct allotted within a marching camp that bears striking resemblance to the marching camps used by Roman armies. This contemporary French map of the battlefield contrasts the power and order of the French forces within their rectangular enclosure with the haphazard arrangement of the Chickasaw houses.

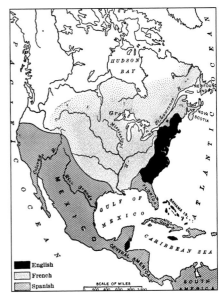

divided along lines defined by race, class, and gender. Increasingly ornate and larger buildings were created as the domain of elite European males. The exteriors of structures both represented and created the power relations between these elites and those they dominated. As Native Americans were pushed farther into the interior of the continent, the colonizers gained control of coastal North America. The space of tobacco and rice plantations became increasingly segregated between the villages of the enslaved Africans and the great houses of the white planters. Women were denied social space in public forums such as county courts, were denied property rights, and were further relegated to the domestic space of the kitchen.

The maintenance of the social order created by mercantile capitalism required that those whose labor and resources were being exploited accept this social order as part of the natural way of things. The European male elites legitimated the seizure of control over land, resources, and people by manipulating space, both physical and social. This manipulation incorporated the symbols of the social order—words, actions, and objects—into the landscape so that the capitalist social order would seem—and still seems—as natural as breathing.

■ JAMES A. DELLE
University of Massachusetts, Amherst

ABOVE LEFT: *North America was certainly not a virgin continent sitting vacant for European occupation. Nevertheless, European understanding of Native Americans and their space was often poor. This early rendition of a battle between the French and the Iroquois at what today is known as Lake Champlain inappropriately depicts naked Americans, hammocks, and palm trees.*

ABOVE RIGHT: *This illustration from an early-twentieth-century school atlas dramatically illustrates the extent of European claims to the space of North America. Notice that the space not claimed by any European power is left blank. No Native American occupation of this space, or any of North America, is recognized.*

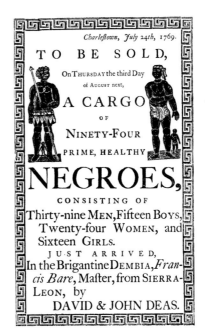

This 1769 broadside from Charleston (then called Charlestown), South Carolina, advertises the sale of men, women, and children forcibly taken from West Africa to work in the rice and indigo plantations of South Carolina. By the time of this sale, slavery was not simply an accepted institution; it was vital to the colonial economy. Broadsides and newspaper advertisements like this helped to legitimate the naturalness of buying and selling human beings—in precisely the same way that draft animals and farm equipment were bought and sold.

A PROFITABLE WORLD: *Personal Identity, Personal Discipline*

People produce profit, not things; their labor is key, not the commodities they make. Yet in the long term, capitalism has regarded people as having qualities like skills and work habits that should be bought and sold as though they, too, were commodities. These skills and habits were taught and self-taught in lessons, lectures, books, almanacs, newspapers, and a hundred other ways in the colonial period. Books and material culture promoted the new colonial understanding of people as profit-producers. And learning how to be punctual, well-groomed, obedient individuals helped to reduce workers to interchangeable parts in a vast machine of production. In other words, these routines transformed the workers themselves into commodities.

Endless how-to-do-it books told people how to eat; women how to be silent and subservient; men how to be numerate and good penmen; and everyone how to reason from empirical cause to effect, not on the basis of miraculous omens or wonderful events. The new rules of society produced behaviors that became progressively more firmly tied to economic standing, ethnicity, and linguistic boundaries. The rapidly expanding world of material culture—encompassing the dishes, knives, forks, razors, tea sets, and clocks that facilitated the new ways of behaving in public and private—introduced a profusion of symbols through which individuals were both differentiated and classified in the emerging capitalist society. And an individual's importance and value to the economy came to be signified by personal possessions and personal traits. The consumer demand for many of the new, mass-produced products could therefore be sustained and even increased by the manufacturers who sold them by linking their use to personal well-being and to professional and social success.

■ PAUL R. MULLINS
University of Massachusetts, Amherst

RIGHT: *Early toothbrushes—like these found at excavations at the site of Reynold's Tavern in Annapolis, Maryland—symbolize the new rules for personal hygiene that became increasingly pervasive in the eighteenth century.*

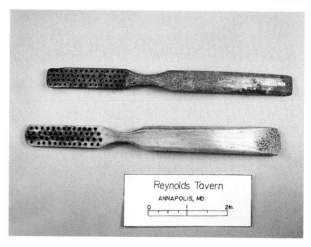

LEFT: *Rule-abiding people are produced in many small but systematized ways: eating habits, toilet training, tooth brushing, time telling, grooming. This late-seventeenth-century barber's bowl features an indented rim specially made to be tucked under the customer's chin. The customary routines of going to the barber and having one's face and hair groomed were accompanied by rules that were taught, learned, and followed.*

In colonial Massachusetts shortly after 1700 and by 1720 in Maryland and Virginia, an individual ate from his or her own plate, not from a common bowl; one used napkins, not the tablecloth or sleeve. One used fork, knife, and spoon in a given order for specified foods. One did not use fingers, but disciplined the mind in order to train the fingers to discriminate between tools applied to tasks over a given period for a known purpose. Eating was rationalized; rules were applied to it, which made it more predictable and widely accessible. Shown here is an eighteenth-century English plate of Tortoiseshell Ware from the collection of the Wadsworth Athenaeum and an early fork from the excavations at Calvert House, Annapolis, Maryland.

LEFT: *Clocks such as this example of the pillar-and-scroll style were not merely artistic or prestige items. Rather, they encouraged and required rules—a discipline—to live by. Of course, a clock keeps time, but in modern society the key is in understanding how schedules and punctuality are learned and will-ingly followed. The clock enables this and is a reflection of it. But it is the mental discipline that divides up time into units and links it to tasks that is so important.*

BELOW: *When common folk learned the rules for tea drinking, they stood the chance of not being common anymore. They also became disciplined, which is to say both acceptable and productive—modern. They were directed and encouraged by books, and they were motivated because the rules appeared to serve a reasonable purpose.*

COLONIAL CHILDHOOD
Travels Through an Eighteenth-Century Looking Glass

It is in the quiet and forgotten cemeteries that they are best remembered. Their tiny slate markers and appropriately brief epitaphs often bear the sole testimony of their existence on earth. In surveying these morbid silhouettes, one is struck by how many children of prerevolutionary America lie buried. In row upon row, the dangers of birth itself, infectious diseases, and the accidents of the everyday in the seventeenth and eighteenth centuries are made real again. According to contemporary estimates, these markers represent over half the human beings born in this time and in this place. In other words, childhood was for the majority of American colonists the final as well as initial stage of life.

Despite this fact, the story of these eternal children and of the rest who would live to become adults has yet to be fully told. This silence is not surprising. It stems from the tacit assumption that children were and are lesser human beings. The inability of these younger individuals to perform some cognitive functions and to reproduce sexually, for instance, is consistently understood to preordain their subordinate position, not only within the societies of which they were a part but in the retelling of history. The "naturalness" of this oppression and silence is deceiving, however. One has only to survey the definitions of who is considered to be a child in different cultures and in different time periods to realize that childhood is largely a social construction, not an inevitable stage.

It is precisely this plasticity which makes the story of children in the past so important. For in understanding how children were perceived, we better understand the values and beliefs that defined and determined the world of adults, both then and now. In seventeenth-century America, for instance, the realm of children was stereotypically perceived as meshing and overlapping with the realm of adults. Not only did very young individuals share similar outfits and carry themselves in the manner of their older counterparts, they also participated in many of the same activities and attended the same events. Even objects described as "toys" were used for entertaining individuals of all ages. This de-emphasized construction of childhood reflected and helped to reproduce general adult belief systems within the seventeenth century that stressed corporate living and unarticulated divisions within time and space.

By the onset of the eighteenth century, however, these adult understandings of community and their surroundings began to shift. The new belief system stressed the individual as well as an ordered segmentation of time and space. Intimately connected to this emergent ethos was a new conceptualization of childhood. Children born during the second half of the eighteenth century, in particular, were understood to be separate from their older contemporaries. It was at this time that toys and outfits began to be produced specifically for younger individuals. It was also in these years that many of the activities that both adults and children participated in began to be carried out by one group or the other.

This headstone marking the grave of Josiah and Nathaniel Smith is located in Cobb's Hill Cemetery in Boston, Massachusetts. A double headstone such as this one is common in colonial cemeteries. In most cases, it memorializes siblings who perished within a short time of each other. Josiah and Nathaniel, for instance, died within two days of each other in November 1721, probably from one of the many epidemics that swept the colonial port.

In contrast to the adult demeanor of the Mason children, this portrait of Elizabeth and Mary Daggett (c. 1794) reflects the eighteenth-century emergence of an articulated construction of childhood. Posed informally and dressed in loose-fitting garments made expressly for children, the sisters are depicted playing with a doll—a prop that by the end of the eighteenth century had become closely associated in portraiture with little girls.

In noting a relatively deemphasized childhood for the seventeenth century and an increasingly specified period and condition of childhood for the eighteenth century, the essential nature of adult belief systems can be traced. Yet what did these colonial American children believe? The answers to this question are elusive, for aside from the occasional journal or letter, picture, or handmade toy, these younger human beings were rendered as silent within their own societies, as they have been by later historians. Thus, when we return to our cemeteries, it becomes clear that, despite earlier allusions, the headstones and epitaphs commemorate not so much the children who lie beneath them but stand in testimony to the silence of their voices and their status as the most consistently and "naturally" subordinated group in history.

■ AMY ELIZABETH GREY
University of California, Berkeley

Although the Mason siblings were all under the age of ten when this portrait was executed in 1670, their clothing, postures, and props are exactly the same as those of seventeenth-century adults of similar rank and gender. This suggests that at least among the seventeenth-century elite, children were introduced early on to the conventions of adulthood.

This eighteenth-century Queen Anne–style doll is not unlike the one the Daggett sisters are depicted playing with. Although this toy and others were linked specifically with children by the end of the colonial period, they often carried distinctly adult messages. This doll in her meticulously sewn outfit presented young girls with a miniature template of the ideal colonial woman, while the watch found chained around her waist suggests then-emergent trends toward the segmentation of time.

ANCESTRAL HOMELANDS, NEW FRONTIERS
The Transformation of New England's History

I t is to be noted that the Indians do reserve for their use their present planting field and a privilege of fishing at the Falls." This provision, in a 1702 deed, makes obvious that Native American peoples were still an integral part of Connecticut's social landscape as the eighteenth century began. By then the colonists, numbering more than thirty thousand, lived primarily along the coast and in the broad valley of the Connecticut River. Affordable land was becoming scarce as affluent merchants and farmers continually enlarged the size and value of their private holdings. Scarcely propertied people, sometimes in concert with speculators, petitioned colonial governments for permission to

An early-twentieth-century photograph of the falls at Meticha-won where native peoples continued to fish and visit the graves of their ancestors long after New Milford was colonized. It is now called Lovers' Leap.

explore poorly known and supposedly uninhabited frontier regions. Unlike their maps, the colonists' reports made clear that many preserved wilderness areas were in fact ancestral homelands long occupied by Indian peoples. Despite the enduring native presence, the colonists, often with the sanction of the General Court, formed groups of town proprietors who decided how the lands of each new settlement would be acquired, divided, and used. Through their actions the Puritan legacy of dispossession was renewed for another century.

In 1702, when the earliest proprietors arrived at Weantenock (soon renamed New Milford) along the upper Housatonic River, they found a traditional homeland settled more than fifteen centuries before by the Weantinock, Pootatuck, Schaghticoke, and Mahican Indian peoples. Well-known to, and contested by, Dutch and English fur traders and trappers since the 1640s, this homeland encompassed more than ten square miles. In its core, centered along a stretch of the river about four miles long, were numerous small wigwam settlements, sacred spaces including cemeteries, fishing sites used for generations, and meeting places where respected clan leaders lived. A network of paths linked native peoples to their kin who lived throughout this homeland and nearby ones in eastern New York and southwestern Massachusetts. The ancestral cornfields of the Weantinock were of special interest to the colonial settlers. Then more than five hundred years old, these fields, dozens of acres in extent, were worked communally by local communities and clans. At first native peoples shared their planting fields; in less than ten years, however, New Milford's colonial settlers surveyed the better-drained floodplain soils into four-and-one-half-acre lots. Fifteen acres, identified as "land improved by the Indians," were reserved for native use. Soon even this parcel was taken and subdivided into twenty individual pieces, each less than one acre in size. By 1730 the Weantinock and their kin no longer had legal title or access to the fields

ABOVE: *These flaked and ground stone hoes are similar to those which would have been used in the Weantinock's cornfields.*

LEFT: *A reconstructed native village at the Institute for American Indian Studies, Washington, Connecticut. There were dozens of such settlements, consisting of bark- and thatch-covered wigwams and lodges, in each traditional homeland in Indian New England.*

where they and their ancestors had grown corn for centuries.

This history was repeated often as successive generations of colonists appropriated parts of ancestral homelands and planting fields along the many frontiers of eighteenth-century Connecticut. In New Milford, the Weantinock never completely abandoned their homeland. Some moved their wigwams to less accessible ridgetops and upland valleys where they lived intentionally invisible lives. Others resettled with kin at long-used meeting places such as Scaticook in nearby Kent, still the site of a reservation community. For more than a century and a half after 1730, native peoples continued to travel to the falls at Metichawon in southern New Milford. There they fished for eels and shad and visited the graves of their ancestors, continuing the traditions recognized in the 1702 deed. Despite their enduring presence, the town's histories written after the Revolution ignore the Weantinock and their kin. Instead the courage, fair-mindedness, and economic successes of New Milford's colonial settlers and their descendants are celebrated in paintings and stories that do not challenge us to remember what happened in the planting fields along the river.

■ RUSSELL G. HANDSMAN
University of Rhode Island, Kingston

The grandson of one of New Milford's early colonial settlers, Daniel Boardman was a successful merchant in New Milford and New Haven during the revolutionary era. His family's wealth depended, in part, upon the agricultural productivity of lands which Boardman's ancestors appropriated from the Weantinock people. Part of his family's property is shown in the background of this 1780s portrait.

THE PUEBLO REVOLT
Resistance and Cultural Survival in the Southwest

Before 1680, the Spanish colony of Santa Fe depended upon corn and cloth taken as tribute from the Pueblo Indian villages. A declining population due to disease and overwork meant that tribute demands had to be increased on a per capita basis to maintain the flow of goods. No less oppressive to the indigenous peoples of the region was the official prohibition of native religious practices—a policy common to all the Spanish colonies in America. The Franciscan missionaries at Santa Fe objected to the Pueblo Indians' masked *katsina* dances, their handling of snakes, and the ribald performances of ritual clowns.

Resistance was not long in coming. In 1680 a group of Pueblo priests under the leadership of the "Pope" of Santo Domingo Pueblo met in the northern pueblo of Taos (see illustration on page 55) to unite the Pueblo peoples and drive the Spanish out. They agreed that the Spanish would be allowed to leave and that only those who resisted would be killed. By agreement and with the support of the Pueblo population, the revolt began on August 10, 1680, and the Spanish were quickly driven to the capital of Santa Fe. Besieged in the plaza of Santa Fe by the Indians for eight days, the Spanish forces (and approximately three hundred Christianized Isleta Pueblo Indians who chose to remain with them) were allowed free passage south to El Paso. With the evacuation, the triumphant Pueblo occupied Santa Fe and sought to wipe out all vestiges of the Spanish presence.

The victory was not to be permanent. In 1694, the Spanish colonial official Diego de Vargas, sensing weakness among the Pueblo leadership, mounted a military expedition from El Paso to recapture New Mexico. After fourteen years, the unity of the Pueblo revolt had disintegrated and Diego's forces easily retook Santa Fe. As Diego de Vargas's troops moved back north to recover the region, the Pueblo sought security in different ways. Some appeased the Spanish in return for their lives and lands. Others removed their villages to isolated mesas until the Spanish cajoled or drove them down. Still others fled to join the Pueblo villages at Zuni in present-day western New Mexico and Hopi in Arizona.

LEFT: *The Christian Isleta Indians that accompanied the Spanish to El Paso built the village of Ysleta, where their descendants live today. They adopted the Spanish Matachine dance, shown in a photograph from the early 1900s.*

FACING PAGE, TOP RIGHT: *Tourists and a monument to the veterans of the Indian Wars now occupy the plaza in Santa Fe where Spanish families huddled during the week of August 13, 1680.*

FACING PAGE, BOTTOM RIGHT: *After the fall of Santa Fe, the Pueblo Indians transformed the Spanish governor's palace into a Pueblo apartment block. Archaeological excavations revealed the foundations for these changes under the existing floors of the palace.*

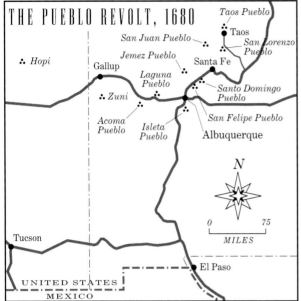

THE PUEBLO REVOLT, 1680

Taos Pueblo

Taos

San Juan Pueblo

San Lorenzo Pueblo

Jemez Pueblo

Santa Fe

.: *Hopi*

Gallup

Laguna Pueblo

Santo Domingo Pueblo

.: *Zuni*

Acoma Pueblo

Isleta Pueblo

San Felipe Pueblo

Albuquerque

N

0   75
MILES

Tucson

El Paso

UNITED STATES
MEXICO

RIGHT: *The Franciscan friars objected most to the masked dancers, or katsinas, of the Pueblo religion. The modern Hopi make dolls in the form of these dancers to instruct their children and to sell to tourists.*

The Spanish soon pursued these refugees west. At Zuni, the people grudgingly gave nominal allegiance to the Spaniards. At Hopi, the Spanish established a mission and converted the population of one nearby village to Christianity, but within a year other Hopi descended on the village, burned the mission, and killed the converts. The Zuni and Hopi resistance succeeded, the Spanish withdrew, and these people lived free for over two hundred fifty years until the United States asserted control over them. Even then, they continued to hold their sacred *katsina* dances in public—as they still do today.

Meanwhile, in the Rio Grande Valley, although Spanish control had been restored and the Pueblo became nominal Christians, resistance continued. Behind the appearance of allegiance to the secular government, the Pueblo still honored the sanctity of their priests, who held the real authority. In the pueblo, on sacred days, masked horsemen appeared (and still appear) to drive out any non-village residents so that *katsina* dances and other ceremonies could be performed. This pattern of resistance acknowledged Spanish domination, but also allowed the Pueblo to survive on their own terms up to the present day.

■ RANDALL H. McGUIRE
State University of New York at Binghamton

"CLASS WARFARE": *The American Militia System*

The notion of the citizen soldier, exemplified during colonial times by the militia, has had a long grasp on American images of the past. Citizen-soldiers subdued the Indian threat, helped Great Britain extend her empire into Canada, and ultimately overthrew a coercive royal government, defeating its regular army.

Even in the seventeenth and eighteenth centuries, independent yeomen were thought to provide the first line of defense for political freedom against external threats. A standing army was viewed as a serious danger. Formed out of lower class, propertyless men, such an army was both a tax burden on property owners and a potentially oppressive force for political control. The only alternative to a standing army was a volunteer army, made up of independent property holders who could be called on in an emergency. A volunteer militia seemed the ideal solution to the public defense.

In many New England colonies, where threats

The archaeological remains at Wolstenholme Town, an English settlement destroyed in an Indian uprising of 1622, reveal the threat against which English colonists first organized. Excavations by archaeologist Ivor Noël Hume uncovered the postholes of the original timber palisade. The slave quarters of the later plantation at the site, Carter's Grove, illustrate part of the shifting threat against which later militias organized in the south.

from Indians and the French were real and long-lasting, these militia units tended to be such an active defense. By contrast, in some southern colonies, the Indian threat had diminished considerably by the end of the seventeenth century, and the size of the slave population had begun to rise. There, the militia became important as a means of controlling slaves, and also served to contain other restless elements of the population. Militia helped Governor Berkeley of Virginia suppress Bacon's rebellion of 1676, subdued the rebellious North Carolina Regulators at Alamance in 1771, and put an end to Shay's Rebellion in 1787, and the Whiskey Rebellion of 1794.

Whatever the ideal, the real makeup of the militia was not static. When called up for serious conflict in the eighteenth century, it usually wasn't the propertied citizen who responded. The need for longer commitments was often met instead by companies of propertyless men, led by lower-ranking officers. Those who formed the peacetime militia stayed with their farms and businesses. We can thus see the emergence of two parallel forces. One, which approached the myth of the day, was made up of propertied, politically franchised segments of society. They participated in regular, socially reinforcing meetings (muster days), which reflected civilian social relationships, with the middle and upper class officered by the "better sort," the social and political leaders of the area. The other force, called upon only when external threat required, was made up of propertyless men who could be spared from daily pursuits and business.

During the Revolution, the Continental Army mirrored this latter force and was made up predominantly of men without prospects. It was this army that did the vast bulk of the fighting. The Revolutionary militia, on the other hand, was dominated by men of property. It functioned primarily to control the countryside by keeping the Loyalists in check, and it actually performed quite poorly in real battles.

Traditional images of our past have generally remembered only one half of the equation, the

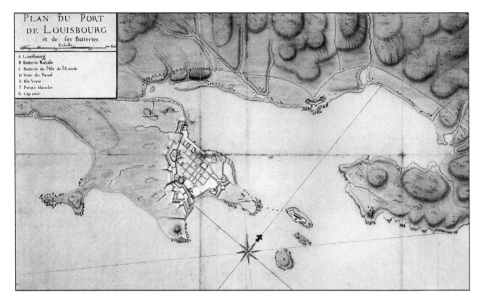

PLAN DU PORT
DE LOUISBOURG
et de ses Batteries
Echelle

A Louisbourg
B Batterie Royale
C Batterie de l'Isle de l'Entrée
D Tour du Fanal
E Isle Verte
F Pointe blanche
G Cap noir

LEFT: *The Fortress of Louisbourg is shown here in a 1755 plan. In the myth of the invincibility of the yeoman soldier, successes were long remembered and defeats quickly forgotten. In 1745, Gov. William Shirley of Massachusetts led a force of colonial militia in an audacious attack on French-held Louisbourg in Nova Scotia. Strongly positioned on remote Cape Breton Island, Louisbourg was thought by many to be unassailable. The American success was remarkable and did much to encourage Americans in their view that militia were the only form of defense that free men required.*

RIGHT: *The Old Barracks, in Trenton, New Jersey, seen here after renovation in 1925, are the last remaining examples of five barracks built in New Jersey by British colonial authorities during the French and Indian Wars. The presence of regular British troops, especially so far from the scene of conflict on the frontier, deepened the colonists' fears that a standing army might someday be employed against them.*

"invincible yeoman." The dominance of this view was made necessary by the linkage of popular sovereignty to the strength of the propertied classes. In the fiction, it was the people who threw off external threats to freedom. Maintenance of the myth then gave added power to the propertied. In addition to removing the real or imagined threat posed by a standing army, the militia helped control the lower elements of society. It encouraged consent to government by the elite by acting as a "school of subordination." It also served as a cheap substitute for a professional army, thus minimizing taxation and preserving property and capital, the very basis for political freedom. When the myth collided with the necessities for defense, however, it yielded to a proxy: defense by the propertyless, the expendables. Although most conveniently forgotten once the fighting was done, this was the reality. It gave new meaning to the term "class warfare."

■ JOHN SEIDEL
University of Maryland, College Park

The image of the farmer-soldier depicted in this nineteenth-century textbook, ready to leave field and family at a moment's notice, is at the heart of the militia concept. The notion of the farmer as defender emphasizes the connection between the ownership of land and property to individual and political freedom. Yet in the Revolution, most "minutemen" were actually propertyless.

MILITARY INDUSTRY IN THE NEW NATION
Henry Knox's Park of Artillery

One of the best examples of the logistical or industrial successes of the Revolutionary War comes from historical archaeology at Pluckemin, New Jersey. In the winter of 1778–1779, Brig. Gen. Henry Knox stationed his troops in this small town and began activities of great consequence for the army.

As early as 1776, Knox had asked Congress to approve the construction of military academies and supply depots around the country. He recognized that a trained army, supported by industrial production, was essential to winning the war. Congress ignored his pleas and in late 1778, Knox did what he could to put the plan into action on a smaller scale.

One of his first moves was to build warehouses, which made Pluckemin the hub of a large network of supply. Hundreds of wagonloads of supplies rolled into these warehouses over the winter. In one December shipment alone, nine thousand round shot for cannon were delivered, along with seventy-eight tons of grapeshot. Over the course of the winter, close to ninety thousand rounds of small arms ammunition were collected, outstripping British supply by a comfortable margin. At the start of the next campaign, Pluckemin supplied the American army with new and repaired muskets, bayonets, and cartridge boxes. Even mundane but necessary items such as horseshoes were produced and collected there, with orders for twenty to thirty thousand sets (four shoes to a set) placed at a time.

What Knox built at Pluckemin was more than a mere collection point. Archaeological excavations have shown that he built barracks for troops and craftsmen, along with an academy in the center of the site, flanked by a variety of workshops and warehouses. Tinsmiths, blacksmiths, armorers, and other artificers repaired equipment and churned out new supplies in these shops. Knox's "laboratory" alone produced almost two hundred thousand rounds of small arms ammunition, and the armory repaired hundreds of muskets. The excavated remains of blacksmith shops and gunsmith shops show that large numbers of smiths were at work. In the armory, skilled smiths were backed up by less-skilled laborers who did the rough filing of parts, shaping of stocks, and grinding of bayonets. The division of labor clearly improved efficiency.

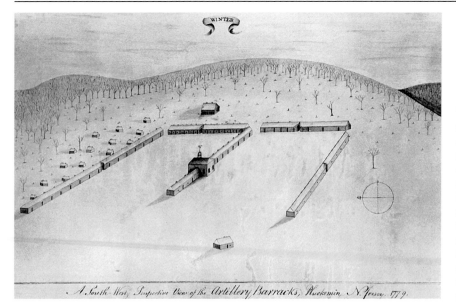

A South-West Perspective View of the Artillery Barracks, Pluckemin N. Jersey 1779.

With a layout based on European military designs, the Pluckemin artillery complex, pictured here in a 1779 engraving, was a sophisticated engineering accomplishment rather than the motley collection of log cabins more commonly illustrated. From the 450-foot-long barracks to the left, to the military academy in the center, and the workshops and warehouses on the right, the site highlights the technical and industrial capabilities of an American army in the field.

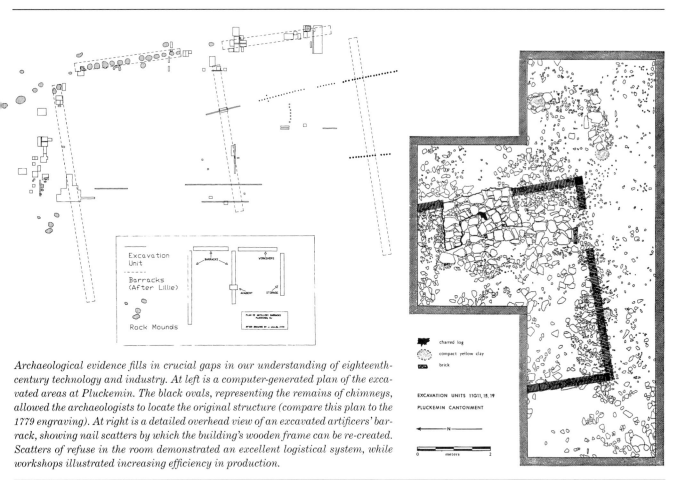

Archaeological evidence fills in crucial gaps in our understanding of eighteenth-century technology and industry. At left is a computer-generated plan of the excavated areas at Pluckemin. The black ovals, representing the remains of chimneys, allowed the archaeologists to locate the original structure (compare this plan to the 1779 engraving). At right is a detailed overhead view of an excavated artificers' barrack, showing nail scatters by which the building's wooden frame can be re-created. Scatters of refuse in the room demonstrated an excellent logistical system, while workshops illustrated increasing efficiency in production.

In addition, parts were mass-produced elsewhere and shipped to field units for use. Blank cocks for muskets, for example, were produced and then stockpiled for later use. Although this was a form of mass production, true interchangeability had not yet arrived. Each of these pieces had to be individually fitted to a broken gun, but prior production was an important first step.

The picture that has developed at Pluckemin is one sharply at odds with conventional views of the American army during the Revolutionary War. It bespeaks sophisticated organization, effective production and transport, and a much improved material status for the army. It also helps explain American successes far better than a shallow invocation of a just cause and a corrupt enemy.

"Armory practice" was established at Pluckemin and at Springfield and Harpers Ferry armories, and is but one example of the impact of the military on domestic industry—and one of the most profound. The military had broken the barriers to mass production of machined metal; uniformity of parts spread rapidly and widely. Armory practice expanded unskilled tasks and increased specialization. Expansion of the labor force required greater discipline in the workplace and encouraged stricter and expanded management. All of these changes spilled over into civilian industry, with deep economic, social, and ideological consequences. For example, men from Springfield Armory helped establish the American Watch Company at Waltham, Massachusetts, and cheap mass production of timepieces tapped an enormous market; their example was followed by scores of other industries.

■ JOHN SEIDEL
University of Maryland, College Park

4

CHAOS AND CONTROL

1781–1865

WITH CONTRIBUTIONS BY

David W. Babson

Amy Elizabeth Grey

Dana Holland

George C. Logan

Paul A. Shackel

John Michael Vlach

David S. Brose

Russell G. Handsman

Barbara J. Little

Charles E. Orser, Jr.

Dell Upton

We begin this section with illustrations of society's instability, not to indict our early heritage as an independent nation but to describe the mix of people and relationships that the new country had to deal with. We focus on instability in order to view the structure that the new United States inherited and the practices and institutions it put into place up to the Civil War to deal with conflicting and contradictory forces.

Consider this picture from the period we call the Federal Era in the French Quarter of New Orleans, which Dell Upton describes on pages 136–137. At a time when we have been told the fledgling nation was beginning to industrialize, expand west to the far side of the Appalachians, and enjoy the widespread popular democracy, a visitor to New Orleans could meet and mingle freely among West Indians, Native Americans, Sephardic Jewish traders and professionals, Northern commercial agents, European speculators, and both free and enslaved African Americans. Contrary to the popular picture, the United States was far from homogeneous even at this early date, and in New Orleans ethnic diversity was an accepted part of life.

Along the old levee, or riverfront, African American laborers gathered for work or leisure. The levee was also the domain of the Irish screwmen, a group of elite, organized workers who had the dangerous job of mechanically packing cotton onto steamboats. In the nearby streets, chain gangs of slave men and women, conscripted for punishment or rented to the city by their owners, performed the dirtiest and most onerous public works maintenance. On Sundays, free and enslaved African Americans gathered in "Congo Square" at the end of Orleans Street. Though they lived and worked in rear courtyards and service buildings throughout the French Quarter, the greatest concentration of free black households was in the adjacent faubourgs, or suburbs, Trémé and Marigny, behind and downriver of the French Quarter.

Was the controlled chaos and racial diversity of New Orleans really so strange in the early decades of the independence of the United States? During the years from around 1780 to the mid-1820s, when the central government was finally established firmly, the nation faced severe social crises brought on by the extensive use of slaves, a high portion of some states' total population; by a government of rich and powerful landed gentry; by the restriction of voting rights to only a tiny part of the population—property-owning males. In addition, social tensions were caused by the presence of a Tory

In the streets and public square of New Orleans, merchants, laborers, and aristocrats of many races and ethnic groups mixed freely— in dramatic contrast to conventional images of the cultural uniformity of Early America. Pictured here is a street scene in Faubourg St. Mary, circa 1821.

remnant who could neither be expelled nor really punished for fear of loss of their wealth. The national government continued to be feeble. Early death and migration continued to weaken family bonds. The slowness of established churches to adjust to national independence was offset by a popular fascination with radical, newly founded religious movements. All these forces produced a rapidly changing social landscape in cities and rural areas alike.

A now-famous exhibit at the Smithsonian's National Museum of American History called *After the Revolution* highlights the severe social problems of the period of Madison, Monroe, and John Quincy Adams, noting the high divorce rate, low rate of affiliation with organized churches, frequency of illegitimate births, and abuse of alcohol. These are historical realities—long left out of schoolbook histories that deal mainly with issues of foreign policy and westward expansion—and demonstrate the incoherence, unpredictability, social breakdown, and forces of transformation at work in a period that is popularly thought of quite differently.

Yet if the French Quarter of New Orleans can represent the chaos of diversity, commerce, and contradiction that the establishment of effective governmental institutions were meant to control, Dr. Upton shows us on pages 138–139 that the Quaker city of Philadelphia was a community where the forces of control struggled more aggressively with those same destabilizing factors. Philadelphia was always, in fact, a center of experimentation with "therapeutic" institutions for repairing faulty citizens. Enlightenment belief in the human ability to analyze, order, and reorder held forth the possibility of "fixing" deviant citizens, including criminals, the young, paupers, lunatics, deaf mutes, the aged, and the infirm through rational means, thus perfecting and ensuring the future of republican America.

The Pennsylvania Hospital of 1751 and the Walnut Street Jail of 1772 were but the first of a series of public and private institutions built around the city's margins in the early nineteenth century. From 1814, when the Friends' Asylum for the Relief of Persons Deprived of the Use of their Reason was organized, these institutions adopted the gridded plan of cells along a corridor as a way of organizing inmates analytically according to their afflictions or crimes—"separation and classification" were the standard terms—and of individualizing treatment. Over the quarter century from 1815 to 1840, reform-minded Philadelphians pushed their government to build a pioneering state penitentiary, a county prison, a naval officers' home; to complete the eighteenth-century almshouse, and to erect a second almshouse. A peculiar system of public funding of privately organized and operated institutions was responsible for completing the Pennsylvania Hospital, building a separate insane asylum under its auspices, and founding a "house of refuge" (we'd call it a reform school), a lying-in hospital, an eye hospital, as well as asylums for the deaf and dumb, the blind, orphans, and widows, and a "Magdalen asylum" for reformed prostitutes. As Dr. Upton points out, many of these institutions were designed by the same architect, John Haviland, and he applied a celled plan to most—a plan labeled by one group of prison reformers as "moral architecture."

We have long considered such institutions a part of modern life—a feature of our society in which people suffering from illnesses or social "afflictions" will be effectively treated by professionals, rather than be allowed to roam the streets and suffer with their disabilities. A watching, and presumably caring, society dominated the theory of the Federal Era, characterized by the symbol of the all-seeing eye. This occurred not because there was an idea of a big, caring government but because reason was supposed to be applicable to nature and society. The latter was a "body," and like the human body, it was operated by fixed rules. These rules could be discovered and applied to restore society to "health."

Certainly in the case of organic diseases, the institutions of Philadelphia pioneered medical techniques. But there is another side to these institutions of which Dr. Upton cautions us to be aware: the personality-transformation techniques practiced in the public institutions and asylums of early-nineteenth-century Philadelphia can be said fairly to be precursors of the even more regulated crimi-

nal and psychiatric institutions of the twentieth century. This is an idea called "panopticism," which calls for society to be watchful over people, and also requires people to learn routines and practices of self-discipline wherein they watch themselves. Techniques of self-discipline were learned in schools, homes, libraries, hospitals, and all sorts of public "asylums," which meant institutions that induced healthfulness. This is not a jailer's suffocating mentality, but rather one wherein citizens of a new republic learned natural laws for governing themselves.

The contrast between life in New Orleans and Philadelphia could not be plainer—between the spontaneous, constantly fluctuating chaos of human struggle on the one hand and the urge for order and control on the other. That is certainly not to say that in New Orleans there were not elites that sought to maintain their powers, nor disenfranchised groups who were subjected to oppression; nor is it to say that in the streets, taverns, and workshops of Philadelphia there were not vibrant diversity, resistance, and the disorganization of everyday life. It is rather to say that the constant struggle between chaos and control is an important element of American history, especially in the coun-try's growing cities. Rapid change is a given in capitalist society. Although some will argue that traditional relationships between ethnic groups, genders, and economic classes are enduring and changeless, we will try to show that they are neither and never have been.

THE HOME AS A CHURCH

The internal contradictions of the Federal Period were masked by quite convincing ideas and practices even at the time, such as democracy and "moral architecture." Another powerful concept was that of domesticity. We choose it here because it spoke to half the population, namely women, and ultimately to everyone. Domesticity is the idea that a woman's place is in the home. As Amy Grey notes on pages 140–141, it is one of the central ideological developments of the period. Yet it is of far more than purely historical interest, because this ideal remains powerful and pervasive in American life and its remnants are everywhere, from magazine racks filled with copies of the *Ladies' Home Journal* and *Good Housekeeping* to the corporations that refuse to grant maternity leaves. Either a

The civilized man can measure the size and distance of the heavenly bodies, which the savage ignorantly worships as gods. Civilized nations rapidly advance in knowledge, for they maintain a constant communication with each other, and with the remotest parts of the earth. They have colleges, churches, hospitals, and many other useful institutions.

CIVILIZED.

HALF-CIVILIZED nations have definite political divisions and large towns. They practice the manual occupations with great skill, but have only a limited knowledge of the professions. They have Mohammedan, Buddhist, or Brahman religions and narrow education. They are jealous of strangers, and have very little communication with foreign countries. For this reason they make but little progress, and continue for centuries in the same condition.

HALF-CIVILIZED.

3. In the **Barbarous State** men are somewhat more advanced than in the savage. They have indefinite political divisions, patriarchal or tribal government, nomadic occupations, Pagan or Mohammedan religion, and meager education. They pay little attention to agriculture, but generally derive their support from their flocks and herds, and from hunting and fishing.

BARBAROUS.

2. Savages are the lowest and most degraded class. They have no political divisions or towns, few and rude occupations, cruel or weak government, degrading religion, and no education.

SAVAGE.

woman acts like a man and is a worker, or she acts like a woman and remains a homemaker—the ideology of domesticity suggests, with a tone of authority that falsely presumes to express a natural, rather than a social reality—and it is up to women to make a final, definitive choice. The ideological images associating women with domesticity have long been powerful; they were employed against the struggle for female suffrage in the late nineteenth and early twentieth centuries, and again in the late twentieth century, in the opposition to the Equal Rights Amendment.

Beginning in the late eighteenth century, the "Cult of Domesticity" was articulated in novels and portraits, sermons and newspapers, even in house plans and styles. Each form expressed the now completely familiar belief that the home was the proper sphere for women, that it was woman's natural domain, while the world of work, commerce, and politics was the realm of men. The catalysts for the articulation of these central tenets of domesticity can be found both in particular events and in long-term trends. The Revolutionary War, for instance, had a profound and immediate impact on the metaphors Americans employed to understand the social relationships of the family. With the rejection of the concept of monarchy, for instance, the idea of a hierarchical, father-headed household was weakened. This, combined with the effects of war, increased mobility, and territorial expansion, served to erode the customs and values surrounding extended family life. In its place there emerged a concept of the family that drew its self-image from the ideology of the new "democratic" nation. This more recognizably modern nuclear family emphasized the importance of children and affectionate ties among family members. Within this context women became "Republican Mothers," charged with the patriotic duty of raising responsible citizens. However, this new preeminence for

In the late nineteenth century, the "science" of anthropology was developed by Europeans to classify the numerous peoples they had conquered, not only in North America but on a global scale. Native Americans were portrayed as "the lowest and most degraded class." Scientifically classified as savages, educators derided their social, political, and religious institutions.

women was largely illusory, since the exaltation of motherhood was accompanied by the exclusion of women from direct access to political power.

Another important catalyst stemmed from long-term economic trends that were slowly eroding the importance of traditional commercial relationships. Where once women and men produced raw goods and finished items for their communities, the beginnings of industrialization and the growth of consumerism eroded the importance of household production, and thus the products of women's labor in the home. The creation of a distinct "domestic sphere," then, acquired the added dimension of serving as a place of shelter and respite from the increasingly unpredictable and anonymous landscapes lying beyond—the factories, mill villages, urban tenements, and workplaces divorced from home. The division was double-edged, for while these economic trends helped to place women as the directors of the domestic sphere, their labor there was uncompensated. Most women who did not themselves become factory workers or hired help became economically dependent on their husbands or fathers. Associated with this basic idea was the formalization of women's roles as mothers. Prescriptive guides such as *The Mother at Home* emphasized the great responsibility women bore in raising the future (read: male) citizens of the young nation.

One of the ways that the "Cult of Domesticity" was widely disseminated throughout the country was through the popularity of the Gothic Revival style of building, which John Michael Vlach illustrates on pages 142–143. In its characteristic use of tracery, steeply pitched roofs, pointed spires, ornate finials, lancet windows, and a host of other decorative devices, the Gothic style represented the asymmetry, the delicacy, and elaborate spontaneity of nature. These qualities—in sharp contrast to the order, strength, and stability that were associated with the male temperament—came to be associated with femininity. Moreover, since Gothic structures were rooted in the design of medieval European cathedrals, the popularity of the Gothic Revival and its feminine associations were fueled by its obvious religious associations. Popular guidebooks such as the Beecher sisters' *The American Woman's Home* (1869) stressed that

a mother's highest calling was to provide religious instruction. The ideal housewife was "to rear all under her care to lay up treasures, not on earth, but in heaven." Thus, no better context for such actions could be imagined than a home or cottage decorated with features typical of a church.

TEMPLES AND CLOCKS

If the Gothic house came to represent the organic, the natural, the religious, the feminine, and the domestic, it responded to the slightly earlier style known as Greek Revival, described by Dr. Vlach on pages 144–145. In the earliest decades of the nineteenth century it came to represent the rational, the public, the powerful, and the masculine. While the terms *classical revival* or *neo-classical* would be more accurate labels, nevertheless the association with ancient pagan Greece remained preeminent. This was and remains so because the facade of the typical classical revival building is essentially a replica of a temple, complete with pediment and columns. Although this is an image that was supposed to conjure up visions of the Acropolis in Athens, many actually owe their origins to Rome and many more are unique American hybrids that combine both Greek and Roman features—suggesting the spiritual and intellectual links between the new American republic, the Roman Republic, and the golden age of Greek democracy.

These images of democracy, a foundation in Greek antiquity, and a leadership managed by men were the chief ideas used to drive the organization of the Federal Era. Thomas Jefferson, one of the main political architects of early American independence, is credited with initiating the classical movement in American architecture when he designed a temple-form structure to serve as the Virginia state capitol in Richmond, completed in 1792. Jefferson's apparent inspiration was a Roman temple dedicated to Augustus in the French city of Nîmes, which he had visited while serving as the U.S. Minister to France. Other prominent American architects during this period were also designing structures in the classical mode. Their creations were, for the most part, used in public buildings—

churches, banks, colleges, and courthouses—where the impression of order and antiquity reinforced these institutions' modern authority.

As Dr. Vlach shows, the first decade of the nineteenth century saw classicism become an important element in the national architectural vocabulary, and the Greek Revival achieved even greater popularity in the 1830s and 1840s when temple-form buildings began to be used more commonly as residences for the middle class. Its main message—for individual homeowners no less than for college presidents or bank directors—was the autonomy and right of the Republican male individual, who had been at least superficially schooled in the classics, to possess and display private property, including personal knowledge.

There was, of course, another element of material culture central to the early-nineteenth-century American character and to both Greek Revival and Gothic Revival styles: the Yankee clock. Russell G. Handsman, on pages 146–147, uses this underappreciated item to illustrate the ideology of universal time, which was new to the era. Many of the most famous styles of mantel clock adopted elements of the Greek Revival style, such as fluted columns and triangular pediments, in their own architecture. But whether the clock stood on a mantel, sat on a table or cupboard, or was installed in a factory tower, it was more often than not made by the same company in New England. More to the point, all kept the same time, which was measured and internalized in the same way by all users.

Like the notion that people should be segregated by race or gender, or that space could be ordered by formal architecture and city planning, clocks presented the public with something that was passed off as inevitable, natural, and most important of all, unchangeable: universal time. With the relentless progress and precise segmentation provided by all the revolving hands and swinging pendulums, people came to learn from childhood that clocks reflected the turning of the heavens and were thus indicators of a force of nature—like the weather vanes installed on the top of every barn—brought home in an inexpensive form.

But there was something very different about the clock: Both it and the time it kept were manu-factured. The division of the day into hours, and the hour into minutes and seconds, was a human convention that was neither natural nor inevitable. Far less precise systems of timekeeping had always been sufficient. Farmers and townspeople had regulated their lives through the seasons, moon phases, and the position of the sun. But now, in an age in which time was money, and in which the duration of labor had to be measured precisely for wage calculations, clocks and the meticulous system of timekeeping they represented served as instruments, like the imposing facades of Greek Revival banks and government buildings, to make a newly established social and economic order seem eternal and unchangeable.

The place of women, Gothic and Greek Revival architectural styles, and Yankee clocks are all ideologies of the Federal Era, which have some life in them still. These examples show how ideology can be manifested in concrete form—as products, behaviors, and systems of reference—and it is in the direct, everyday impact that it has on peoples' lives that ideology's real power lies. Preparing meals in a modern kitchen, closely timed to standard, clock-determined mealtimes, and consuming that meal of industrially processed food on mass-produced plates and with mass-produced silverware, helps to maintain a certain way of life and promote the stability of the larger society.

These routines existed—and continue to exist—to maintain or promote certain social behaviors and relations of power. Even though they are often trumpeted as human "virtues" that are timeless and politically neutral, these ideas or ideologies have often been used to rationalize women's unrecompensed labor in the home, to romanticize unequal wealth and power, and to raise mass consumption to unprecedented levels, making all these practices either a part of commonly accepted culture or an unprotestable given of daily life. In this period, the use of mass-produced products and behaviors resulted in the mass production of millions of laboring men and women at home and in the factories. The subtle communication of ideology through material culture shows how widespread and influential ideologies can become. And artificial landscapes, dinnerware, and mantel clocks show

RIGHT: *The ubiquitous two-room, story-and-a-half house can be found even on the West Coast. This example, from Tacoma, Washington, was built in the last quarter of the nineteenth century, and although it was modernized with contemporary picture windows, it still reveals by its steep central gable the transcontinental reach of the Gothic style.*

BELOW: *The Marden House in Newburyport, Massachusetts, is an example of a typical eighteenth-century New England house that was slightly updated to accommodate the demands of Greek Revival fashion. Decorative elements surrounding the front door suggest a cornice supported by columns. Their presence is almost entirely symbolic as they clearly do not do much to transform the appearance of the building.*

Clocks were only marginally intended as decorative items. They showed how to tell time and how to keep time. They introduced the finely divided day and, when combined with a lamp, they allowed time to be kept at night. Many clocks, such as this early pocket watch, were inexpensive and widely sold.

how common, how vernacular, and how invisible the action of ideology can be.

PLANTATIONS AND COMPANY TOWNS

"The South" is often thought of as having been a homogeneous entity before the Civil War. Yet the familiar images of elegant living, hanging moss, and *Gone With the Wind* romance not only mask the reality of slavery but also conceal the fact that the South was a socially diverse region, organized on local rather than sectional administrative levels. As Dr. Vlach illustrates on pages 150–151, it was an agrarian, export-oriented economy, not yet devoted to urban manufacturing, mass production, or wage labor. It was still largely a colonial economy. The county was the chief unit of governmental administration. Economic regionalism was therefore affirmed and perpetuated through local political structure. State governments exercised little interference in local affairs. Local perspectives and associations had practical political and economic meaning; national union was a more abstract moral and sentimental attachment. Across the South people tended to be locally or regionally self-sufficient, without the practical or perceptual need for goods and services from outside.

The plantation has become the most visible symbol of the antebellum South, and as David W. Babson shows on pages 148–149, there is indeed much to be learned from the material remains of plantation life. Take the Middleburg Plantation, northeast of Charleston, South Carolina, for instance. During the one hundred fifty years that preceded the Civil War, this plantation produced highly profitable crops of rice, cultivated and harvested by African American slaves. The economy of rice in South Carolina rested not only on the labor of these slaves but, also, much more important, on their knowledge and skill.

The African American slaves who worked Middleburg Plantation and the hundreds of plantations scattered throughout the South were closely controlled by an ideology that held that they were not skilled farm workers at all but a form of higher animal, taken from the African wilderness and incorporated into American culture as useful, domestic beasts. Because this ideology was an important prop for the entire plantation system—and because it was false—plantation owners attempted to suppress this essential contradiction by manipulating the landscape. This was done through denying the slaves their humanity by destroying their familiar cultural forms. Slaves were forced to live in European-style cabins or barracks, arranged in distinctly un-African patterns, near large, classically proportioned plantation houses. The visual impression of enormous power and authority stemming from the main plantation house was unmistakable, as was the dependence of the slave quarters to it. The physical landscape was thus arranged so as to enshrine and naturalize a system of exploitation that was clearly human in origin.

In the North, the company town created a similar landscape of power, in which workers both labored and lived. Control here was both direct (using company-issued scrip for money, allowing company stores only, and engaging in union busting) and indirect, through the physical layout of the streets and the location and design of the workers' housing. As Paul A. Shackel stresses on pages 152–153 and as David W. Babson notes on pages 148–149, landscapes as well as objects and rules of behavior were used to incorporate new social relations into republican and agrarian settings in ways that helped to make them acceptable.

Living in the planned landscape of a plantation or factory town had the same kind of subtle effect on everyday life and consciousness as did living in a Gothic or Greek Revival house. Both landscapes and architecture created or facilitated actions that embodied ideologies of the time: namely, productive farm or factory work in a class-divided setting, in which productivity was defined by owners, investors, and managers. The link between technology and landscape, between power and wealth, can be seen in the homes of those who led industrialization by building their mansions right beside the factories and railroads—elegant and orderly in their outside appearance and interior divisions—yet masking their real connection to the smoke, noise, pollution and social dislocations that those machines produced.

CONTESTING THE DOMINANT ORDER OF THINGS

The people who were constrained by these factory and domestic landscapes and routines resisted them to varying extents and in various ways. For example, nineteenth-century American females were not passive victims. In many ways women helped to shape the concept of domesticity in their favor. The common experiences and understandings afforded by the "domestic sphere" allowed women to establish bonds among themselves. This emergent collective consciousness, in turn, made possible the first meeting of feminists in Seneca Falls, New York, in 1848. It was here that women selectively employed elements of the "Cult of Domesticity" to argue for an expansion of their rights and roles.

On plantations, there was an active effort among slaves to preserve African culture. In some circumstances, it appears that slaves were able to hang onto the only thing they could bring with them—their own beliefs and values. After their arrival in America, their customs must have changed considerably, but as George C. Logan discusses on pages 154–155, recent archaeological discoveries show that slaves kept a recognizable form of their own religious expressions alive and that some traditions remained a part of daily life through slavery and into freedom.

Sites from all over the southeastern United States contain material about early African American belief systems. The artifacts recovered to date represent a wide range of material culture, including pottery impressed with religious pictographs, altered glass decanter stoppers, and quartz crystals. On two known sites, these transparent, six-sided prisms called rock crystals had been purposely buried near corners of houses. Other objects buried like this include cowrie shells, blue and transparent cut-glass beads, pierced metal disks, pierced bone disks and coins, buttons made of metal, bone, and oyster shell, black polished stones, and butchered animal bones. Archaeologists now believe that constellations of such objects held religious meanings for their African American users—meanings that were largely unknown to Anglo-Americans, but which existed for centuries in rituals among tribes throughout West Africa.

Other workers saw their own exploitation and acted in various other ways to address it. One of the ways, as Charles E. Orser, Jr., points out on pages 156–157, was to found utopian communities. Modern Western history is replete with examples of like-minded individuals who defied the conventions of their societies by joining together in discrete alternative communities. These were often based on religious, moral, or even economic precepts to which communities' members strived to be faithful in their everyday lives, with their ultimate goal being to build a just and better world. For many, the search for a utopia on earth was inexorably linked to the abolition of private property and personal ownership, and many utopian communities inculcated elements that today might be termed "socialist," since they promoted common ownership of wealth and the means of producing it. In most

Despite a lifetime of oppression and terrorization by the brutal system of slavery, Renty, born in the Congo and later employed on the plantation of B. F. Taylor outside Columbia, South Carolina, still possessed an air of quiet dignity and strength when he posed for a daguerrotype by J. T. Zealy in March 1850.

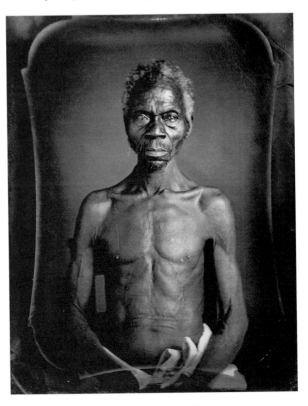

RIGHT: *Regularity of production is one of the key factors in industrial capitalism. People accustomed to an agricultural way of life had to be trained to work according to artificial rather than seasonal schedules. They were forced to work indoors in unhealthy surroundings, and often at night, as this nighttime view of a nineteenth-century New England cotton mill shows.*

BELOW: *These quartz crystals and one black polished stone were excavated from an area of the ground story of the Charles Carroll House in Annapolis, Maryland, now believed to have housed slaves. Associated with the crystals were English ceramics, bone disks, a 1773 George III Virginia halfpenny, and an 1803 Liberty large cent.*

BELOW: *This round fieldstone dairy barn was constructed in the 1820s by the brothers and sisters of the Shaker community at Hancock Village near Pittsfield, Massachusetts. It housed fifty-two cows in radially arranged stalls. As an expression of the Shaker talent for innovation, this barn's unique circular design allowed maximum efficiency for feeding, milking, and cleaning.*

FACING PAGE: *Violent conflict between Native Americans defending their space and the Euro-American invaders was endemic from first contact in the early seventeenth century to the twentieth century. Conflict began to intensify in the decades before the Civil War when United States troops were organized to "tame" the West.*

cases, however, the quest for utopia on earth centered around a generally well-formulated concept of freedom, the exact meaning of which varied with each community and with the views of its founder.

As Dr. Orser points out, the spirit of utopian communalism was strongly felt in the American Midwest as many groups—including Shakers, Mormons, Zoarites, Harmonists, Jansenists, and Amana colonists—settled on its vast prairies, drawn by the region's wide expanses of fertile ground and its sparse population. The common thread that ran through the plan of each of the utopian communities was the desire of their members to resist what they perceived were the harmful effects and tendencies of industrial capitalist society. Within the first few decades after the War of 1812, it became clear to some people that the United States would become a power based on industrialization and some measure of social inequality. The utopianists wanted to remove themselves from a mainstream society that promoted such ideas. Their efforts involved building workable societies based on nonwage labor, strong interpersonal relationships, family ties, and sometimes unshakable religious convictions. The utopian communities represent a nonviolent attempt to resist the goals and aspirations of the national societies within which they lived. Utopianists wished to create their own environments and realities within rigidly established boundaries that they could control.

Throughout the period covered by this chapter, Native Americans also continued their resistance to domination or total assimilation into Euro-American society. While some native peoples were exterminated, confined to resource-poor reservations, or forced to accept the cultural and economic norms of the mainstream, others managed, against all odds, to maintain their identity and autonomy. As Barbara J. Little shows on pages 158–159, the Cherokee nation attempted to craft a unique cultural synthesis of European technology and native traditions. Although most of the Cherokee, along with other Southeastern peoples, were forcibly exiled to the distant Arkansas and Oklahoma territories by the United States government in the late 1830s, a portion of the Cherokee nation evaded deportation and their descendants have preserved tribal traditions to the present day.

Each of the instances of resistance mentioned in this chapter has a different history, and few, if any, of the movements saw themselves as allied with other protestors. Even so, the sheer range of these protesting groups, each of which found the industrial and commercial development of the country to be unacceptable, is, in itself, a provocative commentary on the supposedly inevitable and natural course of American history.

WAR BETWEEN THE STATES

The Civil War represents the triumph of factories, wage labor, mass production and mass markets,

investment capital, and all the rules and behaviors accompanying them. The war is often thought to have been a conflict between North and South, fought to save the national union of states and subsequently freeing African Americans from the institution of slavery. Another perspective on the war is that it was less about notions concerning the immorality of slavery or the natural virtues of union than about forging a modern and unified industrial nation.

Selected places historically associated with the Civil War are preserved today to communicate quite specific and restrictive historical information. Many of these places are museums and national parks that commemorate a particular northern or southern victory, describe military strategies, and convey the human cost of the battles in terms of material destruction, military and civilian casualties, and territory lost or gained. Typically, the Civil War is presented as the composite of four years of battles and bloodshed. Nostalgia and historical romanticism aside, the particulars of specific struggles on the battlefields have only limited social or historical implications for us today. It is rather the outcome of the far more pervasive social, ethnic, and economic struggles that were waged in small towns, urban centers, and farming communities throughout the Civil War era that set the country on a course leading to our present society and national state of affairs.

The bloody, armed conflict of the Civil War was merely the first stage of the transition to a more homogeneous and unified nation, capable of functioning coherently under a national economic policy. With the eventual northern victory in the war, labor and society in both North and South were reorganized in

Military production was an important factor in the industrialization of the United States. Along with Harpers Ferry, Virginia (later West Virginia), the gunsmithing works at Springfield, Massachusetts, were established as a national armory in 1794. By 1800, specialized machines for production were being introduced and interchangeable parts produced. Exceptionally precise parts were turned out. Along with new systems of labor organization, these armories helped to transform American industry. The vast number of other mills and factories in the region around Springfield highlights the connection between arms production and industrial growth. The Springfield Armory is shown here in a mid-nineteenth-century view.

The construction of railroad systems throughout the eastern United States was an important logistical advantage to the Union forces during the Civil War. Pictured here is a troop transport train making its way through Harpers Ferry, West Virginia.

accordance with a national industrial agenda. Communication and transportation networks, which were expanded around the time of the Civil War, shortened overland distances and conquered local orientations. These actions encouraged continuous growth and a philosophy of further expansion.

A national economy required a social atmosphere in which workers held attitudes consistent with efficient work practices. The ideology of the melting pot developed to give credence to the idea of perpetual social homogenization. Tax-supported public schools taught a national perspective and appropriate work discipline. Poor whites and slaves were no longer bound to an aristocratic tradition, but efficiency and the quest for profit became their new masters. In the South, tenant farming and racism served to perpetuate some of the inequitable social relations that existed before the Civil War.

As Dana Holland indicates on pages 160–161, the North's triumph in the Civil War rendered harmless those relations and social traditions deemed threatening to industrial growth and national progress. Americans had free choice only to choose to partici-

pate in the national economy or to be marginalized. And as David S. Brose points out on pages 162–163, in his examination of the industrialization of Cleveland in the decades around the time of the Civil War, the social implications of "modernization," or "progress," could be painful for those groups who were restricted to certain niches in the nation's economic life.

We depict the Civil War as a victory for homogenization, with industrialism conquering all forms of resistance—southern, Native American, African American, and utopian. The Civil War swamped the Shaker communities by forcing them into mass production. The Republicans declared that Mormon plural marriage was, along with slavery, a relic of barbarism and sent Federal troops in to occupy the Utah Territory. Former southern slaves became tenant farmer serfs, in many cases for several generations. Many Native American groups were extinguished or permanently impoverished as wards of the state, and the South itself began slowly to be industrialized. The way was now open for the creation of what some would later call a modern corporate capitalist society.

NEW ORLEANS: *Domestic Social Space*

The French Market, now sheltered by a WPA portico and enclosed to accommodate tourist-oriented businesses, was built in 1813 as the butchers' hall of a market that stretched along the levee and, until 1819, extended into the Place d'Armes (now Jackson Square). Its varied people and goods and cacophony of languages unmistakably demonstrated New Orleans's role as the commercial crossroads of North America.

The 400 block of Decatur Street contains a good collection of the commercial building types that could be found in most antebellum American cities. The granite-piered fronts allowed the ground floors to be opened up, extending the shop into the street and drawing the street into the shop.

FACING PAGE, BOTTOM LEFT: *The Gally double house and slave quarters, 540 Chartres Street. The mixture of residential and commercial space in houses like this lasted longer in the French Quarter than in the "American" sector of New Orleans.*

FACING PAGE, BOTTOM RIGHT: *900 (odd) block of Dumaine Street. A node of antebellum urbanized development in a sector of the city characterized until the late nineteenth century by low, wooden houses and extensive open space.*

In the early nineteenth century, many visitors to New Orleans recorded their dismay at the ease with which various ethnic groups, men and women, blacks and whites, met and socialized in the city's French Quarter. Along the levee in the evening and at the French opera, casual socializing was customary among the French-speaking residents of the city. Outsiders were shocked and fascinated most of all by the commercial ballrooms of the French Quarter

Ostensibly segregated by race and strictly regulated for respectability, these ballrooms nevertheless allowed white men wide latitude for extramarital and interracial adventuring. At the same time, above and behind the open shopfronts, complex micro-landscapes of residences, courtyards, domestic service buildings, and slave quarters housed a mixed population that held a patchwork of ethnic groups and social and economic classes in close proximity, while carefully maintaining social barriers. Outsiders, fascinated and a bit baffled by this unfamiliar mixture of openness and seclusion, could only imagine this active entrepreneurial cityscape as utterly alien to orderly American society—as part of the disorderly, degenerate Old World—and that is why they named it the "French" or "Latin" Quarter.

Even today the architecture of the French Quarter retains many characteristic elements. In the Galley House on Chartres Street, for example, the ground floor was (and is) commercial. The second floor was the main living floor, as indicated by the taller windows and iron balcony. Pay careful attention to the back building, noting the careful way minute architectural adjustments maintain social distinctions. The slaves and their work were relegated to this separate building which, however, stands very close to the main house. By staggering the floor levels between the buildings and holding the upper floor of the back building lower than the windows of the upper floor of the main house, privacy was maintained for main house residents. Similarly, by setting the service building parallel to the rear lot line, leaving its back wall blank or

LEFT: *Salle d'Orléans (1817), 717 Orleans Street. John Davis's ballroom, with its associated (now demolished) theater and gaming hall, was the premier commercial ballroom for white patrons. One for free people of color stood nearby at the corner of Orleans and Bourbon streets. The* bals parés et masqués *held in these rooms conspicuously distinguished French from American New Orleans.*

nearly so, and building a high wall connecting the buildings at the street line, a small, very secluded courtyard (visible from inside the barroom) was created.

The 900 (odd) block of Dumaine offers a good view of the urban social and functional mixture that could be controlled by such microscale architectural devices. At the corner of Dauphine Street is a row of two-story brick houses built around 1833 as rental properties. Behind them stand their back buildings, as at the Gally house. The latter turn a blind rear wall to the largest house on the block, a two-story house (raised to three stories in the 1860s) with a passageway to the rear main entry and service yard, an arrangement favored by Creole builders until the 1830s. Next to this is a smaller house of the same type, followed by a group of two-and-one-half-story row houses similar to those found in northern cities (and in the American parts of New Orleans), built in 1837 as rental housing. This row is broken by an older, one-story wooden Creole cottage, a remnant of the smaller-scale development of the area.

■ DELL UPTON
University of California, Berkeley

PHILADELPHIA: *Health, Reform, Control*

In considering the civic character of Philadelphia in the early nineteenth century, in its preoccupation with the control and discipline of people whose behavior was considered aberrant or abnormal, we should reflect on these contemporary descriptions of the Eastern State Penitentiary. In layout and constant surveillance of inmates, this Philadelphia institution can be seen to be typical of all the rest:

> In the centre of the area stands an observatory, from which ... seven corridors ... radiate. ... The cells are arranged on either side of these corridors, with which they communicate by a square aperture, which may be opened at pleasure from without. There is likewise a small eye-hole, commanding a complete view of the cell, and attached to each is a walled court, in which the prisoner may take exercise. ...
>
> A convict, on arriving at the prison, is blindfolded, and conveyed to a room, where his hair is cut, and after a complete personal ablution, he is led with the same precaution [blindfolding], to the cell destined for his reception. He is thus kept in ignorance of the localities of the prison.
>
> —Thomas Hamilton,
> *Men and Manners in America*, 1834

> An address is then uttered by one of the functionaries of the institution, in which the consequences of his crime are portrayed, the design to be effected by his punishment manifested, and the rules of the prison, as regards the convicts, amply delineated, and he is then locked up and left to the salutary admonition of a reproving conscience, and the reflections which solitude usually produce. In about two weeks they begin to feel the horrors of solitude unemployed. ... Ennui seizes them, every hour is irksome, and they supplicate for the means of employment of the most abject humility. They consider labour as a favour, not a punishment, and they receive it as such.

> They are also furnished with a Bible, some religious tracts, and occasionally other works, calculated to imbue their minds with moral and religious ideas. ...
>
> There is an admirable arrangement in this prison—no man is known by his own proper or baptismal name. On his reception, he receives his own number; ... which is marked over his cell door, and on his clothes. This is known as his prison name, and by which he is usually called or addressed.
>
> —Thomas B. McElwee,
> *A Concise History of the*
> *Eastern Penitentiary of Philadelphia*, 1835

■ DELL UPTON
University of California, Berkeley

There was little development west of Broad Street when John Haviland's Deaf and Dumb Asylum was built in 1824. Their disabilities were thought to make deaf mutes morally vicious. The niches in front were intended to contain statues of sign-language inventors Abbés de l'Épée and Sicard, with their names spelled out below them by brass hands. The building now houses the University of the Arts.

FACING PAGE, BOTTOM LEFT: *The Eastern State Penitentiary (Haviland; 1822–1835), the first and most rigorous experiment in solitary confinement for prisoners, was studied and emulated worldwide. It was part of a therapeutic enclave. Just east on Fairmount Avenue was the 1827 House of Refuge (Haviland), and a few blocks north stands the extant Girard College (1833–1848) for "poor white orphan boys."*

BELOW: *The United States Naval Asylum (1827–1833) housed ill and aged sailors. Its architect, William Strickland, also built the city's third almshouse, immediately across the Schuylkill River at Blockley in 1831 (visible in the background), as well as Friends' Asylum for the Relief of Persons Deprived of the Use of their Reason.*

ABOVE: *Pennsylvania Hospital was founded in 1751, but only its east wing was completed in the initial construction. The west wing was built in 1796 and its center block, with its top-floor surgical theater, was completed in 1805. It was an old-style, uncelled building. Nearby, in the 1000 block of Pine Street, was the city's second almshouse.*

GROUND PLAN OF ASYLUM BUILDING.

ABOVE: *The Friends' Asylum for the Relief of Persons Deprived of the Use of their Reason (1815–1817) was the first of the celled institutional buildings in Philadelphia. A small hand-powered railway that was installed in the front yard in the 1830s and widely imitated at other insane asylums allowed energetic lunatics to drive themselves around in circles during the hours they were not confined to their cells.*

A JOURNEY EMBROIDERED: *Gender Redefined*

Sometimes in making a journey, the route you take is less important than whom you travel with. In moving through the landscapes of nineteenth-century America, for instance, male artists have traditionally been the guides. We, as their companions, come to know New England, the southern states, and the western frontier through their eyes. But what if we traveled into the past and through these places not with Charles Currier and James Ives but with Hannah Stockton and Martha Cannon Webb? How would our understanding of past landscapes and the people who inhabited them change?

In one sense we might better realize that the apparent divisions within early-nineteenth-century landscapes and societies were not natural or inevitable, but were constructed by male-dominated ideologies. One of the most firmly entrenched and seemingly natural of these boundaries, for instance, was the white middle-class belief that a woman's place was in the home, while a man's place was in the world abroad. Many of the depictions of nineteenth-century male artists implicitly stressed this division between the "domestic sphere" and the "public sphere." Women, on the other hand, often highlighted the connections between public and private, male and female, in their renderings of the world.

This is clear when we make our new journey through the nineteenth-century landscape. The places we are taken and the views we are shown by these white middle-class women are hardly limited by the narrow confines of the home. Instead, we are presented with scenes from stereotypically male realms such as the commercial harbor of Stockton, New Jersey, and the Providence, Rhode Island, State House.

In depicting these landscapes within such quintessential domestic forms as needlework and watercolor painting, this appropriation of male realms gains added significance. For in juxtaposing public and domestic male and female themes and forms, Stockton, Webb, Burr, and Keys, whose work is presented here, implicitly collapsed the boundaries that the dominant ideology of the "Cult of Domesticity" held to be natural and inevitable.

To return to our original question, then, by traveling with women we come to know that nineteenth-century American landscapes were not the peaceful and neutral locales of Currier & Ives prints, but intricately embroidered settings with competing depictions and negotiated interpretations.

■ AMY ELIZABETH GREY
University of California, Berkeley

This unfinished panel was probably created by Martha Cannon Webb and was undoubtedly intended to be part of the border of a quilt. Webb drew from a variety of sources and traditions, making her work typical of many other female and folk artists. Her portrayal of ships and the battery continued in a tradition of eighteenth-century engravings and watercolors of Charleston's waterfront.

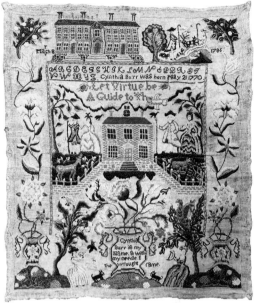

ABOVE: *This sampler was created by Cynthia Burr in 1786 at Polly Balch's school in Providence, Rhode Island. Not only did Burr depict the main building of Brown University but she also wrought the Providence State House. Despite the hours she spent stitching these structures, both of these institutions would have excluded Burr on the basis of her sex. Her decision to make them the topic of her sampler illustrates the manner in which the stereotyped boundaries of public and private, male and female, could be overcome.*

ABOVE LEFT: *This bedcover is believed to have been created by Hannah Stockton around 1830. It probably depicts the harbor and commercial areas of her hometown of Stockton, New Jersey. In portraying these ships and various businesses, Stockton often sacrificed the "realistic" perspective employed within mainstream depictions in favor of the rhythm of repeating shapes and colors.*

LEFT: *This scene of Lockport, New York, was painted by Mary Keys during her attendance at a local ladies' seminary in 1832. Despite the differences in media, Keys's brushstrokes often mimic stitches, and her use of repetitive shapes in the hills and patterns within the dam and houses echoes the patches of fabric in quilts. This continuity between needlework and painting is common in many female works. Indeed, embroidery, watercolors, and cutout forms were frequently all combined in a single effort.*

GOTHIC REVIVAL ARCHITECTURE

During the early nineteenth century, the Gothic Revival style was confined mainly to churches, but by the 1840s it had found a wide popular audience. Some of its success was due to the fact that already familiar building types could be transformed with but a few touches of Gothic embellishment, usually pointy dormer windows and some jigsaw scrollwork along the eaves. For those homeowners with more money to spend, it was possible to build larger houses with asymmetrical, and therefore more "natural," plans. Buildings of this sort, when decked out with lacy barge boards, finials, and brackets, plus the appropriately Gothicized moldings, truly satisfied the romantic premise of the style and provided what Mark Twain called "a bewildering and soul-satisfying spectacle."

The town of Newburgh, New York, can be properly said to incarnate the popular response to Gothic Revival architecture in the United States. It was here that Andrew Jackson Downing, gardener and author of architectural guides, ran his mail-order architectural and landscape design business. From Newburgh his books, filled with elevations and plans drawn up by his architect colleague Alexander Jackson Davis, carried his vision to all parts of the country.

Moving south from the Hudson Valley, where, incidentally, there are plenty of Gothic-style houses, this architectural style spread throughout the Middle Atlantic states. However, when the Gothic mode came into vogue, it was sometimes manifested merely by decorating already existing houses with the appropriate scrollwork motifs. Further south in Athens, Georgia, we find evidence that later in the nineteenth century there was greater acceptance of the Gothic program. Dwellings were not only decorated appropriately but also were given the irregular, asymmetrical floor plans that Davis and Downing often recommended. Swinging out west to Ohio and Missouri, one is sure to note repeatedly along the way the most common vernacular response to the Gothic—a single steeply roofed dormer centrally positioned just over the front door.

■ JOHN MICHAEL VLACH
George Washington University

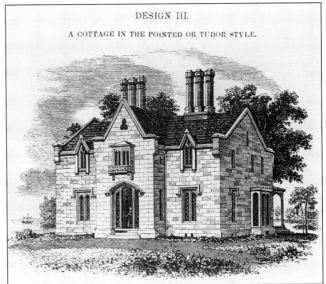

FACING PAGE: *The Merk House (c. 1890) in Athens, Georgia, takes its plan and decoration, like so many dwelling houses of its period, from a pattern book. Here, however, the chief hallmarks of Gothic temperament are an irregular plan and unbalanced projecting gable roof lines.*

ABOVE: *An illustration from Andrew Jackson Downing's Cottage Residences (1842), published while he was living in Newburgh, New York. Although the recommended building plan was little more than a variation of a standard and very widespread folk type, the exterior was graced by several features of the up-to-date Gothic, or "pointed," style, including lancet windows, diamond-shaped panes of glass, and steeply pitched gables.*

LEFT: *The owner or builder of this very plain story-and-a-half house in Centerburg, Ohio, signaled his or her desire to be in step with the Gothic mode with only a single, steep gable—a common strategy in the Midwest, where people tended to negotiate cautiously between the often contradictory attractions of fashion and tradition.*

RIGHT: *The owner of this house in Stoutsville, Missouri, went further down the Gothic path than his or her counterpart in Ohio. The stubby finials at the peaks of the gables and lacy scallops along the eaves suggest a greater degree of comfort with the ideas and values associated with the fashion.*

GREEK REVIVAL ARCHITECTURE

The Greek Revival mode would eventually span the nation from coast to coast, at least in the major cities, where the style was commonly used on public and government structures. Classically styled houses had an equally widespread distribution among the well-to-do, but most temple-form houses were relatively plain buildings built for farmers and small-town merchants.

Versions of temples, usually fashioned in wood and often without the full complement of columns, capitals, friezes, and other classical motifs, were built everywhere, although they dominate most in rural New England, upstate New York, and the upper Midwest near the Great Lakes. Citizens of these regions, it would be fair to say, were generally literate people who paid considerable attention to the dictates of such printed arbiters of taste as fashion books, farmers' journals, and architectural pattern books. Extensive networks of railroads, turnpikes, and canals gave this group relatively easy access to the presumed benefits of cosmopolitan living, so that they, more than other Americans, were especially avid participants in changing trends. Certainly the Greek Revival's well-delineated, freestanding forms bespoke a fierce individualism. Its other features—cleanliness, order, efficiency, novelty—were also deeply embedded American values. Greek Revival architecture, a reminder of the presumed apogee of Old World civilization, had become a grassroots expression of American character.

To view these buildings, one might begin in Richmond, Virginia, at the state capitol, the first temple-form building in the United States, and then move north to Arlington, Virginia, to view the first temple-form house. Then it is on to Newburyport, Massachusetts, to inspect old New England houses built during the colonial period that were somewhat transformed into Grecian houses by the application of a few classical details to their exteriors (as illustrated on page 129). As we follow the spread of the Greek Revival mode through upstate New York, we will frequently encounter the full-blown temple house (a building with a frontward-facing gable flanked by one or two wings). Farther to the west we find a slightly altered version of the temple house. This is the so-called "up-right and wing" building in which the "temple" portion and the wing are the same height. In houses of this configuration, the "wing" is often considered the main part of the house.

■ JOHN MICHAEL VLACH
George Washington University

The construction of Arlington House, begun in 1802, was not completed until 1818. The building was designed by George Hadfield for George Washington Parke Custis and later became the home of Robert E. Lee, commander of the Confederate army. The house, while actually modest in size, seems much more imposing because of the massive scale of the Doric columns that support the front porch.

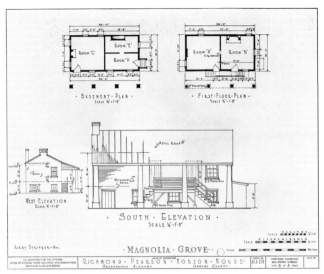

TOP LEFT: *A nineteenth-century illustration of the capitol building of Virginia in Richmond. Designed by Thomas Jefferson, who may have been following the lines of an ancient Roman temple in Nîmes, France. Today the pure temple lines are somewhat obscured by the addition of newer office wings.*

TOP RIGHT: *This structure stands behind a prominent temple-form mansion on the outskirts of Greensboro, Alabama. Here in the Kitchen Quarter the meals for the residents of the "big house" were prepared. Cooking tasks were carried out in the two rooms (A and B) on the upper level, while the cook's family was quartered in the largest room (C) in the semisubterranean basement. Of the remaining storage spaces, Room E served as a wine cellar. Inescapable here is the irony that servitude was cloaked in the architectural wrapping of democratic ideals. There is an attempt here to make chattel slavery more acceptable by setting the labor of slaves behind a row of naively executed Doric columns.*

ABOVE: *The builder of this farmhouse in Oswego County, New York, clearly understood the major elements of a "proper" Greek Revival house. The tall central temple section has the required forward-facing gable and is flanked by symmetrical wings. While there are no corners or cornices, they are nevertheless indicated by wide boards and moldings used as decorative trim. The house is a temple constructed on a farmer's modest budget.*

RIGHT: *The Newton House in Boone County, Illinois, is a common midwestern variant of the temple-form farmhouse. Here the plan is asymmetrical, with only one flanking wing. Moreover, since the "wing" is often larger than the temple section, the temple may look like an addition rather than the central design element of the building.*

EVERYONE WATCHES TIME

By the late 1830s, western Connecticut clockmakers in the Upper Naugatuck Valley had started to mechanize and reorganize their production methods. More sophisticated water-powered technologies and the growing use of brass parts were combined with ideas about labor specialization, in which clocks were to be made "by as many men and women as there were pieces." Despite these innovations, the scale of clockmaking did not alter noticeably; many of those employed in 1850 still worked in small shops with fewer than twenty laborers. Nevertheless, as production was made more efficient and economical, the price of clocks fell. Chauncey Jerome, a well-known manufacturer, boasted that clocks were now cheaper than watches. "No family is so poor," he insisted, "but that they can have a time-piece which is both useful and ornamental." Yet it was shortly after Jerome's retirement in 1860 that Yankee clockmaking was truly transformed into a highly competitive capitalist industry as clocks were made for everyone and every place.

One important center for later-nineteenth-century clockmaking was the Seth Thomas Clock Company of Thomaston, Connecticut. Beginning in 1860, the company enlarged an existing factory complex and built several rows of workers' hous-ing. By 1870 three hundred women and two hundred men were employed, producing 133,000 clocks each year. Most of these clocks were meant to measure time more accurately than earlier ones, so the differences between minutes were marked more clearly in standard units seen on the dials. Clocks were also made to link this more accurate time to other, already familiar systems of reckoning. For example, calendar clocks consisted of two dials, the upper one with hour numbers and minute graduations and the lower with thirty-one days as well as mechanisms for the days of the week and the months of the year. All of these dials were actuated together, so that as hourly time passed, so, in turn, did each day, week, month, and year. These clocks' importance in organizing and managing more efficient households was celebrated in a local newspaper in 1874: "The [Seth Thomas] companies are shipping clocks to all parts of the world—including Japan, Cuba, New Jersey, and other heathen lands. It isn't the fault of Thomaston that meals are ever late in this procrastinating world."

Still other Seth Thomas clocks, outside the home and workplace, helped to standardize time and remind people constantly of its passage. Street clocks, with as many as four illuminated dials facing

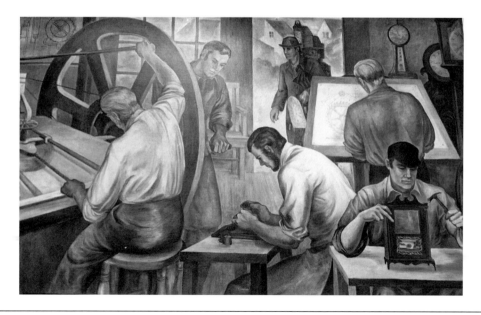

LEFT: *The Seth Thomas movement shops in the early twentieth century. The mechanisms for tower clocks were manufactured here from the early 1870s onward. For Seth Thomas, time was money, and the huge clock face on the factory wall never let the company's employees forget that fact.*

in different directions, were placed along the sidewalks of the commercial centers of many late-nineteenth-century cities. By continually checking such clocks, people reminded themselves to be prompt and punctual, "on time." In the same way, tower clocks were built by the Seth Thomas Company for municipal and factory buildings, churches, schools, and railway stations across America. "Thousands of travelers," it was reported, used the clock in the terminal in Ogden City, Utah, to see "the correct time day and night." And in the *Springfield Union* newspaper, a new tower clock's accuracy was celebrated: It was said to be "capable of regulating the doings of the people of a city as precise even as Springfield, Massachusetts." By the early 1890s, Yankee clocks had become indispensable to the future growth and differentiation of capitalist societies around the world, thereby fulfilling Chauncey Jerome's dream. But clocks had also become symbolic of capitalism's darker side:

> *The tick of the clock is the boss in his anger.*
> *The face of the clock has the eyes of the foe.*
> *The Clock—I shudder—Dost hear how it*
>   *draws me?*
> *It calls me "Machine" and it cries [to] me*
>   *"Sew"!*

> ■ RUSSELL G. HANDSMAN
>   *University of Rhode Island, Kingston*

By the end of the nineteenth century, the clock—far more than the sun or stars—marked time for most people. Pictured here are street clocks on Main Street, Springfield, Massachusetts, in the 1890s.

FACING PAGE, BOTTOM LEFT: *Connecticut clockmaking in the 1830s. This mural shows how clocks were made by small groups of workers, each of whom had a specific job to do, in the days before production became mechanized and industrialized.*

FACING PAGE, BOTTOM RIGHT: *Calendar clocks made by the Seth Thomas Clock Company for homes and offices regulated the lives of those who owned and watched them, dividing their lives into carefully measured months, days, hours, minutes, and seconds. Before the nineteenth century, few people kept such close track of time.*

PLANTATIONS AND RESERVATIONS
Nature Controlled and Standardized

Historical landscapes are a form of nature united with culture for a concrete purpose. The creators of landscapes, particularly plantation owners, had definite purposes in constructing grand conglomerations of nature and culture. The person who had to labor and live within one of these created landscapes was expected to react to it as if it were natural. The author attempted to control the people who were forced to use it, and to make control seem natural and unalterable. In various ways, the people who were constrained by a landscape resisted its domination, and sometimes this resistance could be expressed in alterations to the landscape.

Middleburg Plantation grew rice on the eastern branch of Cooper River, northeast of Charleston, South Carolina, before the Civil War. This highly profitable crop was grown by African American slaves. They were forced into houses of Euro-American form, arranged in un-African patterns, near large Georgian plantation houses that stood amid great alleys of live oaks, giant trees transplanted by the order of the planter and through the labor of the slaves. Resistance took many forms, including efforts to preserve African culture and efforts to get away from the main house, to live in areas not so directly controlled by the planters. This cultural battle persisted, on this and thousands of other plantations, until it was transformed into the active violence of the Civil War, and the more subtle violence that came after emancipation.

Following the Civil War, another problem of American culture seemed to be on its way to being resolved. The last Native Americans, who had fought for four hundred years to preserve their land from European appropriation, were defeated and forced onto reservations in the last series of "Indian Wars." One veteran of these wars, General Richard Pratt, sought to make this victory more complete through forcing the rising generation of "wild" Native Americans to adopt Euro-American culture. He created the Indian School at Carlisle, Pennsylvania, for this purpose, transforming a Civil War army base into a school that would educate the children of Plains and Southwestern tribes to the nineteenth-century values of work, obedience, and docility. The campus, squares, quadrangles, paved paths, blocks of buildings, and solid permanence contrasted utterly with the mobile life these people were born to, as did the military discipline and the haircuts the male students were forced to undergo. Some Native Americans resisted this, by resuming Native culture when they returned to their homelands; others became the Euro-Americans that Pratt desired them to be. Ultimately, this experiment failed, and Native American culture was not entirely "domesticated."

Control of people and culture through control of a

The hierarchy of power on every Southern plantation was instilled not only by the physical layout of the buildings, but in the customary behavior of its inhabitants. In this 1856 engraving, the mistress of a plantation is dutifully welcomed by her slaves after a trip away from home.

ABOVE: *Carlisle Indian School, in Carlisle, Pennsylvania, late nineteenth century. Native American students gather on a campus quadrangle bounded by military barracks, now used as their dormitory. In a Euro-American landscape, Native Americans learn to be "good" Euro-Americans.*

CENTER RIGHT: *In the combined first- and second-grade class at the Carlisle Indian School, the uniformed students of varying ages practice formal penmanship and English composition under the watchful eye of their teacher.*

BOTTOM RIGHT: *Middleburg Plantation. Slave quarters were immediately east of the main house in the late eighteenth century, though some quarters were far to the south of the house, in the Smoky Hill area. In the early part of the nineteenth century, the alley of live oak trees was planted, leading from the public road to the front door of the main house. Tradition holds that some of these trees were up to forty feet tall when they were transplanted, and that the job took more than five years to complete.*

landscape involves the incorporation of a subject people into a defined place within the culture of their masters. People have always resisted such domination, and their resistance has also contributed to the American landscape, albeit in a more subtle way than the landscapes of control that we notice immediately. This conflict has created our present landscapes, artifacts of nature refined through culture, and the ultimate scene for our history.

■ DAVID W. BABSON
Illinois State University

LANDSCAPES OF SLAVERY: *Regions and Commodities*

Southern plantations, where close to two-thirds of the North American slave population lived in 1860, were centers for the production of five major commodities for export: tobacco, rice, sugar, cotton, and livestock. Each of these commodities required a particular climate, particular soils, and a specialized mode of production. As a result, several distinctive plantation "zones" evolved across the region, each with its own appearance and organization. Among those southern plantations that have survived since the nineteenth century, it is still possible to experience the domains that plantation owners controlled but that slaves often felt rightfully belonged to them.

Green Hill plantation in Campbell County, Virginia, is a former tobacco estate that represents the nineteenth-century expansion of the agricultural commodity that had proved profitable from the earliest colonial period. Farther south, in Georgetown County, South Carolina, Friendfield plantation, with its extensive slave village, provides a good example of the kind of centralized estate with a large slave work force that was required to produce the rice of coastal Carolina.

The heart of cotton country runs through the center of an Alabama region known as the "black belt" because of its dark, fertile soil. Typical of the nineteenth-century cotton plantations is Thornhill in Greene County, established by former Virginian James I. Thornton in the 1830s. Farther west, along the Mississippi River, sugar plantations were among the largest and most impressive holdings, and many of them, like Evergreen, are preserved.

The plantations of the Bluegrass country around Lexington, Kentucky, represent yet another type of slave-based agriculture. Here were raised the horses and mules needed to conduct agricultural operations in the sugar, cotton, rice, and tobacco plantations of the other regions of the South. Estates in this part of the state consisted then mainly of pastureland, subdivided by the distinctive rock "fences," laid up without mortar by slave craftsmen, whose contribution to these and other southern landscapes is not often acknowledged today.

■ JOHN MICHAEL VLACH
George Washington University

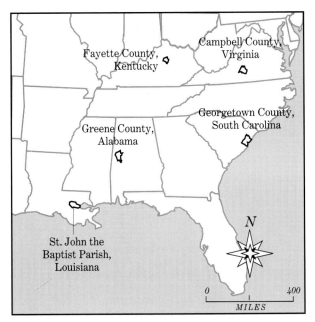

ABOVE: *A segment of twenty slave quarters still standing at Evergreen Plantation in St. John the Baptist Parish, Louisiana. This sugar estate, which fronts the Mississippi River, was established around 1840 by the Becnel family, who owned as many as 102 slaves. Large rows of slave cabins like these are very rare today; had there not been a concerted effort by the present owners to maintain these buildings (particularly after extensive hurricane damage in 1965), the site would no longer provide so clear an image of life in the former slave community.*

FACING PAGE: *Green Hill Plantation, as seen from its fields looking past an ensemble of slave houses, kitchens, and other work buildings to owner Samuel Panhill's residence in the distance. Established in 1797, this tobacco estate grew to almost five thousand acres by 1864, when it was home to eighty-four slaves.*

RIGHT: *View of a typical tree-shaded horse pasture surrounded by a typical rock fence made with limestone in Fayette County, Kentucky, the heart of the Bluegrass region. Note that the capping stones are set upright to discourage animals from climbing over.*

BELOW: *View of so-called Slave Street at Friendfield Plantation in Georgetown County, South Carolina, c. 1905, showing a group of ten wood-frame houses clustered near a slave chapel (note the spire in the row of buildings on the right). The rice-growing plantations in this area often required several slave villages to house their extensive work forces.*

MASS PRODUCTION: *Workers and Factory Towns*

Industrial sites are a reminder of America's enterprising past and are usually displayed to teach people about progress and the benefits of material wealth. Often not explicitly mentioned are twelve-hour days, seventy-hour work weeks, and substandard living and working conditions. Craftsmen lost their individuality, and laborers became interchangeable components in a factory system. Nineteenth-century industrial sites show how capitalists explicitly manipulated workplaces and domestic spaces to create individuals similar to one another and who also fit into the industrial system.

In Manchester, New Hampshire, in 1839 the Amoskeag Manufacturing Company planned an industrial community and relied on women for its labor base. Manufacturing provided one of the few opportunities women had to become independent of the male-dominated farm structure. In the late nineteenth century the Amoskeag Manufacturing Company became the largest textile mill in the New World. Although the New England textile industry collapsed in the twentieth century, the industrial buildings survive.

Lowell, Massachusetts, is built on a standard grid plan and contains nineteenth-century boarding houses. By 1850 Lowell had become the largest cotton textile center in the nation. Today the Boott Mills of Lowell are under adaptive reuse, housing a National Urban Park that interprets lifeways and industry in the nineteenth century—stressing the challenges faced by the "Lowell girls" who worked in the mills in the first half of the nineteenth century and by the later immigrant workers, who began to arrive in the 1840s and 1850.

Another important scene of industrialization is Harpers Ferry, West Virginia, which began operations in 1799 as one of the national armories under federal government supervision. For decades many armorers were allowed to practice their craft in a traditional way, rather than participate in wage labor. Armory workers in Harpers Ferry believed that working by the clock and on the assembly line

The Musket Factory at Harpers Ferry. This 1810–1820s landscape, painted near present-day Hilltop House Inn, shows an early musket factory along the Potomac River. Today the musket factory no longer stands; about one third lies under the railroad embankment. While many of the factory's architectural features were constructed in a symmetrical and standardized style, workers adhered to a craft-oriented system of gun manufacturing and resisted the new technology and the manufacturing system associated with it.

ABOVE: *Boott Cotton Mills at Lowell, Massachusetts. A nineteenth-century litho-graph of the Boott Mills shows the harmonious coexistence of industry and pastoral setting envisioned by early industrialists. While middle- and upper-class residents of Lowell are shown in the foreground, the laborers themselves are invisible, pre-sumably at work within the noisy, dangerous, and unhealthy environment of the industrial complex.*

ABOVE RIGHT: *Space was also segregated along class and gen-der lines, as can be seen in this nineteenth-century engraving. In industrial New England, the space and time of production were controlled by white males. Poorer women were often given the most menial jobs in factories, since employers were able to pay women less than men for similar work, a tradition that still continues.*

demeaned their skill and position. Workers actively resisted these innovations, yet by the 1840s their protests carried little weight. With national secu-rity and efficiency considered more important than workers' self-esteem, the arms factories were gradually rebuilt on a standardized plan.

A drive through the existing residential portions of the town today, however, attests to the persis-tence of individual identity, as early residents built their own homes of different shapes, materials, and sizes. Not until workers openly resisted factory dis-cipline in the 1830s did the government begin to standardize both work and domestic facilities in the armory town.

■ PAUL A. SHACKEL
National Park Service,
Harpers Ferry National Park

ABOVE: *Amoskeag Manufacturing Company at Manchester, New Hampshire. This nineteenth-century photograph taken within the mill complex shows how standardizing not only affected the indus-trial process but also the architecture and landscape. The railroad tracks serve as a graphic reminder of the transportation infrastruc-ture that conveyed goods produced in the factories. Railroads neces-sitated the standardization of time between places in the nineteenth century in order to facilitate commerce.*

AFRICAN RELIGION IN AMERICA

Eighteenth- and nineteenth-century travel accounts reveal that slaves throughout the West Indies practiced the religions of their ancestors, but recent archaeological discoveries in the southeastern United States show that this retention was much more widespread, and in some places survived slavery.

Slaves in South Carolina established strong pottery-making traditions. Not only do a number of the fragmentary pots express African forms but some, like those found at Middleburg Plantation near Charleston, were inscribed with cross marks similar to signs for the cosmos created by the Bakongo people of Africa. Objects found buried inside three contiguous ground-story rooms of the Charles Carroll House in Annapolis, Maryland, suggest that slaves living there held beliefs similar to those of the South Carolina potters. In Manassas National Battlefield Park, on a house site occupied by an African American family soon after 1870, archaeologists recovered a cache of quartz crystals much like those from the important Carroll House find. Stones like these, as well as polished black stones found on several historic African American sites, are spiritually powerful objects in traditional Bakongo practice.

Lone blue beads, important for protection from malevolent spirits according to African beliefs, were recovered from this and other sites in the park, and from a slave quarter site at Thomas Jefferson's boyhood home, Shadwell, in Virginia. During excavations of slaves' quarters at Jefferson's nearby Monticello, archaeologists found a multifaceted potsherd, cut to highlight a star design. It is similar to the painted star, or asterisk, on a shard found with the crystals in the Carroll House. Also on the Monticello site was a cowrie shell, a pierced coin, and a rock crystal. On a slave quarter site at Jefferson's summer home near Lynchburg, archaeologists found a crystal, smoothed black stones, and another pierced coin.

Belowground remains from these and other sites throughout the eastern United States are changing the way we think about the region's past. It is clear now that early attempts to silence slaves' native cultural expressions and religious practices failed in the American South just as in the West Indies, and that some ritual practices survived into the late nineteenth century.

■ GEORGE C. LOGAN
University of Maryland, College Park

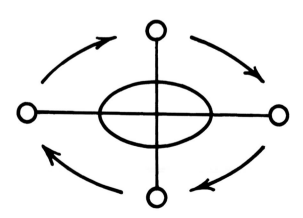

LEFT: *In 1991, an archaeological excavation inside the ground story of the Charles Carroll House in Annapolis, Maryland, revealed that the East Wing room (right-hand side beneath chimney) was occupied by slaves from the late 1700s until Charles Carroll of Carrollton moved to Baltimore in 1820.*

BELOW: *This collection from the East Wing room provides material evidence that the slaves living there kept their African heritage alive inside the Carroll House, by using pierced coins, disks, and crystals that were religiously significant objects in Africa.*

ABOVE: *This cache of quartz crystals and a quartz spear point (3500 B.C.) was excavated from the Nash family site within Manassas National Battlefield Park. It is directly comparable to the collection of Carroll House crystals, and together the two discoveries suggest that African-based traditions were long practiced by African Americans in the mid-Atlantic region.*

FACING PAGE BOTTOM: *Originating in the Kongo region of Africa, variations of this sign for the cosmos, or cosmogram, have been identified in both Africa and the Americas. These symbols represent the universe's most basic divisions and connections. The horizontal line separates the realm of the living, below, from the realm of the dead. The vertical line represents the pathway of power and communication between the two worlds. Archaeologist Leland Ferguson of the University of South Carolina has excavated a number of marked colonoware pots, such as the bowl base pictured at left, from historic African American sites. Scholars argue that these New World cosmograms prove that African Americans retained their ancestral beliefs and values.*

ABOVE: *Archaeologists at Thomas Jefferson's Monticello discovered these pierced coins, cowrie shell, and horn ring during excavations of slave quarter sites on Mulberry Row. Their presence on house sites lining the plantation's main street suggests that evidence of deeply rooted West African traditions were visible even on one of America's most famous plantations.*

MIDWESTERN UTOPIAS

The American Midwest presents a natural environment composed of gently rolling prairies, remarkably flat bottomlands, and densely wooded riverbanks. Aboriginal peoples, who lived in this environment for thousands of years, found it to be incredibly rich. American entrepreneurs came to this environment in the early nineteenth century eager to establish towns that would become profitable in the expanding American economy. During the early expansion of the new American nation, supporters of American business and economic growth came to characterize this apparently inexorable westward march of the American frontier as ordained by God. Clearly, the destiny of the American nation was to stride the two oceans that placed natural limits on the North American continent.

Within this same environment, however, other Americans—utopianists—saw God's will differently. These visionaries of religious achievement, rather than of capitalist success, built largely functional and symbolic landscapes instead of capitalist ones. The ordered, neat landscapes they created in the Midwest were intended not for the pursuit of earthly profit but for the attainment of heavenly glory. These landscapes—among them, a symmetrical, highly symbolic garden in Ohio, a shrubbery maze in Indiana, a massive temple in Illinois—were intended to assist true believers in their lifelong search for moral perfection and godliness. These creations on the prairies stood in stark contrast to the soot and noise of the steam locomotive and the steamboat—those visible symbols of American enterprise—and presented an alternative vision of American life.

The paradox of the utopian communities was that to survive, they too had to be economically feasible; the difference for the utopianists, though, was to also seek success in Godly lives. And just as the landscapes of the nineteenth-century capitalists—abandoned rail lines, dry canal beds, empty grain elevators, and all their modern variants—still dot the Midwestern landscape, so too do the remnants of the utopian communities remain visible.

■ CHARLES E. ORSER, JR.
Illinois State University

New Harmony, Indiana. This reconstructed hedge, The Labyrinth, was designed by Harmony founder George Rapp. In addition to being the only amusement permitted the Rappites, this maze has a deeper meaning. The tower is intended to symbolize that heaven is attained only after the difficult journey of life, symbolized by the maze.

NINETEENTH-CENTURY UTOPIAN COMMUNITIES

Amana, Iowa •

• Bishop Hill, Illinois

• Nauvoo, Illinois

Zoar, Ohio •

Watervliet,
Ohio

Whitewater, Ohio • • Union Village, Ohio

New Harmony, Indiana •

Pleasant Hill,
Kentucky

N

0   200
MILES

BELOW: *Nauvoo, Illinois, the great city of the Mormons, as it looked to a German artist in 1857. The Temple on the heights overlooking the Mississippi not only symbolizes the spiritual power of the Mormons but, when juxtaposed with the small settler's cabin in the foreground, shows the distinction between them and the local settlers.*

BELOW: *Zoar, Ohio. This plat, published in an 1875 county atlas, shows the neat plan of the Zoarites. The prominent garden is intended to symbolize eternal life and the quest for heaven.*

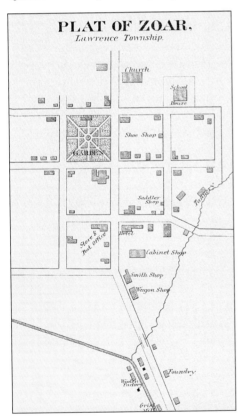

RIGHT: *Bishop Hill, Illinois. This building, called Big Brick, was constructed in 1851; it measured 45 feet wide and 200 feet long and was the largest structure west of Chicago at the time. It demonstrates the communal spirit of the Jansenists, as most people, adult and child, lived there.*

THE CHEROKEE: *Adaptation and Survival*

A trip through the present-day territory of the Cherokee reminds us that many of the native inhabitants of what is now the United States did not obligingly disappear when their traditional way of life was challenged or when their land was taken from them.

The prehistoric site of Etowah (also described on page 40) exemplified the dynamic and complex native cultures, which were eventually seen by Spanish, and later, other European explorers and settlers. The Cherokee, an Iroquoian-speaking people who inhabited the area of present-day western Carolina, northern Georgia, and eastern Tennessee, maintained complex religious ceremonies and supported themselves through intensive agriculture. Long allied with the British, they were initially hostile to the newly established United States but established treaty relations with the federal government in 1794.

During the early nineteenth century, the Cherokee struggled to adapt to Euro-American civilization while preserving their native identity. Centered at the town of New Echota, which was established as their capital in 1825, the Cherokee nation resisted the destruction of their culture and attempts by missionaries, government agents, and others to define a new way of life for them. An important cultural innovation was the invention of a Cherokee syllabary in which their language could be written. Their newspaper, the *Cherokee Phoenix*, printed in both English and Cherokee, promoted literacy, but insisted on the equal status of its two languages and cultures. The title was taken from Greek mythology, but refers to the rebirth of the Cherokee people out of the ashes of a way of life that had become impossible to maintain.

In the 1830s, however, threats to the physical existence of the Cherokee nation intensified. By the Treaty of New Echota (1835), a tiny minority of the nation sold seven million acres of its land to the U.S. government. This act paved the way to the forcible removal in 1838–1839 of fifteen thousand Cherokee to the Arkansas and Oklahoma territories in a brutal forced march supervised by the U.S. Army that became infamous as the "Trail of Tears."

A small group of Cherokee escaped removal by fleeing into the Great Smoky Mountains. Late in the nineteenth century, their descendants formed a tribal corporation and were eventually allowed to settle in a small reservation in western North Carolina. Though the Eastern Cherokee now number only about seven thousand, their story is one of change, survival, and the preservation of a distinct national identity.

■ BARBARA J. LITTLE
National Park Service, National Capitol Region

The site of Etowah was one of several political-religious-social centers for peoples participating in what archaeologists call the Southeastern Ceremonial Complex. These cultures, which flourished after A.D. 1000, were marked by impressive earthen mounds and a characteristic decorative style. The peoples that carried on these traditions were ancestral to the Cherokee and Creek.

ABOVE: *The permanent capital of the Cherokee nation established at New Echota in 1825 endured until Removal on the Trail of Tears in 1839. Pictured here is a reconstruction of the printshop of the* Cherokee Phoenix *newspaper. The newspaper was printed in both Cherokee and English and embodied the struggle to retain a separate, independent nation.*

LEFT: *Sequoya (c. 1760–1843), also known as George Gist, invented the Cherokee syllabary. Submitted to the council in 1821, this alphabet of eighty-five characters allowed Cherokee to become a written language.*

BELOW RIGHT: *At the Oconaluftee Indian village, a Cherokee woman continues the tribal tradition of beadwork. Though the materials and designs are modern, the techniques have been handed down from earlier periods of Cherokee history.*

ABOVE: *Cabins such as this one were a common residence for many Cherokee during the early 1800s. This adaptation of Euro-American culture was part of the larger determination of the Cherokee nation to create a new way of life while retaining its traditions and identity.*

THE CIVIL WAR: *Economic and Social Battlefields*

We set aside places like Gettysburg, Antietam, and Manassas national historical parks to commemorate and learn about the Civil War. Although that war is usually defined as a military event and the focus of interpretation at Civil War sites is primarily on battlefield movements and military technology, the war was also a contest between certain contentious ideas and incompatible interests—even beyond issues of slavery and states' rights. There are naturally many sites and issues that are overlooked in conventional accounts.

Harpers Ferry, West Virginia—mentioned earlier in this chapter—was the scene of early military industrialization and is usually included in accounts of the Civil War in connection with the strategic importance of its arms production facilities; the story of John Brown's famous 1860 raid on its arsenal; and subsequent Confederate attempts to capture the site. Yet Harpers Ferry was also the scene of struggles over the introduction of northern ideas of how industry should be organized and run. It was there that mass production took the place of craftsmanship in providing weapons for the armed forces of the United States.

Antietam National Battlefield Park presents the human and military story of the Battle of Antietam. The underlying theme of the presentation is that in battle and in death, soldiers, northern and southern, were made equal. However, ethnic and social minorities in the North and South were not equal during the Civil War era. In the North

ABOVE: *African American soldiers played an important role in the operations of the Union army. Shown here are the guard detail and guardhouse of the 107th U.S. Colored Infantry at Fort Corcoran, near Washington.*

FACING PAGE: *The intensive industrialization of American warfare can be seen best at Harpers Ferry, West Virginia. Seen here in a photograph taken around 1860, the appearance of the town had been transformed dramatically from the bucolic landscape pictured on page 152.*

BELOW: *This photograph of casualties of the Irish Brigade is one of the few known photographs of unburied Union dead after the Battle of Antietam, near Sharpsburg, Maryland. In 1988, archaeologists of the National Park Service unearthed the remains of members of this immigrant unit who fell on what has become known as the bloodiest day in American military history.*

during the mid-nineteenth century, a huge influx of immigrants—including large numbers of Irish Catholics—settled in urban areas. These immigrants came to the United States to claim freedom, but once here their opportunities were limited by their low social position and refusal to melt into the pot of homogeneity. As the lowest-paid free white laborers in the market, the Irish were routinely discriminated against.

Soon after the outbreak of the Civil War, General Thomas Francis Meagher recruited thousands of these Irish immigrants from New York City to form the "Irish Brigade." Meagher intended to use the troops' American military experience as training for a future war to free Ireland from English rule and thus restore the freedom of the Irish people in their own land. However, the massive casualties suffered by the Irish Brigade at the Battle of Antietam in September 1862 ended the independent existence of the brigade and put an end to the plan to fight for Ireland. And although a northern victory in the Civil War was intended to establish freedom and equality in the South, inequality and lack of eco-nomic opportunity continued in the North even after the war for those immigrant workers who refused to lose their nationality and integrate socially and culturally.

The role of African Americans in the Civil War, as slaves in the South and as soldiers in the Union army, has often been highlighted. Yet for many African American veterans and former slaves, the war accomplished little. In the South, they faced racial segregation and tenant-farming conditions that preserved many of the characteristics of the pre-Emancipation period. In the North, they faced more subtle—but no less pernicious—forms of discrimination in housing, legal rights, and economic opportunity.

The Civil War created a national state out of the individual states, yet this happened not only by the gun but also through the destruction and peripheralization of other regional or ethnic visions of what it meant to be American.

■ DANA HOLLAND
Washington, D.C.

INDUSTRIAL CLEVELAND: *Neighborhoods and Development*

Though Cleveland was still a largely agricultural community in the 1830s, the opening of the Ohio Canal and the construction of a gunpowder factory (pictured here in the foreground) and other industrial facilities on the banks of the Cuyahoga River were to have far-reaching effects for the economic life and demographic makeup of the city.

The 1832 completion of the Ohio Canal, a water-level route connecting Portsmouth, Ohio, on the Ohio River, to Cleveland on Lake Erie, opened the Midwest to the cash markets of the Atlantic seaboard. Cleveland's primitive and constrained economy of subsistence farming, distilling, and land speculation quickly changed to a concentration of market agriculture, banking, and transportation. Within a generation, railroads and lake freighters increased access to production facilities and markets for urban manufacturers. Northern Michigan iron and southern Ohio coal made Cleveland the nation's leader in heavy industrial manufacturing by the 1860s, significantly increasing its demand for new capital and labor. The far-reaching effects of these transformations can be seen in the changes to the ethnic makeup and physical layout of the city, beginning in the mid-nineteenth century.

Though horsecars ran along some of Cleveland's major streets, most businessmen and workers walked to and from home several times a day. As a result, the city's neighborhoods were initially de-fined less by income or ethnicity than by job opportunities nearby. Thus, impressive houses often stood in close proximity to modest single family homes or boardinghouses for workers. By the time of the Civil War, however, this pattern of neighborhood diversity began to disappear, as small companies were gradually replaced by larger, consolidated corporations. These companies employed ever greater numbers of immigrant workers who were housed in multiblock sections of the city—characterized by street after street of closely packed, single family houses near factories and mills.

Thus emerged a distinct pattern of ethnic- and class-based segregation, as many central areas of the city, losing upwardly mobile middle-class populations, experienced an early version of neighborhood pauperization. A case in point is the residential development of the area immediately to the west of the Cuyahoga River, a neighborhood that came to be called Irishtown Bend. Populated primarily by immigrant workers and their families, this area suffered from economic and municipal discrimination.

BELOW: *After 1851, the western Cuyahoga riverbank between Detroit and Columbus Streets became Irishtown Bend. Two generations of new working class Americans lived in eighty one-and-a-half- and two-story wooden frame houses. With no sanitary facilities, railroad tracks down Riverbed Road to the east, and the steep hillside to the west, the neighborhood was gradually depopulated by the outward and upward mobility of its largely immigrant residents.*

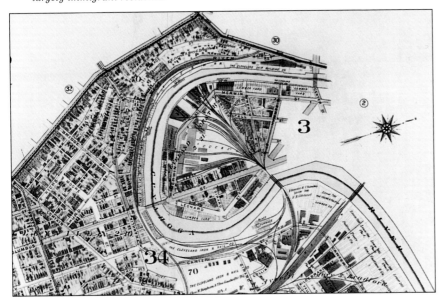

BOTTOM: *This planned working-class neighborhood, developed by Leonard Case, Jr., as early as 1878, stretched east and west from Case Avenue (now E. 40th St.) and from Superior Avenue north to the lakeside docks, mills, forges, factories, and railyards. In this area, small north-south streets packed with single-family dwellings (often two or more deep on the same lot) crossed avenues with schools, churches, and stores. Pictured here is nineteenth-century workers' housing on Belden Street (now E. 42nd St.), with the old Brown Hoist Factory in the rear.*

BELOW: *The earlier mixture of residences of bankers, day laborers, lawyers, clerks, journeyman craftsmen, and wealthy merchants in Cleveland's neighborhoods was gradually brought to an end by the 1860s. This fine 1847 brick house of Henry Merwin, owner of several warehouses and lake schooners, was moved in 1869 from West St. Clair to Prospect Avenue because the increasing commercialization of the neighborhood resulted in the widening of its streets—and the consequent reduction of private yards.*

Late-nineteenth-century fire insurance maps delineate individual buildings right up to the borders of Irishtown Bend; the area inside its borders was usually left blank and marked with the words "Shanties Beyond This Point." Yet recent archaeological excavations of foundations and construction materials here prove that these "shanties" were as substantial as the structures that were classified as houses in other neighborhoods. The significant factors in this differentiation seem to be the inhabitants' economic status and—no less important—their ethnic identity.

An important process can be observed in the neighborhoods of mid-nineteenth-century Cleveland, in which discrimination and internal social differentiation among the city's inhabitants intensified precisely at a time when the economic system of the United States was becoming increasingly homogenized.

■ DAVID S. BROSE
Royal Ontario Museum

5

THE MAKING OF A MASS CULTURE

1865–1917

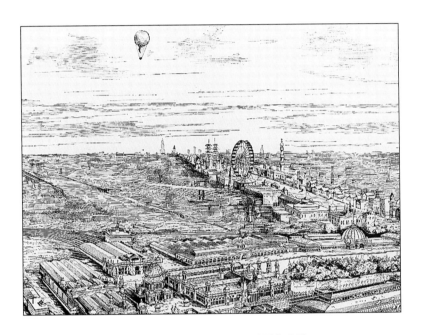

WITH CONTRIBUTIONS BY

Elaine S. Abelson

Jeremy Brecher

Eileen Gatti

Kathleen Hulser

Charles E. Orser, Jr.

Margaret S. Purser

Robert W. Snyder

Karen Zimmerman

Mark Bograd

Mark S. Cassell

David Glassberg

Paul H. Mattingly

Adrian Praetzellis

Robert W. Rydell

Suzanne Wasserman

Larry J. Zimmerman

We want to characterize the technological changes and social struggles of the half century between the assassination of Abraham Lincoln and America's entry into World War I by looking at transformed landscapes, novel Victorian notions of urban life, tenant farming, and immigration. All these are aspects of industrialization that changed the United States irreversibly. The technologies and values that triumphed with the Civil War began to dominate the country and were expressed in cities, regions, towns, and a whole way of life. The advance of new technologies—many of them given impetus by the requirements of the Civil War effort—made cities monuments to capitalist values. The separation of workplace and living place had already occurred, but now there were new spaces expressly designed for relaxation, pleasure, and escape. While in some regions of the country older forms of agriculture continued, industrialization and industrial-style agriculture spread and dominated much of the continent. This far-reaching transformation was not due to an inevitable march of progress or the sudden dawning of modernity. Rather, it is the result of the triumph of the profit-making way of life.

In this chapter we will describe some of the ways in which the American city was reshaped to accommodate millions of immigrants and how the culture of consumption was taught to them by the great department stores and mail-order catalogues. While this was going on, the most brutal outcome of the European "discovery" of America—the extermination of the Native Americans—was being completed on the High Plains. And culminating the period were the great World's Fairs, the spectacles of the century, which glorified "Progress" and made it seem inevitable.

The nineteenth-century urban establishment—owners and manufacturers—sought to mold American society to its own image, to supplant and

A craving for appearances of order, propriety, and stability characterized the urban culture of late-nineteenth-century America. These posed photographic portraits, printed from glass negatives excavated by historical archaeologists Adrian and Mary Praetzellis in Sacramento, California, were taken around 1890 by Julius Asher of the Opposition Studio.

modernize the mores and traditional values of immigrants, southerners, Native Americans, utopianists, and the working class and to rationalize for them the "business of doing business." Modernizing meant utilitarian public works, including the laying out of public parks in the midst of urban areas, and of residential neighborhoods—suburbs—outside strictly business or factory districts. For example, on pages 184–185 Adrian Praetzellis describes the reshaping of the libertarian Gold Rush community into a well-regulated, homogeneous commercial society as the supreme challenge for California's industrialists. The owners of the mines, railroads, and factories were so successful that mass-produced consumer goods and their civic symbols came to dominate the city visually. Taste and style in everything from architecture to tableware became uniform and was supposed to symbolize the achievement of a moral consensus. But they also provided a cultural standard that was not accepted wholesale by all classes of people.

CITIES AND CONFLICT

As Jeremy Brecher discusses on pages 186–187, the major American cities became industrial complexes specializing in the production of certain kinds of products: brass, clocks, hardware, carriages, steel, and so on. Hundreds of independent entrepreneurs were pushed out or bought out as increasingly large industrial concerns emerged. Backyard workshops where owner and apprentices once worked together grew into block-long factories, operated by huge work forces of immigrants from rural areas in America or elsewhere, and supervised by a class of administrators distinguished by the white collars that they wore. Many farm villages became mill villages and eventually industrial cities and towns. Individual proprietorships or partnerships became corporations. Mergers and acquisitions melded local companies into a system of giant national corporations, a handful of which dominated the national market—and eventually the world. By the middle of the twentieth century, 40 percent of all the world's manufacturing was done in the United States.

In the sooty asphalt-and-brick centers of industry, mass production by machine increased productivity and reduced the cost of products enormously, allowing a further expansion of the market. The rise of manufacturing transformed self-employed farmers and craftsmen into employees who did not own their own tools and materials and had no way to make a living except by selling their capacity for labor to others. The burgeoning factories attracted millions of immigrants, one of the greatest challenges to the privately owned American industrial system was keeping the growing workforce under close supervision and control.

The exploitation involved in the factories and mines produced a series of major strikes and labor-organizing efforts from the 1820s through the 1940s, which was often met by violent resistance from private guards, police, the National Guard, and even the regular army. The attainment in the United States of even the most basic levels of job security, minimum wage scales, pensions, health insurance, and other bases for a higher standard of living were won by workers only after bitter struggles and at great cost.

Industrialization and immigration focused on cities, but they both had major impact on the American West—as a source of raw materials and as a place that sustained the ideology of escape, personal freedom, and unlimited economic possibilities. These uses of the West produced profound conflict between Native Americans and Anglo-Americans and within the Anglo-American community itself. In our national mind's eye, the wide open spaces and excitement of the West seem so different from the sooty, closely packed industrial cities of the Northeast. Yet both regions can be seen as parts of the same expanding and intensifying industrial economy. Certainly there are similarities in the movement of people to both the eastern and western regions of America; they attracted immigrants fleeing older societies to find better-paying jobs. And as Margaret Purser points out on pages 188–189, the epic "westering" process was not restricted to covered wagons or ponies. Many came to the ports of the West Coast by the same kinds of steamships that brought others to the eastern factories. These immigrants, as Dr. Purser shows,

These silk workers, taking time out to pose next to their machinery in a Paterson, New Jersey, factory, 1890–1910, are representative of the industrial labor force that made the rapid expansion of the American economy possible.

were certainly not all English-speaking cowboys or pioneers, and they had a bewildering variety of final destinations: railroad work camps, construction crews for newly established towns, mines, Indian territories, and isolated homesteads. People moved West because the expanding industrial economy of the United States in the nineteenth century needed workers to extract and process valuable natural resources—not only because of the freedom of the frontier.

In fact, the "West" shifted location constantly as new pockets of fuels and metals, timber and agricultural commodities became technologically accessible. The West was created, not discovered—Dr. Purser further notes—as vast stretches of land were transformed into property, and as peoples and cultures were connected to labor and markets. In that sense, the "winning" of the West was strikingly similar to the "discovery" of the New World. The driving force of such conversion was profit. Land speculators, railroad agents, town boosters, and labor contractors sold what they described as an empty, unclaimed land of individual freedom, regional autonomy, and limitless opportunity to eager immigrants and investors. Of course, the

lands west of the Mississippi were not empty in the mid-nineteenth century, nor did the subsequent process of settlement permanently fill this territory in a single flood of manifestly destined pioneers. Rather, the industrializing West became populated with an intricate mix of competing cultures, classes, and communities, many long established. The result was an ethnically and socially divided populace subject to highly unstable local economies, simultaneously dependent on and alienated from the larger national and international cycles that dominated daily life. Yet masking it all was the image of the independent, self-reliant cowboy and pioneer.

As we've seen again and again, the static nature of many of our images of the American historical scene conceals a complex history made by people, not impersonal forces of national destiny. The industrialization of the Northeast and the winning of the West are two important examples. The South's Plantation Belt is another example of a transformed economy hidden by myth. On pages 190–191, Charles E. Orser, Jr., notes that the image of faded elegance—cemented in the public mind through movie images and restored plantation

Unlike the Hollywood myths of the twentieth century, the people of the Old West were both more heterogeneous in their origins and less free to forge independent lives. The Dewey Saloon, in Paradise Valley, Nevada.

The system of tenant farming and the intensive cultivation of cotton as a cash crop continued the legacy and economic inequalities of the southern plantation system long after the Emancipation Proclamation declared African Americans of the South to be free. This photograph of cotton fields and tenant farmers' shacks was taken by Marion Post Wolcott in 1940 for the Farm Security Administration.

houses—is deceptive in that it highlights only one element of the plantation system. Until recently, the mansions have been the primary object of expensive restoration and reconstruction projects; slave quarters are only now beginning to attract attention by some restorationists and archaeologists. Even more significant is the fact that the study of the material culture of the postbellum plantation—namely, the distinctly unelegant and unromantic culture of tenant farmers and their landlords—is still in its infancy. Yet as Dr. Orser maintains, the evidence of the postbellum plantations, both archaeological and historical, is essential to understanding the economic development of the South in the late nineteenth and early twentieth centuries. It was in this material matrix that the replacement of slavery with serfdom created intense racist violence at the turn of the century and the tide of African American migration to northern cities in this century.

The study of tenant farming as outlined by Dr. Orser provides testimony that freedom from slavery did not necessarily mean freedom from poverty or the immediate introduction of equal economic opportunity. It shows that, in the years after the Civil War, both blacks and whites throughout the South fell victim to the strictures of plantation tenancy. Although postbellum plantations are generally viewed as less romantic than slave plantations—and are therefore less attractive as tourist spots—they are certainly not less significant. After 1865, even though many of the South's wealthiest planters were forced to beg, persuade, or otherwise convince former slaves to move onto their property as agricultural workers, the system of tenant farming that developed during Reconstruction was hardly less restrictive than slavery itself. Though the tenant farmer was technically a free person, technically free to buy and sell property and to determine his or her future, the basic relations of power that had existed before the war were not questioned. After the war, the largest planters still possessed considerable wealth and power. In fact, the image of the Defeated South proved to be a powerfully deceptive, and useful, ideology—employed to prevent the institution of meaningful change.

MASS-MARKETED MYTHS

The inherited ideas and desires that lie behind modern consumerism are among the most successful American ideologies. Mass consumption of increasing numbers of products and services in late-nineteenth-century America was accomplished through the relentless use of the art of persuasion on an unprecedented scale. Fences, sides of barns and of tenement houses, park benches, billboards, and streetcars were painted and plastered with the seductive claims of manufacturers and retailers. One could not open a newspaper or leaf through one of the new magazines without scanning the vivid illustrations and fantastic claims promised by the ads.

Although advertising was an important element of American newspapers ever since their establishment in the colonial period, it underwent a transformation at the end of the nineteenth century. Instead of appealing to the common sense or practical needs of the consumer through plainly worded announcements, the new advertisements became increasingly based on visual symbols and increasingly dependent on appeals to the emotions. Technological developments in the printing industry made the reproduction of photographs possible for the first time. Yet even more important was the belief of a growing number of American consumers that the products they purchased could change their identity, well-being, or mood.

As Kathleen Hulser suggests on pages 192–193, the merchandising of nineteenth-century patent medicines set a pattern for the selling of almost everything. For rural and urban populations alike, lacking traditional networks of mutual support, medical care, and the basics of nutrition and exercise, patent medicines made fantastic claims for curing multitudes of afflictions. Since the trade was unregulated and labels gave few indications of what a preparation contained, the choice of ingredients was determined largely by cost and the estimation of profit. In some cases, the contents were dangerous; in others, ingredients such as alcohol, opium, and cocaine (the active ingredients of most preparations) relieved symptoms rather than the disease.

HAD WASHINGTON LIVED IN THESE DAYS
HE'D SAY WITH ALL THE REST
"I CANNOT, WILL NOT TELL A LIE,
DUKE'S DURHAM IS THE BEST."

As the "Father of His Country," George Washington—and his ubiquitous image—had the power to sanction manners, bloodlines, and even smoking habits. From an early-twentieth-century tobacco trade card.

Yet, as Dr. Hulser indicates, the profitability of patent medicines and the psychic needs they addressed were so powerful that would-be reformers could do little more than demand some regulation of use. Consumers were led to believe in the effectiveness of the preparations because of their associations rather than their contents. Pictures of healthy, beautiful, and active people were far more prominent in advertisements than descriptions of the contents of the products themselves. Even more suggestive of later developments was the fact that the enthusiastic endorsements of "doctors" with respectable-sounding names were featured on the labels and in advertisements. Few stopped to inquire of the endorser's credentials; for most, it

certainly didn't matter that no one had ever heard of the particular doctor.

The idea of masking the utter worthlessness or even unhealthfulness of a product through phony endorsements of respected names or through positive images pioneered and first perfected by the makers of snake oil and other bogus potions is still very much with us today. In the late nineteenth century, the American public was exposed to a variety of subtle yet powerful ideological messages, and they did not all relate to the purchase of consumer goods. Increasingly, the extraordinarily successful technique of linking visual image and emotion utilized in the retail trade was also used to instill basic perceptions about the "natural" roots and nature of American society.

At that time, with millions of immigrants flowing into American cities from the rural areas of the South and West and from Europe and Asia, the demographic makeup of the population was undergoing a far-reaching change. Italians, Jews, Slavs, and dozens of other ethnic groups became increasingly visible presences on the American landscape. The industrial and commercial elite of the United States had obvious, self-interested economic motivations for permitting and even facilitating this wave of immigration. Yet there was, at the same time, a pressing need to preserve certain values, to make clear to the new immigrant exactly who was in charge. The result was the identification of the trappings of Colonial America (conspicuously associated with America's "first families") as the standard by which the culture of all Americans should be judged.

The Colonial Revival manifested itself on the American landscape in many ways. As Mark Bograd shows on pages 194–195, the decoration of homes, stores, and public buildings with colonial architectural details and the furnishing of interiors with colonial hutches, sideboards, and high-backed settees was the ritualization of a national cult of the ancestors—in which certain ancestors were canonized and others implicitly despised. The celebration of things colonial and Anglo-Saxon as the true essence of America implicitly condemned the cultures, languages, and lifeways of new immigrants as not American. And more than being simply a matter of taste or style, the Colonial Revival offered the nineteenth-century elite a way to secure their privileged position forever, and it did it through what passed for science—including suggestions about heredity. While colonial status symbols (though of course in cheaper versions) could be used to decorate the living rooms and mantelpieces of immigrant families, none of the newcomers could ever buy a colonial pedigree. The prominence and visibility of genealogical organizations such as the Daughters of the American Revolution and the Society of Mayflower Descendants in defining the "true" American character were used to justify the later enactment of restrictive immigration laws.

What's important to remember is that the esteem bestowed upon "colonial" furniture, architecture, and silverware—with its implicit identification of "old" families as the natural American aristocracy—was cultivated in a particular political and social context. In late-nineteenth-century America, with its intensifying economic tensions and rushing, transforming industrialization, an imagined past of pious and respectful English pilgrims and colonists—conveniently shorn of the radical levelers and egalitarian utopianists who populated the period—projected a past that offered both a pious, respectful model for modern behavior and many new categories of consumer goods. Even among immigrant families, colonial styles of furniture and silverware became objects of status and desire. In short, material objects here, too, made subtle ideological points and worked to preserve the privileged position of the powers that were. Indeed, it might be fair to say that the lingering attraction of colonial bedsteads and side tables, and the seductive attraction of the elegant colonial ladies at Williamsburg, is as much a testament to the continuing power of America's nineteenth-century industrial and commercial elite as it is about any quality inherent in the culture of America's colonial period.

Of course, the ideological messages of the nineteenth century did not all flow in one direction. The sheer diversity of cultures and lifeways brought together in the world of American industry created a potent mix that no one could completely control. Outside the sedate cultural spheres imagined and promulgated by the aristocracy were the contrasting and preexisting cultural tastes of farmers and working people. And since providing entertainment that served these tastes could produce handsome profits, the great American show business machine was born. Thus, at the end of the nineteenth century, New York City, the locale of particularly intense ethnic and cultural mingling, became the capital of a new genre of public performance—vaudeville. The stylized, formulaic variety show not only became the most popular form of theater in turn-of-the-century America; it provided a glimpse of the inner lives, emotions, and values of the people who did not come on the Mayflower.

On pages 196–197, Robert W. Snyder focuses on the Union Square theater district in New York City and suggests that the characters, songs, and sketches of vaudeville were important sources of modern American mass culture. It succeeded in cultivating large, dependable audiences of newly urbanized or industrialized working people by offering a fast-paced mix of escapist entertainment and emotion-laden references to earlier, simpler times. In responding to the psychic needs of immigrants (both domestic and foreign), who had been thrust recently into a new economic system of work, wages, and employers, vaudeville offered parodies of the workaday world, fantasies about forbidden sexual worlds, and idealized musical memories of worlds left behind on the farm or in the Old Country. The unembarrassed enjoyment of these images—which was often viewed with open contempt by America's cultural leaders—soon became a subtle brand of resistance. And this kind of entertainment, in its Hollywood incarnation, would go on to claim enormous popularity throughout the rest of the industrializing world. Yet it should be noted that resistance through escapist entertainment never threatened power. Like patent medicine's pretended power to heal bodily afflictions and the Colonial Revival's sanctification of pilgrims, the bawdy jokes, ethnic humor, and dastardly villains of late-nineteenth-century vaudeville diverted attention from the sources of modern social problems—and turned a handsome profit as well.

CREATING NEW SPACES

All these changes took place primarily in people's minds in late-nineteenth-century America; yet, the physical landscape of the continent also underwent a thorough-going change at this time. Here, too, American reality was redefined and the consequences of industrialization were hidden or disguised.

Often we are taught to think of such things as suburbs, subways, and department stores as "modern," a hallmark of the life that is most familiar to us. Yet again and again we have seen that what we have come to identify as modern is a function of a specific economic system rather than of

As trains and trolleys made daily commuting into metropolitan areas possible, suburban communities began to spring up in what had been agricultural areas. Technological advances in construction made homeownership possible for a wider section of the population. A row of houses in Leonia, New Jersey, circa 1905.

technological sophistication or historical period. This chapter shows that even the most superficially neutral innovations had enormous social consequences in shaping and directing the conduct of daily life. In the way that residential areas were patterned and segregated; in the way that most people went to work or to shop, we can begin to see how the interaction of people from different ways of life, different levels of wealth, and different ethnic backgrounds was subtly controlled. Those new interactions influenced how most people conceived of their world.

Take the suburbs, for example, which Paul H. Mattingly examines on pages 198–199. He notes that although the term itself has become associated with the familiar post–World War II suburbs of homogeneous, middle-class tract housing, the historical significance of the suburb extends far further back in time and into realms far more influential than the ex-urbanites' longing for fresh air, green grass, and escape from the grime and danger of city life. In fact, virtually all American

cities had substantial suburbs long before World War II, and they played a vital role in the expansion of industrial society. With their establishment facilitated by new transportation systems—railroad, trolley, and eventually the auto—these new residential concentrations in turn created distinct and often unique social class and cultural mixes. The suburbs are very much a part of the modern industrial city and its distinct separation of economic groups.

In earlier periods of American history, the organization of work allowed urban merchants, artisans, and laborers to live side-by-side, all close to the central commercial district in residential patterns that produced a mosaic of strikingly different enclaves. Continual face-to-face contact of the richest and the poorest was an accepted part of the social order. Yet with increasing industrialization, crime, air and water pollution, and the crowding of the city with tens of thousands of new immigrant workers caused a mass exodus from the central manufacturing districts—for those who could afford it. The wealthy had their private carriages for transport to their country houses and could remove themselves far from the noise and the crowding of the inner city. The growing middle class of white-collar workers could afford the fares of "city cars," or omnibuses, and later of the trolleys to take them to the newly established suburbs. But the workers crowded into "slum" districts had few options for escape.

Eileen Gatti describes on pages 200–201 how urban developments elsewhere in the industrialized world eventually provided a model—and a technology—for the reorganization of the American city's space. The London Underground, successfully opened in 1863, provided a means for workers to be housed in new, carefully planned residential districts, allowing even greater intensification of production in industrial areas. There was also an apparent social benefit to mass rapid transit. The disturbing reports by settlement house workers of the social chaos and unhealthfulness of the inner city served as an incentive for reformers to lobby for the introduction of the subway into the United States. Yet it took decades of political maneuvering before the first subway systems would be built. (Boston inaugurated the first such service in 1897.) The reason was that city governments bowed to the pressure of already existing streetcar companies, which had been granted monopolies. Big-city bosses made hefty profits from granting and renewing such charters—for which they did not demand limits on fares, coordinated schedules, or any regulation of the quality of service.

The dominating ideology of "free enterprise" prevented the government from undertaking subway projects. And the capital required to build subway systems was not easily forthcoming from private sources. Even when city council members weren't bribed or pressured to break the monopolies of the surface-transport companies, periodic economic depressions, particularly in 1873 and in the 1890s, dried up the potential sources of private investment in these schemes. And as Eileen Gatti explains, the "compromises" that were eventually worked out among city governments and private builders at the turn of the century have bequeathed both a complex geography of workers and workplaces and lingering problems in the underground landscape.

The cities were thus slowly girded by a patchwork of suburbs and tunneled under by a labyrinth of subway lines. At the same time, in the heart of the city, another kind of space was created in which order and logic prevailed. On pages 202–203, Elaine S. Abelson describes how, in the long counters, attractive displays, and wide aisles of the great nineteenth-century department stores of America, urban and suburban shoppers discovered new physical and psychological geographies. All across the country, civic leaders boasted about their city's department stores. The vastness of the array of merchandise, the extent and variety of services provided, and the splendor or sheer scale of the buildings were all seen as testimony to the greatness of the city itself. In fact, the department store was, at once, the main emblem and the main arena in the American culture of consumption. It became simultaneously a university and a museum of "things," all of which could be possessed. Because the money needed for purchase had been earned through meritorious labor, the freedom to purchase

The Beach Pneumatic Tube in New York City, opened in 1870, was a short-lived experiment in mass transit. Municipal protection for street trolleys and elevated trains—and the unavailability of private investment funds—doomed further developments for decades. A contemporary illustration from Scientific American.

The grandeur of the great nineteenth-century department stores of the Ladies' Mile in New York City can still be seen, at least in the surviving facades and architectural features of the buildings lining lower Sixth Avenue.

was itself a badge of merit. Mass production combined with mass sales vivified the ideologies of production and personal freedom.

Indeed, there were lessons to be learned in the department store, as surely as they would be learned in the nation's public schools and museum halls. Dr. Abelson notes that after the Civil War, with vast increases in industrial production and with a dramatic increase in the resources available to a new middle class, consumer values revolutionized American society. The department store was one of the dominant institutions in that transformation. With the ability to exploit a vast array of goods, the large stores embodied a vision of trouble-free abundance. The impressive displays of merchandise educated people to understand how one's identity could be shaped by consumer goods. These goods, once possessed, played a crucial role in determining the essentials of middle-class life and aspirations. The stores themselves served as showcases as they became part of a new urban, public culture. Visits to department stores became part of the regular itinerary and urban geography of tourists and residents alike.

Notions of what constituted the basic necessities gradually expanded for all classes, but this was particularly true of the growing middle class. By the closing decades of the century, increasing specialization in the use of clothes—special clothing, for example, for morning wear, street wear, and sports activities—necessitated more time spent in stores accompanied by the effort at knowing how and what to buy. Further, when understood as part of the current definition of a female domestic role, shopping came to dwarf all other activities for urban middle-class women and came to be linked to the supposedly innate, natural characteristics of women. This ideology spread to the rest of the country in the great catalogues of the mail-order houses of the Midwest—encyclopedias of modern tools, toys, and fashions—as farm families across the country learned the lessons of a consumer society, too.

These mass-marketed goods not only spelled out how to be modern, they demanded modern behavior in their proper use, purchase, and display. This is all very much like the ideological project of sixteenth-century European missionaries among Native Americans and the enforcing uniformities of gridded spaces in the first century of European conquest in North America. Both the missionaries and the late-nineteenth-century merchants produced objects, or used mass-produced implements to encourage behavior that appeared uniform and made people "productive."

RESISTANCE: IMMIGRANTS AND NATIVE AMERICANS

To look back on the traditional schoolbook versions of the history of America in the late nineteenth century is to see a story in which technological progress was accompanied by social advancement, a picture in which the inequalities of society were slowly dissolved in a millennium of economic progress and heavy industry. In some important ways, this image is simply a continuation of the colonial metaphor of the "garden in the wilderness," in which human reason was able to triumph over the chaos of nature, and thus demonstrate the virtue—and inevitable position—of those who held power. Yet, as we've seen in both cases, the dominating images were based on a skillful manipulation of things, words, spaces, and actions that concealed other interpretations of what was going on in society. The seizure of land and desire for control over people continued and intensified. Fewer and fewer places on the continent remained beyond the control of market forces and market fluctuations; more and more people were tied ever more tightly to the disciplines of industrial life and the fantasies that it spawned. And as happened in all the earlier periods of American history, some people who clearly recognized the implications of what was happening chose to resist in various ways.

One of the most common reasons for resistance was industrial society's refusal to acknowledge time-honored cultures—ways of life that allowed people to make sense of their worlds and their lives. This became a particularly pressing problem in the historical period covered in this chapter, for the westward geographical expansion, labor unrest, and racial tensions that gripped America at the end of the nineteenth century coincided with the start of a massive wave of foreign (and domestic) immigration. This wave of immigration was much larger than any that had gone before it and brought many older cultures into close contact with the culture of industrial society. The sudden movement of humanity into the nation's big cities, mining regions, and rural areas far outstripped the slow, transatlantic trickle of settlers who had been coming for centuries.

Yet in the closing decades of the nineteenth century, the rapid spread of intensive cash farming methods all across Europe, the use of industries, and the displacement of traditional farmers and villagers set in motion an unprecedented demographic transfer that profoundly changed the character of the population of the United States. And as Suzanne Wasserman points out on pages 204–205, those "new" immigrants (who came largely from southern and eastern Europe in contrast to the "old" immigrants from northwestern Europe), scattered across America in thousands of distinctive kin-based communities, had many strategies for survival. Some hoped to make and save enough money to return, wealthy, to the homeland; some struggled in ethnic-based labor unions to reform the structure of factory work; and some sought to establish the kinds of village-based farming communities that no longer existed in the Old Country from which they had come. Melting away into the mainstream culture was not necessarily these people's primary ideal.

In 1924, the draconian federal Immigration Restriction Act—based partly on nativistic fears that the foreign born would contaminate or dilute America's national character—finally established tight immigration quotas and slammed shut the Golden Door. The lingering effects of 1920s "Americanization" programs and public school civics classes taught that ethnic distinctiveness was appropriate only for family functions or religious ceremonies. The immigrants' fears, struggles, and alienation were gradually replaced by an ideal of good citizenship. As a result, we have the self-congratulatory commemoration of nineteenth-century immigration in schoolbooks and at places like Ellis Island, which now in National Park Service hands underestimates the social problems of immigrants to America.

"The Last Yankee," a cartoon from Frank Leslie's Illustrated Newspaper, *September 8, 1888. Immigration from Asia and Europe concerned many in the United States who feared that "American" culture might be diluted by newcomers. Aside from laws passed to restrict the flow of immigrants, Americanization programs were undertaken to teach "proper" values.*

The industrial "garden" of order, discipline, and increasing production expanded even to the most remote corners of the continent, and there, too, forms of resistance arose. On pages 206–207, Mark S. Cassell examines the far-reaching social and economic impact of the commercial whaling industry, active approximately between 1850 and 1910, on the North Alaska Inupiat Eskimo.

The Eskimo, pressed and enticed by Americans into hunting whales for wages, were paid in canned commodities which left them—supposedly—reliant on American markets and, thus, tied to the new state and all its progressive institutions. They were also to become Christians. However, they managed to maintain some cultural integrity, while Native Americans in the northern Plains were virtually destroyed at the same time in the same quest for profit.

The Plains Indian Wars of the late nineteenth century, which Larry J. Zimmerman and Karen Zimmerman explore on pages 208–209, are among the best-known cases of resistance to the expansion of industrial society, though they are usually framed in explicitly racial terms. The traditional version, even in its most recent and superficially sympathetic incarnation, sees the Indian peoples of the Plains as passive, if heroic, victims of the greedy palefaces that populated the frontier. Yet we must come to understand how both frontier and inner city were parts of the same industrial society, in which the "taming of the wilderness" and the identification of "savages" were the central ideologies. Indeed, many of the Plains Indians of the nineteenth century saw the threat clearly. The violence that they ultimately used did not result from any inherently savage temperament, but as a last-ditch effort to maintain traditional lifeways in the face of relentless, imposed change. As Euro-Americans ventured westward from the eastern seaboard, their inevitable population increase and occupation of territory affected native peoples across the continent, exerting influence long before Euro-American settlers actually arrived. As we've seen, Indian groups forced from their homelands displaced other tribes. And Euro-American trade goods found their way into Indian hands, subtly altering material culture, social organization, and, in some cases, belief systems as well.

The mobile lifestyle of groups like the Sioux and Cheyenne allowed them to survive the early waves of epidemics that decimated settled agricultural peoples. Their acquisition of the horse and gun allowed a concentration on hunting buffalo and caused a cultural florescence. But with the relentless push of industrial society across the Mississippi, the construction of railroads, the subdivision of land for profit and new settlement, and the continuing hunt for exploitable resources, the peoples of the plains were soon overrun. During the Civil War, the plains hunters began to pose a serious military threat, but it was only in the years after 1865

that the United States government could devote its full attention to the problem of the Plains Indians. The federal authorities decided that the most powerful of the native peoples, the Sioux, be gathered and concentrated (by force, if necessary) in a large reservation in Dakota that included the Black Hills. Within only a few years, in the aftermath of the Panic of 1873, the lure of riches led to a violation of even the initial, restrictive arrangement: in 1874, Lt. Col. George Armstrong Custer led a military expedition into the Black Hills, where the discovery of untapped gold resources started a rush of miners to the area.

The conflicts that resulted crushed the Native American groups, reduced them to subsistence at government-created welfare stations, and turned their land over to miners, ranchers, and traders. In this example of a nearly universal process, we can see how, century to century and coast to coast, local populations were captured, land was subject to market conditions, resources were extracted, and a harvest of unequal social relations was left for a subsequent generation to resolve.

IMAGINED FUTURES AND PASTS

From the very beginning of the European conquest of the North American continent in the late fifteenth century, history proceeded on two levels. First was a search for exploitable natural resources and eventually colonization, which held out a promise of a new life for all involved, then also bitterly disappointed those hopes by largely resurrecting the relations of power from which the colonists had escaped. Second was the creation of a story that, despite the painful reality, pictured the conquest of America as a triumph of the forces of good. Any who had not benefited from this great enterprise, the dominating ideology suggested, had only themselves, their lack of ambition or energy, or their supposed genetic limitations to blame. As we have tried to stress throughout this book, there is another story, another version of American history, that can be traced. It is the story of how people in every generation, every period of American history, perceived that objectionable things were going on beneath the surface of the society's dominant ideology. It is also the story of how that realization was usually defused, assimilated, or neutralized.

We have suggested that the genre of vaudeville gave voice to the unspoken hopes, fears, and emotions of the newly arrived industrial populations of the cities, and how its vivid emotions, diversity of characters, and implicit sexuality contrasted so sharply with the frigid "highbrow" tastes of the Colonial Revival. Yet if vaudeville was the "Voice of the City"—as Robert Snyder has called it— another late-nineteenth-century dramatic form, the community historical pageant, was the voice of the small town. On pages 210–211, David Glassberg shows how a triumphant industrial order advertised its origins, its ability to sow goodness, and its productivity through pageants. These seemingly harmless festivals, rituals of success really, occurred everywhere, advertising the success of progress and making it seem inescapable.

Often sponsored by a community's most prominent citizens and staged as part of a civic celebration commemorating the anniversary of a town's founding, the pageant featured local residents in period costume reenacting a dozen or so dramatic episodes from their town's history. Using images of a preindustrial golden age of handicraft and undoubting religious faith, embodied in scenes of Colonial or Pioneer America, it drew a picture of utopian progress to civilization through hard work and community cooperation that the bawdiness and Old Country ethnicity of vaudeville denied. Each community was homogenized in this vision, overlooking differences of accent or attitude, or any prior Native American heritage. Immigrants appeared only briefly in the pageant of local community development, and African Americans or representatives of organized labor were rarely seen at all. And with the resources of the entire community mobilized to produce these epics, they had enormous power to persuade that the myth was true.

As Dr. Glassberg notes, many pageant promoters and participants at the turn of the century viewed historical pageantry not only as a form of local boosterism, patriotic moralizing, and popular entertain-

On June 25, 1876, on a grass-covered ridge above the Little Bighorn River, the last act in the attempt to subjugate the Plains Tribes began. Custer's Last Stand marked the beginning of an intensified military campaign. White tablets mark the places where Custer's men reportedly fell.

ment but also as an instrument for social reform. While pageantry originated among the same self-appointed guardians of local tradition who orchestrated the Colonial Revival in the late nineteenth century, it also included an influential number of progressives, who sought to institute improvements in public recreation and the fine arts. Due to their influence, American pageantry took on a distinctive form—a sequence of historical episodes arranged to show an inevitable path of local community development from past through present to an ideal future. Pageants accommodated a great deal of ethnic diversity but did not question the bases or basic inequalities of industrial capitalism.

By the 1920s, pageant imagery was not so much progress and national history as escape from modernity. Pageants no longer attempted to present the entire sweep of local history, concentrating instead on scenes of an idealized past increasingly remote in time and in sensibility from the present, and thereby used nostalgia to avoid criticism of the everyday world. By the 1930s, the historical pageant had given way to the period village (Greenfield Village or Colonial Williamsburg) or the national military park (Shiloh, Vicksburg, or Gettysburg), which depicted the past frozen in time for tourists rather than linked with a dynamic present and future. At the turn of the century, the display of ideology as entertainment beckoned as an escape from the routines of daily life. Indeed, the messages of the pageant were echoed and reinforced by those of another powerful contemporary institution, the much advertised world's fairs.

Robert W. Rydell explores this social phenomenon on pages 212–213, for after the success of London's 1851 Crystal Palace Exhibition, world's fairs became a characteristic feature of industrial life. America's first international exposition followed quickly on the heels of the Crystal Palace. Held in 1853 in New York, its promoters (among whom was P. T. Barnum), unabashedly called it the New York Crystal Palace Exhibition to stress the connection

In 1886, on the occasion of Springfield's two hundred and fiftieth anniversary celebration, the courage and vision of the city's colonial settlers were praised, as was their conquest of the Connecticut Valley's indigenous peoples. Springfield's elite of merchants and manufacturers presented themselves as the rightful heirs of this history by commemorating the founding fathers with books, statues, and, as seen here, parades. On the first float, colonial settlers are seen purchasing lands from Native Americans.

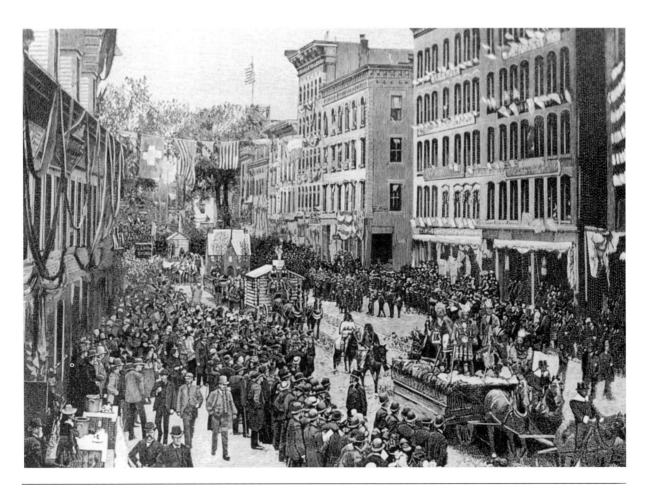

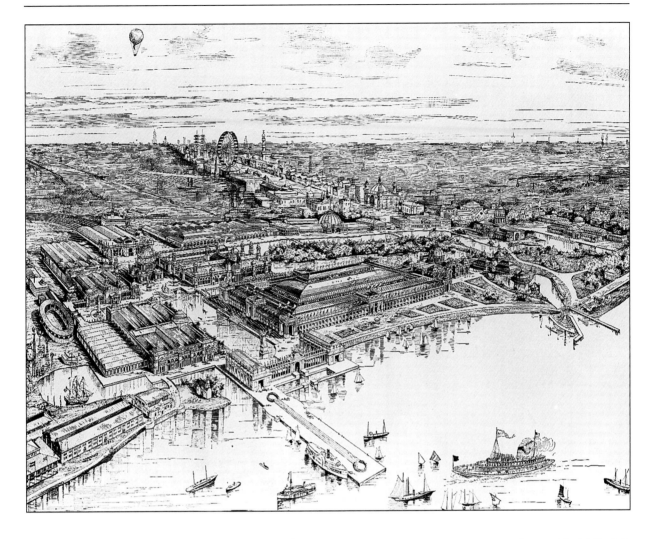

An artist's bird's-eye view of the 1893 World's Columbian Exposition. Bringing together the most modern technology and the most curious and bizarre entertainment attractions, the Chicago fair set the standard for decades. The gleaming buildings of White City, intended as architectural prototypes of the utopian city, were actually constructed of a mixture of wood framing and plaster of Paris.

with its English predecessor. The lessons it taught through arrangement of industrial, ethnological, and amusement areas helped instill the naturalness of the division of Industry, Savagery, and Leisure— the contrasts between Western World, Third World, and Fantasy World that are still with us today.

The Civil War interrupted America's world's fair movement, but as the Reconstruction era closed the federal government, together with Philadelphia business and civic leaders, turned to the exposition medium to commemorate the centennial of American independence as a celebration of both national unity and national industry. So successful was the 1876 Philadelphia fair in attracting crowds and exposing them to America's achievements that civic and business leaders around the country quickly hopped on board the exposition bandwagon to stage their own extravaganzas. By the turn of the century, exposition-going was such a common and significant national experience that historian Henry Adams proclaimed the existence of a new secular religion of world's fairs.

As Dr. Rydell points out, these fairs had multiple effects, not all of them strictly ideological. There is no question that they helped spread awareness of the latest technological advances. A newly improved fire engine pump placed on display at the 1893 Chicago World's Columbian Exposition provided Henry Ford with an idea on how to improve the internal combustion engine. In their carefully designed open spaces and landscaping, the fairs inspired a nationwide "city beautiful" movement, an attempt to regulate the congestion and efficient flow of urban crowds. The "anthropological" displays of such human curiosities as Native Americans and Filipino villagers at the 1904 St. Louis Fair heightened public and even academic interest in ethnology and encouraged the establishment of permanent ethnological museums—Chicago's Field Museum and San Diego's Museum of Man, for instance. In short, the great world's fairs of the late nineteenth and early twentieth centuries left a powerful imprint on the way millions of Americans understood the world.

Like visitors to the world's fairs or participants in community pageants, we are still often taught to see our nation's history as driven by an inevitable progress. Yet, the late nineteenth century can be seen not so much as a step on a ladder of progress propped up for humanity by the Great Creator but also as an era in which certain human interactions created conditions in which subsequent genera-tions would have to live. The utopian art forms of the great world's fairs—fantasies of the order and control of an industrial elite—remain our guiding metaphor in such views of the future as science fiction films, children's video games, and theme parks. The destruction of the lifeways of the Plains Indians would give birth both to a heroic mythology and to an angry response by the survivors. Furthermore, the costs of reshaping the American city to intensify the industrial order had consequences that still refuse to go away. Workers' discipline, intensified agribusiness, and consumer desire have spread everywhere in North America as the dominant forces to live with or to be fought.

We take local pageants and world's fairs with unusual seriousness because they illustrate and reinforce the sense that there was only one way to live: an unreflective life within a society that wanted to absorb everything and everyone into a market. This era is, in fact, the time when North America was finally brought completely into industrial capitalism's orbit. It was also when most everything was commodified, and when the triumph of these forces was announced through vaudeville, department stores, and advertising, and engraved in a steel-and-concrete landscape of subways, suburbs, and factories.

VICTORIAN SACRAMENTO: *Behind the Facades*

Preserved and partly re-created in Old Sacramento Historic Park, the commercial landscape of Victorian Sacramento was dynamic and feverish, but carefully controlled by ordinances that enforced the aesthetic orthodoxy of the age.

America's industrial cities were built with ideas as well as bricks and mortar. In the spirit of Progress, Morality, and Boosterism, the nineteenth-century urban establishment sought to mold society to its own image—to supplant and modernize the mores and values of immigrants and the working class. In the lead in this progressive movement were the proponents and beneficiaries of commercial capitalism, including shopkeepers, merchants, bankers, and newspaper owners, who did their best to ensure that their own ideals became the accepted ideals of society at large.

The industries owned by such people created an icon of Progress in the urban landscape itself, using great public works, streetscapes, and building fronts. In the case of Sacramento, California, the "get rich and get out" ethic of the Gold Rush era eventually gave way to a vision of a stable, prosperous city modeled on the business centers of the settled East. The heart of Victorian Sacramento was its commercial district, where strict building codes rapidly forced the replacement of the wood-and-canvas structures of Gold Rush times by symmetrical brick facades. For this purpose, the Greek Revival style of architecture was the perfect medium and one widely used for public buildings throughout the nineteenth-century American West. Thus was the landscape of the settled East quickly re-created in what just a few years before had been a wilderness of marsh and "wild" Indians.

But some people remained apart, refusing to be absorbed. Sacramento's nineteenth-century Chinese district, tightly controlled by family associations and merchants, clustered along I Street, on the shore of noisome Sutter Slough. In an effort to retain political and economic control of their community, the Chinese merchants actively resisted majority values. While adopting outward symbols of conformity in their dealings with the authorities, they maintained a distinctively Chinese landscape and continued to use familiar Chinese goods to reinforce traditional social relations within their community.

For most Victorians, the uniformity of taste and style in everything from architecture to tableware symbolized the achievement of a moral consensus. Even hidden city backlots, for years filled with filth and debris, moved toward conformity, and were placed behind respectable building facades. All these things were taken by residents as confirmation that Progress, shaped by commerce and accompanied by its attendant values and symbols, was both the natural course of social evolution and the nation's destiny.

■ ADRIAN PRAETZELLIS
Sonoma State University

LEFT: *California's State Capitol building, completed in 1869, was another of Sacramento's public monuments to Permanence, Progress, and Prosperity. Standing on a raised mound at the end of a wide, tree-flanked mall, its symmetry evoked—and still evokes—a sense of controlled power, balance, and stability.*

RIGHT: *A toy tea set found by archaeologists at a site in downtown Sacramento reminds us of the scope of Victorian didacticism. Just as the great public works both preserved and promoted commercialism, so toys taught gender-specific roles to children.*

BELOW: *Chinatown, 1895. Traditional Chinese New Year celebrations in the streets of Sacramento were part of the attempt to re-create the Chinese material world in California.*

THE NORTHEAST: *Brass Valley*

As one of Waterbury's oldest industrial enterprises and as one of the city's largest employers, the Scovill Manufacturing Company was a dominating physical presence. The plumes of thick black smoke rising from its factory chimneys in this 1896 view were perhaps intended to symbolize the company's bustling prosperity; general awareness of the ecological damage being done to the Naugatuck Valley would not come for decades.

To speak of the American Industrial Revolution is to speak of places like Waterbury, Connecticut. In 1802, two brothers and their nine employees began producing buttons by hand at what would become the Scovill Manufacturing Company. Gradually, machines revolutionized production: By 1864, a single machine could produce 216,000 buttons per day. By the 1860s, Waterbury became known as the Brass City—part of a national specialization that made Pittsburgh the Steel City and Detroit the Motor City. By World War I, Scovill employed fifteen thousand workers.

The first Irish immigrants to Waterbury, fleeing the Great Famine, settled on the barren hillside of Pine Hill, known locally as the "Abrigador," in the 1840s. Irish immigrants in greater numbers began settling in the Brooklyn section in the 1860s. In the 1890s, large numbers of Lithuanian immigrants began to arrive in Brooklyn. Yet Waterbury was no melting pot. Each group built its own commu-

nity institutions; St. Patrick's Church was long an Irish institution, while St. Joseph's was Lithuanian. Two Lithuanian social clubs, one closely tied to the church, the other started by freethinkers, stood within a few blocks of the church on Green Street.

With the rise of industry, Waterbury's workers organized to gain greater control over their working and living conditions. In the 1880s, Waterbury workers organized into the Knights of Labor, and women workers conducted many strikes over factory working conditions. For decades there was considerable resistance to this activity; unions were not accepted by the Naugatuck Valley employers, who hired labor spies and kept records on labor activities. In 1919 and 1920, over fifteen thousand workers, mostly unskilled immigrants, conducted two general strikes. In the General Strike of 1919, the Connecticut State Guard occupied the Brooklyn section of the city and set up

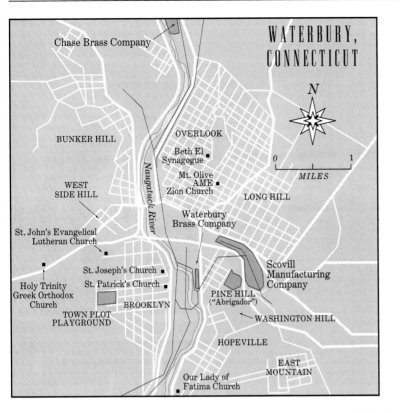

WATERBURY, CONNECTICUT

DRUTUOLIS

J. GILIS

J. GILIS savininkas limonado dirbtuvės nes jau nuo senai žinomas kaipo milžino kovai Waterbury'je ir jau nevieną m susirėmime į porą minutų paguldė savo priešą.

The language and culture of immigrant communities was kept alive in the industrial cities of America. Pictured here is a poster for a wrestling match held at a Lithuanian social club in Waterbury in the early twentieth century.

machine-gun emplacements on the roofs of local stores. The union was defeated and the "open shop" restored until the late 1930s, when companies were finally forced by strikes and workers' elections to bargain with their employees.

The dirty and dangerous toil of Waterbury's industrial workers produced affluence for a tightly knit group of families who owned the city's major brass companies and controlled virtually every sphere of city life, from the building of the railroads and hospitals to the creation of charity organizations to help the poor. Today, the remaining factory complexes of the big three brass companies—Scovill, American Brass, and Chase—can be seen along the valley's streams and rivers. Superimposed on this landscape are the major ethnic regions of the city, each marked by its own large church. Much of this physical skeleton of the rise and fall of American industrialism has so far survived the bulldozer—and is still there to be seen.

■ JEREMY BRECHER
Cornwall, Connecticut

ABOVE: *The button rooms of the Scovill Manufacturing Company, from an 1879 engraving.*

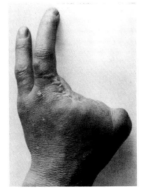

LEFT: *This photo of a work-related injury, labeled "Injured Hand," was taken in the early twentieth century and deposited in the archives of the Scovill Manufacturing Company.*

THE WEST: *The Roads to Paradise*

Paradise Valley, Nevada, was one of the destinations that dotted the densely gridded western speculator's map in the 1880s and 1890s. But most of its settlers never sat in a covered wagon. They made their pioneer trek on the Central Pacific Railroad, got off in the bustling county seat of Winnemucca, and took one of the daily stages north for the remaining forty miles to the valley. Many newcomers actually traveled *east* to reach the town, emigrating from earlier settlements in California and Oregon. Others began their trip to the Nevada desert on a steamship, leaving hometowns in Germany, Italy, and the Basque country.

People made the journey to Paradise with a range of goals in mind, and their rates of success varied widely. Most newcomers spent time working for someone else, either in the nearby mines or on the wheat farms and livestock ranches that dominated the valley economy. They hoped to save enough money from wages to purchase a homestead. But by the end of the century, much of the prime valley land was already privately owned, and declining water tables made much of the rest untenable. For most immigrants, the chances to buy property or to enter a community with any permanence were slim. This was particularly true for the small family groups of Paiute who moved through the valley in summer and fall each year, working on ranches, gathering firewood, and taking in laundry from local households.

You can still make the trip from Winnemucca to Paradise, but you can't take the same road. The new road is higher, faster, and emptier than the old. The old was built for horses, mules, oxen, wagons, and for walking; it was really several stretches of privately owned toll roads, built by local entrepreneurs who ran stage stops at their toll stations—Toll House, Willow Point, and Paradise Hill—providing fresh horses, a meal, and perhaps a bed for the night.

In the town of Paradise Valley, the main stop for the stage was at John Case's store and post office. The commercial success of the stores, hotels, and shops that built the town in the nineteenth century remains visible today. But the only traces of the migrant laborers who moved through Paradise and sustained a large part of its economy are in the memories of its oldest residents, and in the artifacts of rowdy buckaroos and Indians that these residents display in their homes and yards. These artifacts claim, simultaneously, an evolutionary stage beyond, but also a cultural identity with a western past that was, and never was.

■ MARGARET S. PURSER
Sonoma State University

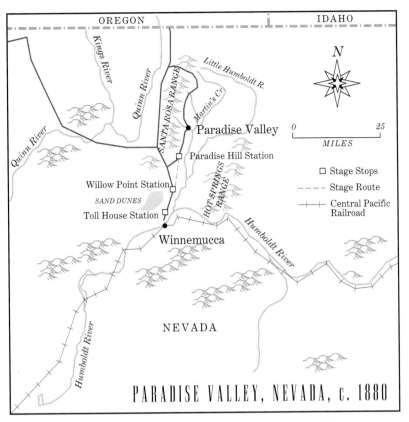

PARADISE VALLEY, NEVADA, c. 1880

FACING PAGE, TOP: *The Paradise Saloon. Such places provided a place to eat, to sleep, and sometimes to hear about available work for the many migrant laborers in the nineteenth-century West.*

ABOVE: *The multiethnic character of the industrial west often gets lost in the dominant motif of an "American" west peopled largely by Anglo cowboys, pioneers, and bandits. Here two recent immigrants to Paradise Valley pose in a photographer's studio as if sitting in a saloon.*

FACING PAGE, BOTTOM: *Daisy Siwash and her children comprised one of the many Paiute family groups that moved seasonally through the valley in the early 1900s on the way to pine nut harvest festivals farther east.*

RIGHT: *The old road to Paradise Valley ran downslope from the new highway, to take advantage of lower grades, on which draft animals could haul their loads more easily.*

THE SOUTH: *The Postbellum Plantation*

When most people think about the plantations of the American South, they envision the huge, white mansions of the wealthiest planters in the years before and during the Civil War. This image, reinforced by popular movies and books, has entered the ideology of American life because it helps to define the South for those Americans who do not live there and have no connection to it.

An important element of the popular conception holds that plantations died with slavery in 1865, but in truth, plantations continued to exist long after. The new, post–Civil War plantation was an adaptation to the changing conditions in which former slaves became tenant farmers and former masters became landlords. Tenants were now free to decide on the locations of their own homes, and on some plantations they seem to have abandoned former slave quarters and selected sites that were far from the landlord's home and close to tenant-farming neighbors.

During Reconstruction, experimental forms of labor such as collective squads of tenants or gangs of free farmers were employed on some plantations. Although former slaves could now sell their labor to an agricultural establishment that very much needed workers, these experimental forms seemed too much like slavery for most. Many former slaves simply became tenant farmers on the same plantations where they had been held in bondage before the war, and they were often kept there by a complex system of debt peonage. Because of the distance to towns or to reliable retail outlets, plantation tenants were often forced to obtain consumer items and commodities from the plantation commissary, typically at vastly inflated prices. In a bad crop year, or when their commissary debts grew particularly large, tenants were faced with the prospect of ever

deeper economic dependence. Those who attempted to flee from their plantations faced stiff legal penalties, harsh vagrancy laws, or assault from white terrorist groups.

Thus, while the plantations of the American South after 1865 were worked by ostensibly free laborers, emancipation did not necessarily mean freedom from poverty. Tenancy became a major social problem in the 1920s and 1930s as it grew increasingly clear that much of the South's poverty, lack of education, and poor land conservation practices were directly tied to a plantation tradition that the Civil War did not alter.

■ CHARLES E. ORSER, JR.
Illinois State University

Waverly Plantation, Clay County, Mississippi. To many Americans, influenced by the Hollywood images of Gone With the Wind, *the elegant mansions of the South seem to go hand-in-hand with slavery. Yet in the case of Waverly Plantation—and many other plantations throughout the South—the system of intensive labor that supported their elegant owners continued long after 1865.*

FACING PAGE: *After the Civil War, plantations noticeably changed their layout and appearance. Before the war, plantation workers—slaves—usually lived in rows of small cabins. After the war, the same workers—now tenants—lived in houses spread throughout the plantation lands. A view of the Millwood Plantation in South Carolina in 1875.*

ABOVE: *Laurel Valley Plantation, Thibodaux, Louisiana. This postbellum sugar plantation still has visible signs of its tenant past preserved in these rows of tenant cabins.*

LEFT: *The Mississippi Delta, an area well above the mouth of the river, is well known for its plantations and its poverty. Although this photograph was taken by Dorothea Lange for the Farm Security Administration in 1937, the architectural style and the economic system depicted here have their roots in the nineteenth century.*

PATENT MEDICINES

Shattered by the Civil War, the South eagerly dosed itself with patent medicines. Traveling peddlers and medicine shows toured most in the fall, when crop sales put a little cash in the hands of rural customers. The unhealthy climate of low-lying areas bred fevers and poverty. Primitive accommodations and haphazard sanitation meant that most children carried worms. Spiritually, the South was in even worse shape, and many remedies seemed to address themselves to a malaise as much mental as physical. Since most popular nostrums contained opium, morphine, or cocaine, dissolved in alcohol as high as 90 proof, patent medicines might relieve a panoply of symptoms, while failing to cure anything. By the 1870s, the United States was importing nearly half a million pounds of opium a year, much of which went into over-the-counter remedies.

One leading fear of the late nineteenth century was the notion that the Anglo-Saxon race was losing its vigor. The lagging vitality of women and the comparatively low birth rates of whites fueled anxieties about the future dominance of Anglo-Saxons. Female regulators, spring tonics, and potions for female complaints addressed themselves to the too-delicate woman, whose health was thought to reside in her reproductive system. For the men, a thousand different concoctions offered to restore the blood, reinvigorate manliness, conquer syphilis, and boost potency. Attitudes toward these medicines paradoxically mixed a reverence for the shamanistic natural powers of roots and herbs (supposedly learned from Native Americans) with a devotion to techniques and substances touted as modern. Often alongside claims for the naturalness of herbs and roots of the American pharmacopeia appeared endorsements from medical men.

The medicine shows that toured the backroads of rural America also had affinities with the religious revival meeting. The smooth-talking patent peddler necessarily needed to command the call and response rhetoric of the inspired preacher in order to hold his audience. His plants among the audience members would testify fervently to the miracle of their cures. The setting, the style of talk, and the manipulation of sentiment mimicked the techniques familiar to any Baptist revivalist. These attitudes combined to make the South a very particular market for patent medicines. Touting southern liniment over Yankee remedies, yet buying blood tonic and hair straightener in vast quantities that revealed regional self-doubts, the white southerner seemed to worry more about improving bloodlines than the local economy.

With its implicit appeal to maintain white supremacist blood-lines, Swift's Sure Specific spoke directly to white southern men who felt their blood and manhood in jeopardy after the Civil War. Made in Atlanta, the nostrum was promoted with trade cards that pictured men in the bold postures of frontiersmen.

■ KATHLEEN HULSER
New York University

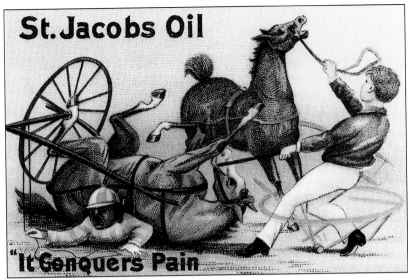

ABOVE: *The Baltimore makers of St. Jacob's Oil distributed trade cards, postered fences and barns, and even plastered ads on a Mississippi paddle wheeler. As a measure of men's attachment to their mounts in the region, St. Jacob's testimonials often featured horse breeders claiming a dose ("one for men, two for horses") could conquer pain.*

LEFT: *Syrup of Figs was claimed to cure biliousness. Southern regional staples of pork, corn bread, sorghum, and gravy interfered with digestion enough to ensure steady sales from the Gulf of Mexico to the Chesapeake.*

ABOVE LEFT: *The Chattanooga Medicine Company distilled Wine of Cardui from the "blessed thistle" and promised that it eased all sorts of women's complaints. Like many other potions of the time, the remedy had supposedly been passed on from the Native Americans; such claims grew in the rich loam of quack entrepreneurship, rather than in the continent's Native American heritage.*

LEFT: *These nineteenth-century glass bottles, recovered in the excavation of the Maynard-Burgess Houses in Annapolis, Maryland, originally contained a variety of patent medicines. John Maynard, a free African American, built the house in the 1850s. It seems evident from the archaeological finds that the longing for miracle cures was common to both blacks and whites.*

THE COLONIAL REVIVAL: *Worshiping the Ancestors*

Take a walk through just about any American neighborhood and you are bound to see a Colonial Revival house. Look for a red brick or clapboard house, with a doorway topped by sculpted pediments and six-over-six paned windows. Not all are fancy copies of famous colonial structures like Mount Vernon or the high-style houses from Colonial Williamsburg; travel downtown and look for "colonial" cupolas on public and commercial buildings. You're as likely to see them on gas stations as on schools.

The Colonial Revival began around 1876, at the time of America's first centennial, when several cultural forces coalesced. First was an anti-modernistic response to the Industrial Revolution and a reaction to the Civil War—a nostalgic desire for simpler, better times. Second, a nationalistic impulse persuaded many that the country needed to return to its roots, toward purely "American" antecedents. Yet what counted as American was

decidedly restricted: America's English and Dutch past was celebrated above all else. This nativism was fueled in part by large-scale immigration.

All these factors resulted in a celebration of things colonial, a movement that began as an elite preoccupation, but soon became popularized. In homes across the country, old-fashioned rifles dangled over mantels and high-backed settees were placed near colonial-looking fireplaces. From hutches to highboys, from hatchets to hearths, the Colonial Revival initiated an interest in things old. It spawned the antiques trade and resulted in the reproductions of colonial furnishings now available in almost any furniture store.

One source of inspiration for colonial Americana was the historic house movement. Throughout the late nineteenth and early twentieth centuries, scores of early homes were saved from destruction by members of genealogical organizations like the Daughters of the American Revolution and the

The interest in things colonial encouraged many to scour the countryside for antiques, but these items were too expensive for the average consumer. Wallace Nutting brought coloniana to the masses, through reproduction furnishings and whimsical colonial photographs for those neither highborn nor rich.

For both social events and fundraisers, patrician Americans seemed to like nothing better than to don colonial costumes. These celebrants from the 1920s are dressed for George Washington's Birth Night Ball in Alexandria.

FACING PAGE: *Washington was a central figure in the Colonial Revival, and his home continues to be a major drawing card. Maintained by the Mount Vernon Ladies' Association of the Union since before the Civil War, the plantation draws over a million visitors a year.*

BELOW: *Washington is known as the "Father of His Country." His house has its progeny as well. From pizza parlors to gas stations to banks, tawdry copies of Mount Vernon are everywhere.*

Mayflower Descendants—organizations dedicated to celebrating American heritage along with their own bloodlines. George Washington and his home became central elements in the Colonial Revival movement; Mount Vernon became a must-see tourist stop. The ultimate revival museum, Colonial Williamsburg, established in the 1920s with millions of dollars from the Rockefellers, created an idealized, self-contained eighteenth-century world that existed only in the minds of its founders. "Williamsburg colors" became synonymous with the palette of the eighteenth century even though they had no basis in historical fact. The Colonial Revival dug up a fictive past, a past colored the way the present wanted it.

■ MARK BOGRAD
*National Park Service,
Lowell National Historic Park*

VAUDEVILLE: *Something for Everyone*

In the turn-of-the-century vaudeville houses of New York City, street-corner comedians from the Lower East Side met stage-door entrepreneurs. Together they turned nineteenth-century theater into twentieth-century show business. Gotham's showmen capitalized on the city's pre-eminence as a center of business, transportation, and theater to make it the center of the vaudeville industry. Their booking offices sent performers on nationwide tours and their theaters defined stardom. From vaudeville sprang performers who defined American popular culture for generations—Sophie Tucker, Eubie Blake, Bob Hope, and Jimmy Cagney—and chains of theaters, like the Keith and Orpheum circuits, that forged national networks of stars and fans. From these foundations were built the twentieth century's structure for film, radio, and television: the core of popular culture.

If vaudeville was the cradle of American mass culture, Union Square was the birthplace of vaudeville in New York City. It was no accident that the vaudeville impresarios gravitated toward Union Square. In the early 1870s, the area was well established as New York's main theater district. The uptown surge of Manhattan's commerce along Broadway and the Bowery reached the square by the 1860s; uptown, downtown, and crosstown trolley lines, plus the erection of the Ninth Avenue elevated train in 1869 and the Sixth Avenue elevated train in 1879, brought more and more customers for stores and theaters around the square. The combination of transit links, theaters, and proximity to shopping on the Ladies' Mile made the square prime real estate for vaudeville entrepreneurs seeking to attract a mass audience.

The three most influential founders of vaudeville—Tony Pastor and the team of B. F. Keith and E. F. Albee—all had theaters on Union Square. There they confronted a common challenge: creating a large and profitable audience in an era when natives and immigrants, middle class and working class, all had different ideas about

Pat Rooney, Sr., was one of the many popular ethnic comedians on the vaudeville stage.

enjoyable entertainment and proper conduct. The solution was to stage variety shows, stripped of their reputation for booze and bawdry, billed under the classier-sounding name of Vaudeville—and marketed to an unprecedentedly broad audience. Each bill had "something for everyone": propriety for the sanctimonious, raciness for the naughty, Old Country sentiment for homesick immigrants, and Yankee Doodle Dandy snap for their children, who were constructing new American identities.

Vaudeville's heart and soul was the invigorating influence of outsiders trying to become insiders—Irish tenors, Jewish comics, black ragtime

Strong emotions, vivid characters, and melodramatic plots were the stock in trade of the vaudeville impresarios. An Exciting Scene at the Bowery Theatre, *1878.*

Eva Tanguay, sprawled seductively, helped make titillation a staple of vaudeville.

Now abandoned and derelict, the Jefferson Theater is a vestige of the heyday of vaudeville.

pianists. Its nerve system was the theater circuit, which embraced everything from tawdry small-time dumps to elegant big-time palaces. Vaudeville flowered from the 1880s until the 1930s, when it was finally killed off by the Depression and the overwhelming competition of sound motion pictures. Today, the landmarks of Union Square are largely destroyed, disguised, or forgotten. But it is still possible to pound the pavements where starving actors once looked for work and gaze at the old theaters that were once the summit of saloon singers' ambitions, and the birthplace of a new, mass-marketed entertainment form.

■ ROBERT W. SNYDER
Rutgers University

OLD SUBURBIA: *Metropolitan Landscapes*

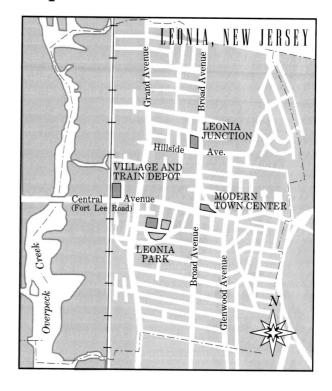

By the nineteenth century, the social significance of the suburb had changed from that of a dangerous, wicked area outside a city's walls to an idyll of domestic repose and leisure. From the mid-nineteenth century to the post–World War II era, every major metropolitan region developed suburbs. But these older, urban-oriented communities bore little resemblance to the regimented rows of boxlike housing associated with post–World War II Levittowns, which have today fixed the image of suburbia in the American mind.

In the case of Leonia, New Jersey, the opening of a train station in 1859 had given rise to a railroad village that depended on both agricultural and urban commerce in its coal-and-feed store, livery stable, blacksmith shop, Chinese laundry, and hardware and general store. By the 1880s, local entrepreneurs created one of the earliest planned suburbs in New Jersey: Leonia Park. Their 1885 plan included a central, winding country lane and individualized houses for local merchants and railroad commuters to New York City.

The introduction of the electric trolley in the 1890s accelerated the development of Leonia Park. A trolley transfer point, Leonia Junction, reoriented the center of town from the railroad depot to a northern and upland section of the emergent suburb. The nickel trolley ride to the Hudson River ferry enabled even working-class consumers to covet the new houses along the main thoroughfare. Such residents helped to transform the character of this suburban community by 1915, so that it had new churches and new business establishments, such as the realty office, the local branch of the A&P grocery store chain, the first town library, the public high school, and sandwich shops for trolley travelers.

During the 1920s and 1930s the availability of automobiles changed the complexion of the suburb again and attracted a professional and artisan class. By the 1930s, most commuters traveled to work by auto or bus rather than trolley or train. The center of town shifted for a third time—to the present-day Broad Avenue and Fort Lee Road. Here one can document another distinctive middle-class imprint: banks, specialty stores with apartments above, and professional offices, all constructed of brick with a decided sense of permanence.

In contrast to the mythology of the bleakly homogeneous suburb, the social structures and physical landscapes of Old Suburbia changed drastically even *within* single communities. As in Leonia, New Jersey, each structure developed its own material culture and cohesive mythologies. Middle-class suburban cultures rarely sought to "escape" the city, but rather to maintain access to it while cultivating a distinctive, newly created form of community life.

■ PAUL H. MATTINGLY
New York University

FACING PAGE, TOP: *No longer standing, the Leonia train station was the nucleus and entry point of the late-nineteenth-century mixed commuter suburb and agricultural village.*

$1000 SAVED ON THIS HOUSE

I have built a score of houses in **LEONIA**. I am my own builder and contractor. I guarantee to put $1000 in any man's pocket who buys of me. This is no dream but a fact.

Wm. P. Richards

LEONIA, N. J.

PHONE 18 W. LEONIA

ABOVE: *This 1909 advertisement, promoting a relatively simple frame house for sale at an affordable price, was meant to appeal to a new kind of middle-class consumer. It also marked the start of a tenuous, even speculative dimension to suburban development.*

ABOVE LEFT: *In this photo of the village (c. 1910), parked Model T Fords, corner sewers, and telephone poles are manifestations of the new suburban infrastructure of the twentieth century.*

LEFT: *Leonia's third town center features a bank and brick stores that anchored subsequent town development and gave it a sense of permanence.*

SUBWAYS: *The Geography of Underground New York*

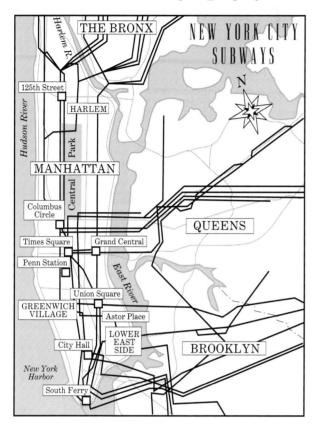

Before the mid-nineteenth century, New York, the "walking city," was concentrated below 14th Street. Later, with an influx of immigrants and a rise in population, the density of residents in Lower Manhattan grew unbearable. Housing reformers decried the lack of public transit, but improvements were slow in coming. Many city bosses had a financial stake in streetcar or elevated train companies, and these forms of transit simply could not transport large numbers of workers from uptown residences to downtown factories.

New York's first subway was built in secrecy beneath Broadway by inventor Alfred Eli Beach, who intended to break the transport monopoly by conveying passengers beneath the city streets in cars blown along tracks by a huge fan. The Beach Pneumatic Tube, equipped with elegant chandeliers and plush furnishings to assuage public fears of riding underground (see illustration on page 176), was

opened to the public in February 1870, but was never extended beyond the initial two stations at Warren and Murray streets. In the aftermath of the Panic of 1873, Beach could find no investors.

In 1894, New York was in a reform swing of its infamous "machine-reform cycle," and municipal leaders were finally persuaded to support a rapid-transit plan. Intense population pressures could no longer be ignored, and tax dollars were being lost as many middle-class residents chose to ride the ferry from New Jersey or Brooklyn rather than live uptown. Yet instead of recommending a public system, the city offered contracts to private builders and operators who would "rent" the road from the city, and sell the subway back to the city after fifty years.

The Interborough Rapid Transit Company, backed by railroad financier August Belmont, won the bid for the initial contract and began construction in 1900. Its first route, which opened in 1904, began at City Hall, ran north to Grand Central Station, where it turned west and met Broadway, then continued up to Harlem on the West Side. A second company, the Brooklyn Rapid Transit Company (later known as the Brooklyn-Manhattan Transit Company) began competing with the IRT in 1908. With fifty-year contracts, the IRT and BMT kept profits up and service down, and left the city with a subway system in disrepair. By the late 1920s, they had stopped expanding their service. The pressing need for more subway lines led the city to establish its own Independent Division, the IND, in the 1930s, extending to areas that had been previously underserved.

The New York subway system remains a tangle of overlapping lines and confusing transfer stations that reflect its builders' quest for profits and the city's reluctance to intervene until it was too late. The decision of city government to leave rapid transit in the hands of private companies created problems it would have to face later, and which even today, despite continuing construction and renovation, remain unsolved.

■ EILEEN GATTI
New York University

LEFT: *Lenox Avenue and 113th Street, 1901. "To Harlem in fifteen minutes" was the slogan during the building of the first IRT line.*

BELOW: *Subway kiosk at Astor Place. These decorative entranceways were a point of civic pride to New Yorkers. Astor Place is the last remaining structure of its kind from the original IRT route.*

ABOVE LEFT: *Bas-relief beaver at Astor Place. Many stations were decorated with representations of neighborhood landmarks or legends. The beaver is a symbol of the origins of the Astor family fortune—the fur trade.*

RIGHT: *Mosaic at Pennsylvania Station, 1909. Each station on the original BMT line was designed with its own color scheme, allowing easy recognition for riders unable to read English.*

DEPARTMENT STORES
Ladies' Mile and the Culture of Shopping

In the late nineteenth and early twentieth centuries, shopping in New York was an unforgettable experience. Nowhere was the activity more concentrated than in the area known as Ladies' Mile. Centered between Union Square and Madison Square, Broadway to Sixth Avenue, this shopping district was home to the great mercantile institutions that made New York the shopping and fashion capital of the nation. So spectacular and extravagant was the architecture of mercantile display in this area that it remained the central location for the city's retail trade for over a generation. Even today, the remnants of Ladies' Mile are impressive.

Ladies' Mile offered a succession of palatial department stores, some of which survived well into the twentieth century—B. Altman and Best & Co.—some surviving even today—Bonwit Teller and R. H. Macy & Co. Others lived only in this heyday, such as Siegel-Cooper, the largest, and final,

addition to the great department stores that lined Sixth Avenue. Calling itself The Big Store—A City in Itself, Siegel-Cooper contained almost eighteen acres of floor space. Customers were drawn into this store as much by the excitement of the great emporium and its legendary array of services as by the variety of merchandise that sought to respond to every need—from fur coats and colored ostrich plumes to bicycles and sheet music.

Walking north on Sixth Avenue, the shopper would be jostled by crowds composed largely of women. At lunchtime and late in the afternoon office workers and shopgirls in long skirts, high-necked shirtwaists, and large hats would fill the already congested sidewalks. The department stores and countless specialty shops in this area catered in large part to the middle- and upper-class woman and her family. Other women—poor, black, immigrant—rarely found their way onto Ladies'

LEFT: The Lace-Room at A. T. Stewart's—The Superb Holiday Display of Valuable Laces. *In this engraving, all of the shoppers are women, all dressed very precisely by rules that helped to enforce more shopping.*

Influenced by the Beaux-Arts style of the 1893 World's Columbian Exposition, the furnishings of the huge Siegel-Cooper store epitomized the extravagance of an extravagant age. Behind the main counter stood the Statue of Justice, modeled on Athena, from the Chicago fair.

Mile; they depended on neighborhood shops, retailers on Grand Street, and merchandise sold from pushcarts and from small stores all over the Lower East Side.

Ladies' Mile is no longer home to the great department stores. As the commercial center moved uptown, retailers went out of business or moved away from the Sixth Avenue area. A number of buildings were ultimately demolished. But many of the original structures, once housing such mercantile giants as Sterns, F.A.O. Schwarz, Ehrich Brothers, Adams Dry Goods, Hugh O'Neill, and B. Altman, survive—refurbished, occupied by new tenants, and serving new uses. The huge Siegel-Cooper building, minus its tower, has become a retail center for the 1990s, housing numerous stores under one great roof.

The Ladies' Mile Historic District became a reality in 1989 and encompasses most of the famous shopping area, particularly the fine old stores on Sixth Avenue north of Seventeenth Street. The commercial palaces of the nineteenth century thus remain part of New York's living history.

> ■ ELAINE S. ABELSON
> *The New School for Social Research*

The architectural opulence of the Hugh O'Neill store remains, even today, on Sixth Avenue and 21st Street. Neoclassical facades promised respectability but abundance; new ways of classifying goods, special lighting, trading stamps, credit or charge cards, elevators, and the juxtaposition of many services generated a whole new experience of spending as a pleasure and a necessary good.

NEWCOMERS: *The World of the Immigrants*

The United States Immigration Station at Ellis Island was opened in 1892 both as a celebration of Columbus and as an efficient human processing machine. In its architectural style and layout, it shared much with other 1890s Renaissance-style post offices, railroad stations, and courthouses, directing the flow of people and things.

Between 1820 and 1940, over forty million people left their homes in Asia, Europe, and elsewhere to come to the United States. Many did not intend to stay, but to work for a certain period, save money, and return to their native lands. In fact, for every one hundred immigrants who came, around thirty left. Immigrants adapted to or resisted the new economic order in many different ways and with many different results. And the loci of commodification and resistance occurred not just at the workplace but at all points of life. Some immigrants chose ethnic cohesion, conservatism, and religion; others chose radicalism; and yet others—but by no means all—opted for a lifestyle of assimilation into the American mainstream.

Ellis Island and the Statue of Liberty celebrate the successes and triumphs of the immigrants who came to America before World War II. But sites in one of the United States' most famous immigrant neighborhoods, the Lower East Side of Manhattan

in New York City, reveal a more complex picture of immigration. These sites can illustrate immigrants' attempts to adapt to, adjust to, or resist life in the New World—at work, at worship, at school, and on the street.

One entry point for immigrants was New York Harbor's Ellis Island, now a National Park Service monument to the immigrant experience. In 1890, Ellis Island became the main receiving station for immigrants. Immigration peaked in 1907; in that year over one million immigrants came through the station. Then restrictive immigration laws, passed in 1924, put a virtual end to immigration through here. The station closed and the island was vacated in 1954. The historical exhibits seen there now highlight those who stayed, though they also acknowledge those who left or rejected mainline life in turn-of-the-century America.

Jews and Catholics often used their worship centers as foci for their new lives. For example, the

LEFT: *Ellis Island processed more than two thousand immigrants during its first day of operation. Federal immigration inspectors weeded out the physically and mentally handicapped, paupers, criminals, prostitutes, and radicals. Twenty percent of immigrants were detained while two percent were deported.*

BELOW: *Pictured in this early-twentieth-century photo of Hester Street on New York's Lower East Side are immigrant pushcart peddlers and their customers.*

LEFT: *Lower East Siders claim that the building now occupied by the Bialystoker Synagogue once served as a stop on the underground railroad. The conversion of the structure in 1878 from a Methodist church to a synagogue added another dimension to its multiethnic history.*

Bialystoker Synagogue at Willett and Grand streets on the Lower East Side illustrates Jewish immigrants' attachment to religion and tradition, as well as the changing face of that attachment with each new immigrant wave. The stone structure was originally built in 1826 as a Methodist church. Yet in 1878, with a new wave of immigration from Eastern Europe, the church was purchased from its original congregants and converted into a community synagogue by immigrants from the Lithuanian factory town of Bialystok. Such adaptation often served to preserve buildings as neighborhoods changed.

While religion stabilized life, the pushcart enabled immigrants to break into closed parts of the economy. Open-air pushcart markets were both center and symbol of immigrants' attempts to adapt to their new urban environment. Newcomers needed neither a large outlay of capital nor a command of English to become pushcart peddlers. Further, with this vehicle immigrant peddlers and shoppers alike operated within a familiar economic and social context. Even though New York City banned pushcarts from its streets in 1938, the open-air markets of the Lower East Side continue to flourish for more recent generations of newcomers to America.

■ SUZANNE WASSERMAN
New York City

ALASKA: *Whales, Work, and Eskimos*

The Western Arctic commercial whaling industry, active between 1850 and 1910, brought Inupiat Eskimos into contact with the ever-expanding world of American industry and influence. American commercial whalers initially sought whale oil, but after the Civil War, with the development of fossil fuels, emphasis shifted to baleen. This flexible, fibrous, plankton-straining material, hanging from the upper jaw of the bowhead whale, was used in the manufacture of corset stays and buggy whips—items in high demand. Until the late 1880s, the whaling industry obtained baleen in commercial harvesting on the open sea and through trade with Eskimos, who for a thousand years had hunted bowheads for food. In the late 1880s, American whalers added a shore-based spring whaling season to the summertime open-sea hunt to compensate for the diminished whale populations caused by commercial overhunting. Shore stations needed workers to run whaleboats. Eskimos, with their knowledge of whaling, were sought as laborers.

Shore stations initially attracted Eskimos by supplying foodstuffs shipped from San Francisco; overwhaling had drastically depleted the Eskimo's primary source of food. Once hired, the Eskimos were paid in the form of canned food and other manufactured goods. By the early 1890s, virtually every able-bodied Eskimo in North Alaska worked for the commercial whaling industry at the many stations along the North Alaskan coast. At the same time that representatives of American industry were trying to create an Eskimo labor force, Federal and Christian mission interests began actively attempting to influence the nature of traditional Eskimo society. Together, these outside institutional forces embarked on a course to "Americanize" the Eskimos, to turn them into good Americans, good Christians, and good industrial workers. Ridding Eskimos of their traditional material goods and encouraging their subsequent accumulation of manufactured items as industrial workers was the method of Americanization.

In a walk through Barrow today, the traveler may be overwhelmed by the preponderance of manufactured things—evoking a nostalgic yearning for those bygone days when *real* Eskimos lived in igloos, wore caribou-skin parkas, and hunted seals with spears. But the outward appearance of a society does not necessarily reflect its cultural essence. Although commercial whaling ended here around 1910, when American industry began to substitute spring steel for baleen, the North Alaskan Eskimo society and heritage proved to be strong. Despite the prevalence of outboard motors, snowmobiles, and rifles in modern Eskimo life, the people of North Alaska are no less Eskimos now than they were before commercial whalers arrived a century ago. Subsistence hunters of bowhead whales today, they are Americans when they want to be or when they have to be, but they are always Eskimos.

John W. Kelly, an early commercial whaler on the North Alaskan coast, at Point Barrow, c. 1891, showing a mix of local and Western equipment. Such men also encouraged the Christian missionizing of Alaskan natives.

■ MARK S. CASSELL
University of Wisconsin—LaCrosse

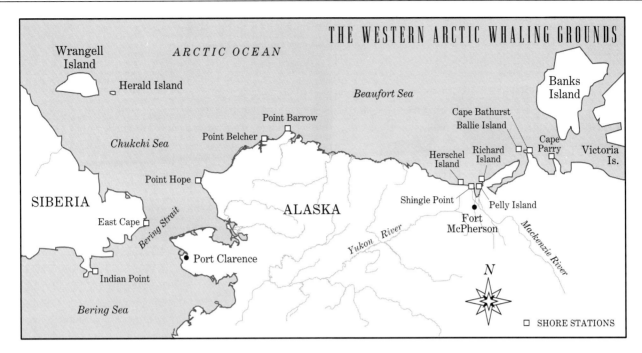

ARCTIC OCEAN

Wrangell Island

Herald Island

Beaufort Sea

Banks Island

Cape Bathurst
Ballie Island

Point Barrow

Point Belcher

Chukchi Sea

Herschel Island

Richard Island

Cape Parry

Victoria Is.

Point Hope

SIBERIA

ALASKA

Shingle Point

Pelly Island

Bering Strait

East Cape

Yukon River

Fort McPherson

Mackenzie River

Port Clarence

Indian Point

N

Bering Sea

□ SHORE STATIONS

LEFT: *Eskimos cleaning baleen at a Point Hope shore station, late nineteenth century. Background and foreground show continued use of native housing, sleds, and clothing.*

BELOW: *"Manner of Cutting-in the Bowhead and Right Whale." Butchering whales was done on board or on shore according to formulas like this one, and according to the commercial uses to which the parts and products were to be put. The uses varied over time and continue to the present.*

BELOW: *An engraving of a traditional Eskimo skin scraper—part of the material culture that the new industrial and religious influences tried to wipe out.*

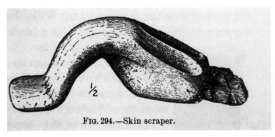

½

FIG. 294.—Skin scraper.

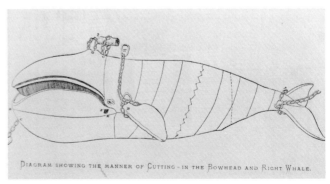

DIAGRAM SHOWING THE MANNER OF CUTTING-IN THE BOWHEAD AND RIGHT WHALE.

ABOVE: *The acquisition of the horse and gun from Europeans allowed groups like the Sioux and Cheyenne to concentrate on buffalo hunting—and made them a military power to be reckoned with, as this petroglyph battle scene from northwestern South Dakota shows.*

ABOVE: *"Last Stand Hill." A grass fire in 1983 allowed archaeologists to use metal detectors and excavations to document U.S. cavalry and Native American movements across the battlefield. The nineteenth-century stone markers designate the places where Custer's men were believed to have fallen.*

INDIAN WARS:
The Trail to Wounded Knee

The Plains Indian Wars of the late nineteenth century are forever emblazoned on the American consciousness. For some, they were stages for acts of Indian and white glory. Others see them as an episode of Manifest Destiny that, whether for good or bad, helped to mold America's character. Many feel guilt or anger that the wars nearly destroyed a noble and free people. Whatever the case, the last half of the nineteenth century was a period of remarkable change on the northern Great Plains, with the Indian Wars as tragic symptoms.

During the Civil War, Indian-White relations on the margins of the Plains began to unravel with the 1862 Sioux uprising in Minnesota. Two years later, Chivington's Third Colorado Cavalry massacred Black Kettle's band of Cheyenne on Sand Creek. Several meetings with Indians at Fort Laramie, with an important treaty in 1868, provided for the great Sioux Reservation, which included the sacred Black Hills. In 1874, Gen. George Armstrong Custer violated that treaty by leading an expedition into the Black Hills. Gold was discovered and a rush of prospectors began. The government, making only token efforts to keep settlers out, demanded that the Indians come to specially designated concentration points called agencies or be considered hostile. Most did not heed the demand.

By the summer of 1876, the Sioux and Cheyenne, under the leadership of chiefs like Sitting Bull, Gall, Hump, and Crazy Horse, camped on the river they called Greasy Grass, also known as the Little Bighorn. A detachment of the Seventh Cavalry under Custer attacked, and the "Last Stand" became a part of American mythology. For the Sioux and Cheyenne, however, the seeds of final defeat were sown in their major victory. In time, the Cheyenne were forcibly moved to Indian territories in Oklahoma. The demise of the buffalo made Sioux resistance impossible. Most moved into the Indian agencies, lived on poor government rations, and suf-

ABOVE: *Red Cloud. One of the important Native American leaders of the Plains Wars, this Oglala chief led resistance to the military, especially on the Powder River. The 1873 establishment of the Red Cloud Agency near Fort Robinson marked the beginning of the gradual movement of the more militant Sioux toward reservation life.*

FACING PAGE, BOTTOM: *The mass grave at Wounded Knee. More than two hundred of Big Foot's people were buried hurriedly after a sudden blizzard hit the "battlefield."*

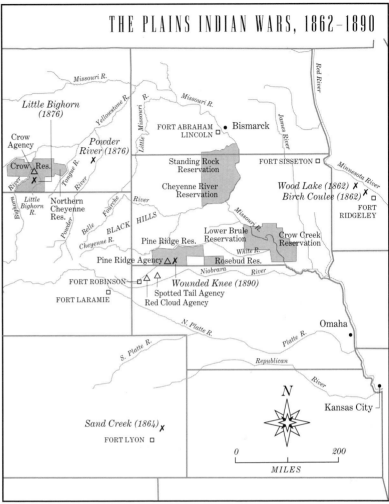

THE PLAINS INDIAN WARS, 1862–1890

fered mightily. By the late 1880s, many of the Sioux, dissatisfied with reservation life, took up the Ghost Dance, a mystical movement that promised return of the old ways. The U.S. military, alarmed at what seemed to be new hostility, insisted that one group, Big Foot's band, move to Wounded Knee Creek to be disarmed. The camp was surrounded, and—for reasons still unclear—the military opened fire, killing Big Foot and more than two hundred fifty of his people.

Today, the desolation of Wounded Knee is overwhelming. At the base of the hill, near the creek, stands an interpretive sign describing the Seventh Cavalry's massacre of Bigfoot's band. In the grave-yard on the top of the hill the visitor's attention is drawn to a wrought-iron fence marking the mass grave that ended the Indian Wars. Though it might now be difficult to imagine the sound of the Hotchkiss guns firing and the cries of the wounded and the dying, the burned-out shells of nearby buildings and bunkers from the 1973 American Indian Movement occupation of Wounded Knee show that the Indian Wars in many ways never ended.

■ LARRY J. ZIMMERMAN
KAREN ZIMMERMAN
University of South Dakota

HISTORICAL PAGEANTS: *Public Epic in the Midwest*

In the early twentieth century, historical pageantry flourished as a form of local boosterism, patriotic moralizing, and popular entertainment, and also as a vehicle for expressing reform ideals sweeping the nation. Pageantry's popularity grew with progressive reform movements at the turn of the century and culminated with the American entry into World War I.

Thomas Wood Stevens's *Historical Pageant of Illinois*, performed in Evanston in 1909, was among the earliest historical pageants in the United States. Stevens taught at the Art Institute of Chicago and believed pageantry would whet the public's appetite for higher forms of dramatic art. His first plot focused on white settlement of the Old Northwest and represented the displacement of Indians as the result of inevitable progress—not red-white conflict. The pageant proved so popular that Stevens repeated it in Milwaukee in 1911 and in Madison, Illinois, in 1912.

Stevens also contributed to the *Pageant and Masque of St. Louis*. Shamed by Lincoln Steffens's articles attacking city government as rife with corruption, and by the loss of Midwestern trade to Chicago, St. Louis city officials wanted to present a different civic image to the nation. They hired Stevens to create a glittering extravaganza in which St. Louis history from the ancient Indians onward would be shown both realistically and allegorically, climaxing in the knight "St. Louis" banishing "Gold" from the civic temple, symbolizing the city's triumph over corruption.

In light of the success of pageants in Illinois and St. Louis, Indiana officials commissioned their own pageants to celebrate the centennial of statehood in 1916. They appointed as state pageant-master William Chancy Langdon, a New Yorker who believed strongly in pageantry's power to join past, present, and future. His dramatic history of Indianapolis from the coming of La Salle in 1669 to an automobile parade emphasized the essential continuity across generations as each participated in the commercial development of the city.

Langdon's success in Indiana led to his being

invited to create a similar series of pageants commemorating Illinois statehood in 1918. But by the time he arrived in Champaign in the fall of 1917, the United States was already at war in Europe. Scrapping plans for a local-history pageant, Langdon instead created *The Sword of America*, a symbolic play detailing the reasons that the nation had entered World War I—and presenting standardized images calculated to unify audiences in support of the war effort.

Out of such pageants grew outdoor history museums. By the 1930s, the popularity of pageants was eclipsed by such locales as Greenfield Village and Colonial Williamsburg, which depicted an idealized past, frozen in time for tourists, rather than linked through anniversary commemorations with the present and future of a specific community.

■ DAVID GLASSBERG
University of Massachusetts, Amherst

LEFT: *Standing before the mimic Mayan temple erected to symbolize the civilization of the ancient Mound Builders, these "water maidens" were among the seven thousand participants in the* Pageant and Masque of St. Louis *(1914). While pageant organizers claimed that this mass participation brought the city together, the virtual exclusion of African American residents (the sole black participant appeared as "Africa" holding a spear) effectively sharpened differences between black and white residents.*

THE·PAGEANT·OF·INDIANA
AT INDIANAPOLIS
OCTOBER·2–7·1916

LEFT: *Indianapolis was among the dozens of Indiana towns to venerate the pioneer on the occasion of the centennial of admission to statehood in 1916.*

BELOW: *In this scene from* The Sword of America *(1917), America rises to do battle against the Germans, declaring, "This is not war! This is the purging of the world!" Author and director William Chauncy Langdon stands at far right, in monk's robe.*

FACING PAGE: *On the cover of the souvenir program for the* Historical Pageant of Illinois *(Evanston, 1909), the Native American prophet "White Cloud" is shown predicting that his race would soon be supplanted by white settlers.*

WORLD'S FAIRS: *Utopian Spectacles*

Between the end of Reconstruction and the beginning of World War I, nearly a hundred million Americans traveled across a cultural landscape torn by mounting class conflict and anxiety about the future to visit the great world's fairs. These huge, highly publicized industrial and cultural expositions, with their overpowering neoclassical architecture, displays of impressive new technologies, and novel amusements, shaped the form and content of America's emerging culture of imperial abundance.

The 1893 Chicago World's Columbian Exposition set the tone for many of the fairs that followed. It consisted of a "White City" of monumental structures housing cultural exhibits and a mile-long "Midway Plaisance" with honky-tonk amusements, George Ferris's Revolving Wheel, and "living ethnological villages." These contrived natural habitat settings for displays of living Eskimos, Africans, South Sea Islanders, and Middle Easterners reinforced lessons about the inevitable course of progress from the "savagery" of the midway plaisance to the "civilization" of the White City.

Chicago's success in attracting over twenty million visitors—and the continuing effects of the 1893 depression—inspired civic leaders in other cities to promote their own fairs. With the help of the Federal government, they constructed fantasy lands of mass consumption. In 1898, Omaha hosted the Trans-Mississippi and International Exposition, which featured an enormous display of Native Americans who were hired to fight mock battles with costumed cavalrymen before sell-out crowds. The exposition concluded by celebrating America's victory in the Spanish-American War—a victory that inspired exposition organizers to keep the fair open in the following year to glorify American imperialism.

No fair was more important for celebrating

RIGHT: *Near impressive exhibits extolling the wonders of modern industry, George Ferris's huge "Revolving Wheel" gave Chicago fairgoers a mechanical thrill in 1893. The thrill continues at modern fairs and amusement parks.*

FAR RIGHT: *With a stern-faced Uncle Sam embracing the globe and pointing to Cuba and the Philippines on this 1899 Omaha Greater America Exposition poster, the fair's main ideological message is clear.*

GREATER AMERICA EXPOSITION

OMAHA U.S.A.
July first to Nov. first

THE WHITE MAN'S BURDEN

★ First Colonial Exhibit ★

In this scene from the 1904 St. Louis Fair, loinclothed Filipinos (on the right) pose with Native Americans to demonstrate the continuity between America's continental and overseas imperial conquests.

American's growing international empire than the 1904 St. Louis Exposition, held to commemorate the centennial of Jefferson's Louisiana Purchase. The fair generated a hit song, "Meet Me in St. Louis, Louis"; covered the greatest acreage of any American fair; and boasted a staggering array of amusements and commercial and industrial exhibits. But the centerpiece of the fair was the Philippines Reservation. Organized by War Department anthropologists, it put over a thousand native Filipinos on display as a vivid demonstration of America's rise as a global imperial power.

The generation of Victorian-era fairs concluded on the West Coast. The 1915 San Francisco Panama-Pacific International Exposition, held to commemorate the opening of the Panama Canal, presented the story of the American West in terms of Social Darwinism and projected a vision of California as a paradise of consumer riches. The San Francisco Fair—like its predecessors—had the effect of making an increasing number of Americans comfortable with what historian William A. Williams called "empire as a way of life."

■ ROBERT W. RYDELL
Montana State University

In 1915, at a time of great anxiety about America's ability to act effectively in the world, the San Francisco Panama-Pacific International Exposition's official poster emphasized the importance of national will—here personified by an American Hercules parting the Isthmus of Panama.

6

CORPORATE AMERICA

1918–2000

WITH CONTRIBUTIONS BY

Richard H. Beckham

Mary Ann Beecher

Elizabeth C. Cromley

Alan Hess

Randall H. McGuire

Maria Praetzellis

James Smokowski

Larry J. Zimmerman

Sue Bridwell Beckham

Steven Conn

Robert L. Hall

Kathleen Hulser

Max Page

Mary Praetzellis

Karen Zimmerman

The asphalt ribbons and concrete slabs of interstate highways and cloverleaf interchanges mark nodes of movement and connection in the late twentieth century. They are among the most characteristic—and certainly largest—artifacts ever placed on the American landscape. Yet, like the maps, atlases, and grids of the sixteenth and seventeenth centuries or the Georgian buildings and Federal banks and capitols of the early nineteenth century, the roads and billboards, neon monuments, and red, white, and blue interstate route markers that accompany them are best understood as indicators of fluid cultural relationships. Our superhighways are material markers of the spread of a powerful economic and social network, hardly less potent in transforming lifestyles than the European and Native American fur traders' routes of the sixteenth and seventeenth centuries. For at a time when the American economy had become powerfully uniform in methods of production and commerce, the next step was to make every American woman, man, and child a potential consumer of industrially produced goods at any place in the country at any hour of the day. Thus the highway moved goods, and, in addition, it made mass consumption possible.

Highways—even more than railroads—both facilitated and symbolized a contradictory reality: the honking congestion of the major cities and the high-speed highway flow among them. The mobility they enabled could often disguise ever more rigid social relations. We emphasize the highway, the automobile, and the often trivialized items accompanying them because they exemplify the contrasting homogeneity of daily life and the supposed independence, mobility, and freedom of choice that highways facilitated. But highways and automobiles also led to intrusion, disruption, migration, high accident rates, personal isolation, and the paralytic conflict between ownership of the means of freedom and the prison of car loans, mechanical breakdowns, and traffic jams.

The automobile was the vessel in which these changes were effected, and the American landscape was dramatically reshaped as roads spanned the continent, garish shops (and, later, shopping malls) were built alongside them, and lurid signs were hung outside to tempt customers. Huge, bright symbols that could be apprehended at high speed and at a distance became a means of expression, and these trademark symbols became more graphic as the network of highways grew. The lure of the road became a metaphor for freedom, but in reality an individual's choices—even at 80 mph in the passing lane—became increasingly limited.

From behind the steering wheel in air-conditioned comfort, the divisions between civilization and wilderness; between the road and its surroundings; between the past and the present; between fantasy and reality became more blurred. And in the increasing absence of these distinctions, the everyday crime, filth, and inequality to which people had always responded directly and personally did not cease, but now appeared as unpleasantness and *other* peoples' misfortune to be avoided, not cured. In fact, the automobile magnified both the social problems of modern America and the difficulty of ever formulating a solution for them. Highly regimented working conditions, planned obsolescence of the finished product, and wasteful utilization of natural resources became part and parcel of the process of manufacturing, selling, and servicing millions of automobiles—with enormous implications for the transformation of the entire economy. No less important was the indirect effect of Model Ts, Cadillacs, Corvettes, and Mustangs on the national consciousness. As cultural icons, automobiles perpetuated the twentieth century's greatest ideological illusion: that the increasingly unavoidable routines and oppressions of the modern world could be escaped, through mobility.

THE AGE OF THE AUTOMOBILE

We have become used to believing that the history of America has unfolded in a neat, almost inevitable progression, from the days of horses and buggies to the days of eighteen-wheelers and convertibles. Yet this change, among the many other changes in American material life, was brought on by the conscious efforts of particular individuals for particular, private ends. Methods and technolo-

The transition to the Automobile Age was not always easy or quick. The Lincoln Highway in Iowa, following the general route of the Chicago and Northwestern Railroad, passed back and forth across the tracks repeatedly. During the 1920s, the Iowa Highway Commission used public funds to build underpasses that eliminated the most dangerous crossings. Within a few decades, the interstate highway system had become the nation's most heavily traveled medium of transportation—and a landscape for national fantasy.

gies of transport, for instance, have long been matters of the highest economic significance; the interests of private owners and operators have clashed repeatedly with the interests of the government since the toll and bridge controversies of the early nineteenth century. In Chapter 5 we have seen how late-nineteenth-century disputes over subway concessions made for lingering difficulties within cities, and how privately funded trolleys and trains made the creation of suburbs possible and profoundly changed the demographic patterning of metropolitan life. And so it was, on an even larger scale, with the highway. In order to make possible an enormous expansion of the economy, far beyond the control of the relatively few, tightly controlled train lines, beyond the effective control of the federal government or the governments of states, counties, and municipalities, the highway offered a vast, ever-expanding network—lined, leveled, and numbered—across the continent of North America.

As Mary Ann Beecher explains on pages 232–233, the concept of the "highway"—the idea of which is so much a part of our geographical understanding today—would have been impossible if groups of private businessmen and investors all across the country had not begun the construction of major roads, and then been able to convince the federal government to underwrite the cost of a national transport network. Before the turn of the twentieth century, most roads were local, only a few interregional. As early as 1902, routes for transcontinental automobile roads were proposed, but none of them was completed, since enormous capital was required. That issue of funding was apparently the main problem, for by 1910, the more than two million miles of American roads that had been established piecemeal adequately demonstrated the enormous profit-making potential of long-distance travel, transport of goods, and automobile sales. Through the next two decades, therefore, an intensive lobbying effort succeeded in achieving an ideal situation for American business: Taxpayers would pay for the roads by which manufactured goods would be offered for sale to them.

In 1916, and more significantly in 1921, Congress appropriated $75 million for use in the development of interstate roads. And by 1922, nine transcontinental routes were under federally funded construction or improvement—making the eventual disintegration of the regional cultures of America just a matter of time. Such disintegration was made up of the movement of people in large numbers across the country, the ballooning of suburbs, the weakening of factory owners' responsibility to workers, and the creation of markets so vast that laws had to be enacted to compel manufacturers to assume responsibility for what their products delivered, or for the consequences if they failed.

The enormous disruption brought about by these highways was often masked by the promise of an urban motorist's visit to the "real" American heartland—or by a carefully designed, nostalgic, patriotic appeal. Such illusions created another source of social instability. Nostalgia allowed people to avoid attempts to explain the disruptive demands of daily life by escaping into an imagined past as seen in the roadside remnants of bygone eras in the countryside. The attraction of "seeing the country" ironically intensified as the reality of the country changed. In its mechanical separation from the natural landscape, the highway proclaimed a new sphere of experience. Often, it was

the act of traveling or the thought of it, not the destination, that became the more significant fact. When one finally got to the "country," the end point was, in many ways, much like the place one had started from.

The highway offered Americans a chance to believe they were escaping. And as tourism grew, so did the competition for the tourist dollar by roadside entrepreneurs and impresarios, who recognized the psychic yearning for sensation and did their best to make a profit from it. Sue Bridwell Beckham explores the tourist attraction in depth on pages 234–235. Roadside colossi—towering parodies of Old World castles, plaster dinosaurs, and pink elephants—as well as amusement parks,

Brainerd, Minnesota's answer to the Lincoln Memorial—a tourist attraction featuring a colossal Paul Bunyan and, in the foreground, his squirrel Henry. This is one of the thousands of roadside curiosities that sprang up all over America in an attempt to lure travelers and vacationers off the road.

DREAMS AND ADVERTISEMENTS AS IDEOLOGY

Immigrants to the industrial cities of America did not all come from outside the country. These new arrivals in Newark, New Jersey, in 1918 came from the rural South.

theme parks, miniature golf courses, and open-air museums offered myriad harmless alternative realities that all shared one thing: They denied the very unpleasantness, conflict, and suffering that could be seen right there on the same highway.

American highways, in fact, became the means, the technology for imposing an economic homogeneity on the nation, channeling skilled workers to regions of labor shortage, manufactured goods to untapped markets, and immigrants from the farms to the cities. This movement, facilitated and sometimes even forced by the nearness of the highways, began long before the 1930s and continues today. Like the immigrants who had come to America from rural areas in Europe, Asia, and Africa on sailing ships and steamships, the immigrants on the highways were brought irreversibly into the world of industrial discipline. For example, the movement of African Americans from the rural South to the industrial North is described by Robert L. Hall on pages 236–237.

The process of national homogenization, made physically possible by the highways, had to be accompanied by a long and determined process of cognitive homogenization as well, with people coming to think alike. In the late nineteenth century, the way had been cleared for the construction of a shared fantasy world by the profit-making requirements of commercial theater; we have already seen how vaudeville producers established nationwide circuits, attracting audiences with similar, melodramatic themes and a constantly culled constellation of stars. At the same time, the lessons of local historical pageants and regional industrial expositions—though commemorating different dates and achievements—all preached the same messages of technological progress, increasing control over Mother Nature and human nature, and the triumph of the American Way. With the coming of the movies in the early twentieth century, such dreams were made part of everyday shared consciousness, no longer dependent on the occasional arrival of an eastern vaudeville troupe or the anniversary of the founding of the town. The early movie houses still found in small towns across America can therefore be seen as monuments no less significant than the remains of other great periods of social and psychological change.

Like the sixteenth-century Spanish mission churches in the Southeast at which native peoples were taught a more proper way of life through visual symbols and repeated recitation about the saints and the apostles, Hollywood movies became an important ideological medium in the twentieth century. Whether the local theater was an ornate movie palace or a modest frame building with wooden benches and a hung sheet for a screen, it was often a focal point of the community's social life. In some places, as Sue Bridwell Beckham and Richard H. Beckham point out on pages 238–239, the size and opulence of the small-town movie palace was rivaled only by that of the biggest local churches. The movies exchanged dreams for petty cash, not prayer or penitence—an attractive, if deceptive, exchange. For a population that was becoming almost entirely governed by the 9-to-5 tedium of work in shops and factories—not the vagaries of drought, tornadoes, and other acts of God—people sought at least psychic escape into other lives that appeared to be more glamorous, exciting, meaningful. As the national networks of film distributors and exhibitors spread across the country, the movie houses of the 1920s and 1930s shaped the belief systems of the faithful, reinforcing ideas about proper conduct and proper gender roles through the images on the screen.

On Saturday mornings children were instructed in cowboy chivalry, outer space heroism, and cliff-hanging jungle escapes. On Friday and Saturday nights, courting couples discovered how love was made, how elegant men treated elegant women, and what they wore. On weeknights, married folk nodded their heads at the homespun charm of Jimmy Stewart and Henry Fonda and the assurance of John Ford and Frank Capra that Americans were, by nature, independent, noble individualists. In fact, despite the exotic locales and glamorous characters, Hollywood movies offered an imitation reality that filled needs very close to home. And in the shifting themes, characters, and stories, one can trace both the changing needs of the American public and the ways in which they were filled throughout much of the twentieth century.

Movies were and remain a way of tying emotions and dreams together in ways so satisfying that reality, when it is confronted again, seems somehow less difficult or inevitable, less in need of being changed. That is the way effective ideology has always worked, be it in architecture, landscaping, or artistic productions, in every period of American history, that is where capitalism operated. Art can and often does call upon idealistic, nostalgic, or false images of ourselves and our communities. Thus, when we think about commercial entertainment at the movies and later on TV, we can see a hoped for alternative to everyday life, a hope that appears realistic but is usually empty.

Movies were certainly not the only ideological images creeping into the life of small-town America. Just as escape into shared fantasies became especially intense during the years of the Great Depression—from our point of view appropriately called the Golden Age of Hollywood—it was then also that the federal government entered the image-making business on a large scale. The most famous of the federal agencies established to underwrite and install conspicuous works of public

The main streets of small-town America centered on shops, movie theaters, post offices, and parking spaces for the ever-growing numbers of automobiles, as seen here on Main Street in River Falls, Wisconsin, c. 1939.

The power of art as public discourse was vividly demonstrated by the Depression-era post office murals. In this contemporary photograph, artist Nicholai Cikovsky and assistants apply the only Civil War mural south of the Mason-Dixon Line to the wall of the Silver Spring, Maryland, post office. Southerners did not care to be reminded of "the War" in their federal buildings, preferring rather to have either earlier history or current prosperity represented.

States could develop a movement and tradition of monumental public art. Thus was born the Treasury Section of the Fine Arts Project, which underwrote the painting of murals in federal buildings constructed between 1934 and 1941.

New Deal officials believed that common citizens needed help to express their pride in their local communities without threatening the larger national ideal. And although the idea was to fund a medium of local self-expression, the hand of the federal government was heavy. Competitions for commissions were run by local art aficionados appointed by the section, who would select the artist to be offered a lucrative job (with fees sometimes reaching as much as $3,000 for courthouse or post office murals in large cities). The care with which the process was conceived, however, did not help to achieve its ideal. By the 1930s, contemporary urban tastes had become the standard by which all artistic production was judged. As a result the officials of the Fine Arts Section often overruled the decisions of the local panels of judges, making the idea of "local" expression a farce.

As Dr. Beckham notes, the kinds of murals commissioned by the federal government in post offices and courthouses across the South provide an illuminating glimpse at the way southern history and southern heritage were officially conceived. Equally significant is the way that southern communities responded to these oil-painted messages. While some continue to be celebrated and remain visible even today, others, considered inaccurate or incompatible with community consciousness, were quickly painted over or concealed. The varying acceptance and rejection show that often there is conflict over ideology, with a region or community capable of dismissing an effort to dominate it with national or outside ideas. (For an example of a post office mural from an entirely different region, see page 146.)

The struggle to maintain distinctive regional cultures was ultimately a losing battle, for even more pervasive than the sedate and often inconspicuous post office murals were the colorful lithographed and painted billboards that sprouted everywhere along the roadside, on the sides of barns, and on the roofs of urban buildings from coast to coast. As Kathleen Hulser describes on

art was the Works Progress Administration. As Sue Bridwell Beckham outlines on pages 240–241, the WPA hired unemployed artists from all over the country to paint murals in public buildings, sometimes according to their own judgment and creativity, sometimes according to a strictly predetermined pattern. Yet, as Dr. Beckham points out, while the WPA has garnered a great deal of attention from historians and art critics, there was another federal project in this period that had a particular ideological goal. Artists and art critics who had the ear of President Roosevelt and his wife, Eleanor, convinced them that the United

WORLD'S HIGHEST STANDARD OF LIVING

There's no way like the American Way

Billboard promises did not always match reality, as in this photograph by Russell Lee for the Farm Services Administration, c. 1936.

pages 242–243, this was a picture language equally intelligible to immigrants, illiterates, women, children, professors, and farmers. It homogenized taste and style across classes. And while the American Automobile Association in some of its earliest membership newsletters recommended that motorists rip down offending signs, as an offense to the natural landscape, other commentators hailed the rows of colorful ads as "the picture galleries of the poor." However, these picture galleries did not attempt to instill a sense of community identity or other such abstract ideals. Telegraphing a message of pleasure and desire to customers, they relied on direct appeals to the need of the individual. Billboards sold the package as much as the product and helped small companies become national by placing their products in stores. And they did it by cementing emotional messages to slogans and trademarks of every imaginable kind of service or good.

Billboards showed people how to be modern, elegant, charming, and successful. Particularly after World War II, Dr. Hulser notes, advertisers rushed to cash in on consumer purchasing power bottled up during the war years. Houses in new development tracts, cars and the gasoline to get there, refrigerators and ice cream to put in them, and of course television were only a few of the products depicted in gigantic scale and garish color on the boards. Even as most messages preached hygiene and normality, the hot colors and exuberant large characters on some billboards sang a more seductive tune. Ads for bathing suits, sports products, and tanning lotions let advertisers expose square yards of realistically painted female flesh. Las Vegas showgirls lounged above blinking neon cocktail glasses in the commercial strips that sprouted across the country. And along with public erotica, billboards also featured sparkling appliances and honeybun housewives polishing the Formica surfaces of their all-electric kitchens in new suburban tract homes.

The television commercial—a hybrid of Hollywood filming techniques and the billboard's instantaneous ability to reach a mass audience with tailored messages—taught us how to purchase and use all these new things. The expression of the American ideology of individualism taught initially in themissions and commercial centers of the colonies, involving recognition of merit and opportunity for advancement, was now facilitated by the purchase of things, often modeled on what was seen on television. The discipline of shopping was the subject that now had to be learned, much as the discipline of work had been taught in previous centuries. By choosing the cultural messages among the repertoire of items on display in department stores and advertised in the national media, the "self" was formed and continual profits were made from the notion. The ideal of growth and plenty for all was expressed in the range of available products. With movies, government-sponsored art, billboards, and TV commercials, ideologies had virtually universal reach.

LIVING SPACES

Changes in the world of the living are often, ironically, to be seen in the changing treatment of the dead. And by considering cemeteries we move now to a material manifestation of ideology. Archaeologists all over the world recognize how the status accorded to people after their deaths can sometimes enshrine, sometimes conceal the relations of power in life. For an archaeologist, changes in living patterns, working patterns, and family patterns find their expression in modern cemeteries. And although our society has largely succeeded in separating the inevitable fact of death from everyday life—through the segregation of the dying in hospitals and hospices and through the Halloweenlike demonization of funeral homes and graveyards—our cemeteries and the cemeteries of all the people who have lived and died before us in our hometowns and neighborhoods can offer us a telling glimpse at the kinds of social changes that have taken place in American society over the last three centuries.

On pages 244–245, Randall H. McGuire explores these themes as he describes the changing monuments in a particular place in America—Broome County in upstate New York. As he notes, the variations in the form of this region's cemeteries reflect changes that can be observed almost anywhere in the eastern United States. Colonial cemeteries, with their strict equality, were often attached to a church and symbolized the unity of a community, the stones more or less the same shape in rows with limited data and religious inscriptions and limited range of motifs. The only size difference was between adult and child.

This forest of tiny angels, many with photographs of deceased children on their bases, is a characteristic twentieth-century Italian-American form of memorial in Calvary Cemetery in Binghamton, New York.

From the 1820s, however, the separation between the dead and the living community began. In reaction to condemnations of church graveyards in urban areas as unhealthful and morbid, cemeteries were moved to the surrounding countryside and laid out as carefully planned parks. Now burial plots no longer signified membership in a certain congregation; gravesites were purchased from cemetery associations like other plots of land and other forms of private property. And Dr. McGuire observes that once purchased—rather than allotted—the privately owned burial plot became a legitimate field of expression for wealth. Toward the end of the nineteenth century, the size and variety of grave markers increased dramatically, with each community's most prominent families vying for attention through the construction of impressive family mausoleums, obelisks, and statues. In this way, the status of the wealthiest citizens (and by comparison, of the most humble citizens) was preserved after death.

To our modern sensibilities, these elaborate monuments of the Victorian period seem self-serving. For most people today, erecting conspicuous burial monuments as symbols of status is not a seemly way to honor the memory of loved ones. Yet that change of attitude has a great deal to do with ideological—and thus with economic—changes that have taken place in American society. It certainly is not the case that wealth has been more equally distributed—quite the reverse—while most grave markers since the 1920s and 1930s have become much more uniform. Rather, the equality of the modern cemetery masks the frequent existence of inequality in everyday life. Not uncoincidentally, the transformation of American cemeteries occurred almost simultaneously with the creation of a new kind of American suburb, located—like the cemeteries themselves—on the former rural or undeveloped peripheries of cities and towns. And the ideology of equality was reflected in their relatively low-density, uniform architectural styles, and their appearance of racial and economic homogeneity.

What was the reason for this far-reaching change in the domains of both the living and the dead? After World War II, the American economy was reshaped, and with it the patterns of consumption and work. The United States government actively supported the building and manufacturing industries by enabling former servicemen to purchase new houses with generous veterans' administration loans. Tax exemptions on mortgage interest also indirectly supported private home ownership in preference to renting, a city form. The post–World War II suburban phenomenon enabled thousands of moderate-income families to own their own houses, and thus to have the kind of stake in the nation's future that property has always been assumed to secure. Just as land ownership afforded the franchise to Federal-period Americans, twentieth-century suburbs made land ownership available to a hugely expanded population. But it also created mass-produced, mass-designed, and homogeneous houses and domestic environments. These were like the homogeneity engendered by the Greek Revival and Gothic Revival houses or mass-produced dinnerware of earlier eras. The post–World War II period, however, created a new kind of separation. The construction of highways and the tremendously expanded production of private cars increased the separation of the factory or office, to which Father commuted, and the homeplace, to which Mother was relegated. Thus, the suburbs shaped a new kind of society.

The number of suburban houses erected after World War II was unequaled, and on pages 246–247, Elizabeth C. Cromley explores the architectural and cultural impact of this development. Large-scale builders such as the Levitt Company in the New York metropolitan area began mass-producing houses, erecting thousands in the years immediately after the war. In 1947, the Levitt Company's four-and-a-half-room basic bungalow sold for $7,000 to $7,500, including appliances and landscaping. Suburban house constellations ranged in size from just one street of homes to thousands in a single development. Yet no matter what their size, the street plan of most of these suburbs—planted in the midst of former cornfields or meadows—was characterized by its extensive use of carefully placed shrubbery, ornamental trees, sharply delineated flower beds, and curving thoroughfares. As Dr. Cromley notes, the ideological echo of the formal gardens of the eighteenth century was unmistakable: Nature could be used to enhance social life.

Depending on income level and particular local mores, individual yards were either fenced and strongly secured or blended together, unbounded by hedges or fences, suggesting an unimpeded flow of children around the neighborhood. The suburb became a park of domestic life in which women's work—consumption and reproduction—was strictly segregated from the men's workaday world.

Despite today's conservative calls for a return to "traditional American family values," we must recognize that those family values were never static and have been constantly reshaped to serve the larger industrial society. Middle-class women in the early 1950s, moving into a suburb for the first time, would not have regarded their lives as in any sense "traditional." Separated from their husbands for the duration of the workday, they were consigned with their children to a world of tightly circumscribed roles and activities: shopping, bridge parties, charity

Dr. Benjamin Spock's Baby and Child Care *was first published in 1946, just in time for the baby boom in the suburbs. Its prescriptions for child-rearing contributed to the crystallizing ideology of post-war suburbia.*

work, and afterschool activities. Dr. Cromley suggests that although suburban homes were meant to be a heaven for mothers (where they could raise children in health and safety, far from the conflicts of urban life), a move to a new suburb separated young families from parents and relatives, cutting off networks of child care and emotional support.

A new ideology of family life was thus needed and it was supplied in millions of paperback copies by the pediatrician Benjamin Spock, in *The Common Sense Book of Baby and Child Care,* published in 1946. Spock urged mothers to have a more instinctive relationship to their children, to become more sensitive to their individual natures and talents, and to be in their children's constant company. For most middle-class mothers of the 1950s, notes Dr. Cromley, there was hardly any alternative than to be at the baby's beck and call, since they were alone to do the job. And more restrictive even than the friendly advice of Dr. Spock or the relentlessly cheerful examples of television mothers and housewives was the physical structure of the 1950s suburban house.

As Dr. Cromley and James Smokowski point out on pages 248–249, the floorplans of the ranch, Cape Cod, and split level houses all subtly contributed to the shaping of the American family form. Their basic configuration of three bedrooms fit—and molded—families with a mother and father who shared the master bedroom and, ideally, a son and a daughter who each had a room. In addition to the sexually segregated bedrooms and one fully equipped bathroom, a basic suburban house would have a living room and a kitchen; and it was there in the kitchen that the mother's proper role was architecturally expressed. They contend that in open-plan, contemporary-style houses, the kitchen could serve as both a work station and an observation post, enabling Mother to see the activities of all the household's inhabitants. What's more, the kitchen was usually positioned in the rear of the house, allowing the homemaker working at the sink to also oversee children's play on the patio, in the sandbox, or on the swing set in the backyard.

This was a world that depended principally on the successful maintenance of American prosperity. The whole suburban population was absorbed in buying, producing, and recognizing the same goods in similar

Beyond the massive portals of a mammoth shopping mall lies an idealized community of consumable experiences, products, and foods. Protected from weather and outdated regional traditions, the mall facilitates the homogenization of American culture and society.

settings, while working in similar surroundings. Moreover, all, or many, believed that they were fulfilling their individualism this way. And, like the 1950s cemeteries whose form and substance they reflected, the post–World War II suburbs both symbolized and created a powerful reality: the baby-boom generation, which also produced the "me" generation. This period of wealth and security derived from an economy that was protected more than ever before from dramatic economic fluctuation. But the era also demanded the full dedication of one's work and thoughts. The intense control exercised by the material facts of suburbs, cars, parking places, malls, stores, clothes, ads, foods, and cemeteries is extremely hard to appreciate. Yet that powerful, socially regulating American culture, which is now so widespread in the world—and is occasionally so violently rejected by political or religious movements in various parts of the world—is the main fact of late-twentieth-century life.

AGAINST THE FLOW

Reacting to this homogenizing environment were and are protesting groups. Recognizing, if not accepting, their status on the fringes and lower reaches of corporate culture, some people and groups rebelled and resisted. Some were violent, some political, some strictly cultural. They exemplify a segment of society that emerged after the crises of the 1970s in which diversity and cultural pluralism, not conformity and assimilation, would be the goals. Those separate protests include struggles waged by the civil rights movement, young people, feminists, and Native Americans—only a few of the many groups resisting their assigned places in society.

On pages 250–251, Robert L. Hall traces the history and development of the civil rights movement, which can be seen as a renewal of the efforts to counterattack an entire economic and political system. The obvious paradox was that the American economy could never do without the labor of African Americans in the 1950s and 1960s, any more than it could in the earliest colonial period or in antebellum times. And yet racism denied this central fact. Resistance centered at first not only on nonviolence but on depriving southern white-run transit systems of revenues from their black ridership, as in the Montgomery and Tallahassee bus boycotts of 1955 and 1956. Gradually, the promise of fully integrated life—implied if not ensured by the desegregation directives enforced by the armed forces after the Supreme Court's historic decision in the case of *Brown* v. *Board of Education* in 1954—became the focus of further political campaigns such as the "Freedom Rides," the 1963 March on Washington, and the Mississippi Freedom Summer of 1964. From this time onward, the civil rights movement entered a phase of sustained militant action, stemming from the failure of local authorities to enforce anti-discrimination statutes—and continued violence and brutality aimed at blacks (or anyone else) who dared to challenge the racial and thus the economic status quo.

The long-standing struggle for civil rights was more than a simple challenge to legalized segregation and white supremacy. For the three centuries of the African American experience, resistance had been conducted most often by cultural and religious institutions, by leaders who often expressed their outrage in veiled and metaphorical ways. But now new organizations such as the Southern Christian Leadership Conference, the Student Nonviolent Coordinating Committee, Black Muslims, and eventually Black Panthers formulated explicitly political programs to achieve explicitly political aims. At least officially, the civil rights movement of the 1950s and 1960s achieved a number of notable legislative victories—particularly the passage of the Civil Rights Act of 1964, the Voting Rights Act of 1965, and the federal commitment to equal opportunity employment and affirmative action in both employment and education. Yet Dr. Hall observes that despite these achievements, the problems of everyday African American life persisted and even deepened, as activists in the civil rights movement struggled with one another and with the federal government to decide how to address the underlying problems of both urban and rural industrialized society—crime, malnutrition, and persistent poverty.

For many middle-class children growing up in the suburbs, the struggle of the civil rights movement as seen on television and discussed at school underlined the fact that a reality of inequality underlay the verities of American life. And even as social protest movements were gaining momentum, a more subtle and pervasive cultural rebellion among the young

people of America was under way. As Mary Praetzellis and Maria Praetzellis trace on pages 252–253, the motorcycles, leather jackets, and bongos of 1950s teenage culture, today often used merely as prompts for *Happy Days* nostalgia, then represented threatening challenges to the sexual and behavioral disciplines of the times. For many parents and social critics, the years from 1949 to 1959 were the Golden Age of Juvenile Delinquency. James Dean and Elvis Presley came to be the patron saints of a new sensibility that cherished an angry, if innocent, conception of personal freedom and sought to overcome the stifling uniformity of consumerist expectation and role definition imposed in the post–World War II years. For the most part, this youth movement was cultural rather than political. Even more seemingly threatening forms of youth protest came in the 1960s with Dr. Timothy Leary's challenge to "Turn On, Tune In, Drop Out." Through the combined media of drugs, music, art, street theater, and political protest, the youth movement desperately—and not often successfully—sought a degree of spirituality, independence, and open sexuality that was antithetical to the requirements and standards of modern industrial life.

Behind all this, however, was the deeper cultural phenomenon of teenagers themselves. For teenagehood was a novelty that American society created; and the category (no less than the rebellion against it) should be our main focus. Otherwise, we have misidentified cause and effect. Society determined that it was necessary to keep a certain group out of the workforce, sexually neuter, and politically neutral while preparing its members to be conventional consumers, workers, family makers, and mainstream participants. "Teenage rebellion" can therefore be seen as not a fact of nature but as a response to very specific historical circumstances in which sexually, physically, and mentally maturing young adults rejected the roles they were given— and acted out their resistance in a subtle cultural revolt that continues, in changing form, today.

In time, the trappings and cultural tastes of the American youth movement spread around the world, as a symptom of the vastly reduced power of young adults that industrial capitalism enforced everywhere. Yet the rebellion against the routines of conformity was not conceived so as to be able to exist independently. It was made possible by the relative prosperity of its leaders, middle-class white suburban youth. And when, from the 1970s, the economic expansion of the postwar years began to crumble, the culture of the "Flower Children" gradually faded and changed. The rebellious consciousness lost focus and became confused with its physical trappings, and with the musical forms and costumes it inspired. Hippiedom gave way to disco to punk and eventually to the African American youth culture of rap. By the 1990s, teenage identity—like all the others—could be, had to be, purchased at the local mall. The same corporations once attacked as symbols of the establishment now skillfully mounted advertising campaigns to sell products like designer jeans, sport shoes, and stereo systems—marketing identity and authenticity (even at times in a cynical, self-mocking tone) to the young and not-so-young.

The glaring inequalities of the post–World War II years, about which everyone knew but was reluctant to speak, were hidden by numbing conformity. Family patterns, residential patterns, and employment patterns were structured to preserve and enshrine certain kinds of relations between men and women, adults and children, employers and workers, blacks and whites, immigrants and the native born. Anyone who challenged the *Saturday Evening Post* consensus risked social ostracism, accusations of political subversion, and, worst of all, the destruction of any chance of participating in the quest for the American Dream. Only in the fantasy realms of cowboys, spacemen, monsters, sex kittens, and teenage rebels—slickly packaged and sold in the movies, on TV, in records, and in the form of ephemeral memorabilia—could Americans find the freedom to imagine other societies and other ways of life. The mythic West, as Randall H. McGuire explains on pages 254–255, was one such make-believe world—one that contrasted sharply with the realities of the peoples and cultures of the western United States in the late twentieth century.

On pages 256–257, Larry J. Zimmerman and Karen Zimmerman explore the cultural and political activism of Native Americans in the twentieth century. Unlike the status of African Americans, immigrant workers (legal and illegal), and suburban women, who were meant to remain in closely circumscribed, inferior economic positions, the peoples of Native America were supposed to disappear. Those indigenous groups who first met Europeans in what would later become the eastern United States—and who were not devastated by disease or killed in military operations—were eventually relocated to the West, for the most part.

The renaissance of late-twentieth-century Native American culture, and its integration with aspects of Euro-American culture, can be seen in the hundreds of intertribal wacipis *or powwows held across the continent.*

Other groups on the Plains, in the Rockies, and in the Far West also struggled through disease, wars, and destruction of their livelihood only to be confined on reservations, which were generally established on land non-Indians simply didn't want. There they were subjected to a concerted reeducation program carried out by churches, philanthropic groups, and agents of the Department of the Interior's Bureau of Indian Affairs.

In the 1960s, in the context of other challenges to authority—protests by African Americans, teenagers, and women among others—the imperative of "civilizing the Indian" took on a hollow, almost ridiculous ring, and began to backfire on the ideology of conformity behind it. From the stereotyped Indians of 1930s films and 1950s TV series, the image of the Native American underwent a far-reaching (if not total) transformation in American society. As avatars of the environmental movement and victims of campaigns of conquest, Native Americans came to symbolize, at least in the minds of others, the various ideals of the 1960s countercultures. Naturally, the problems of Native Americans themselves were far more concrete.

For some Native Americans, valuable resources such as oil and natural gas, unknown or undiscovered at the time of the establishment of nineteenth-century reservations, became in some cases the economic underpinning for a powerful resurgence. In addition, the younger generation prepared to confront powerful government agencies on their own terms. Groups such as the American Indian Movement and the Native American Rights Fund, using tactics ranging from militant to legalistic, helped to forge a powerful Native American political identity.

In recent years, Native Americans have had to meet the challenge of using the political power they have gained. Some of these protesting voices coalesced and intertwined from the 1960s on and have become respectable causes and subjects for comment, neatly summarized and inserted in the flow of schoolbook history of recent decades. Yet, it is important to remember that while the most famous heroes of those movements became celebrities, the struggles they represented were often diverted rather than won. The injustices and inequalities that they protested could be ended only with a long and painful reorientation of American society, one which none of these groups' leaders would say has occurred.

MATERIAL CULTURE, IDEOLOGY, AND SOCIETY

This chapter concludes with an exploration of two of the most conspicuous material symbols in our society: the fast-food franchises that have become fixtures of everyday life in every part of America and the soaring skyscrapers that have become the characteristic cultural markers of every community that considers itself to be an important modern city rather than an out-of-the-way small town. Yet behind the surface appearances of the neon, stain-

Rising above the noise and grime of modern city streets—here, in Philadelphia—are monuments to corporate power: the modern and postmodern skyscrapers of late-twentieth-century America.

An ubiquitous symbol of uniform consumption, this modern McDonald's in Des Plaines, Illinois, is the end result of decades of architectural and technological development. It is located across the street from the first midwestern outlet, which became a museum in 1984.

less steel, and plastic of the drive-ins, and of the girders and plate glass of the skyscrapers, lie some of the pervasive social and economic processes through which modern homogeneity has been created and sustained. The streamlined drive-in restaurants of the 1930s must be seen not only as a campy image but also as a more profitable and efficient way to distribute food products, ultimately—as Alan Hess discusses on pages 258–259—making the cuisine of the entire country more or less homogeneous, perhaps less healthy, but certainly more profitable for those who would dish it out.

Finally, on pages 260–261, Max Page and Steven Conn examine the symbolic statements made by the skyscraper towers of one major American city, with their appearance of elegance and power. They are seen by many as the purest expression of modernity, yet this too can be perceived as a manifestation of ideology that misrepresents the cruel paradox of the typical American cityscape. For the spires and towers of glass and steel that etch the silhouette of nearly every urban horizon almost inevitably rise from an inner city of crumbling highways and bridges, homelessness, and crime. The cultural and economic homogeneity promoted in late-twentieth-century America, and whose way

was prepared by the earlier eras of our history, usually fails to address or even acknowledge the social tensions and profound economic assumptions on which it is based.

Thus, we see in this most recent century of American history illustrations of a larger dynamic that has been present since the European "discovery" of America. The official emphasis is on development, expansion, control, and profit. Yet we do not necessarily see "progress"—the steady movement toward a freer, happier, healthier, or more prosperous society. Inequality, injustice, and poverty remain with us, and powerful economic and political institutions have developed ever more sophisticated methods of combating or defusing resistance, partly by the discipline of the consensus and partly through the consumer goods that can seduce us into failing to recognize that there is anything else. Our freedom to choose lifestyles, identities, or even living conditions is often restricted to only a few options, determined by the marketplace. In the pages that follow, we will highlight some of the places and artifacts that embody the more recent manifestations of this historical process. And it is here that modern ideologies and economics merge with our history.

AUTOS AND HIGHWAYS: *Conquering Space in Iowa*

Before the automobile could revolutionize American life in the twentieth century, serious geographical and physical obstacles had to be overcome. Because railroads had long been the chief means of interregional transport, local road conditions were notoriously poor in the early decades of this century, making travel by automobile slow and difficult. The Lincoln Highway was one of the earliest transcontinental highways designed specifically for automobile traffic, conceived in 1912 as a gravel road linking New York and San Francisco. Its initiator, businessman Carl Graham Foster, invited the public to join the Lincoln Highway Association for the upkeep of the road and solicited donations from manufacturers of automobiles and automobile accessories.

When the Lincoln Highway was officially established in Iowa in 1913, it was little more than a dirt path that followed the general route of the Chicago and Northwestern Railroad, passing along the edges of fields and pastures. Despite the slow pace of surfacing, the Lincoln Highway—with its promise of linking small communities to the greater centers of the nation—became a focus of civic pride and entrepreneurship. Local business-

men enthusiastically joined the public associations for the promotion, support, and marking of the road. Initially, the registered symbol for the highway, a capital letter "L" on a red, white, and blue field, was painted on trees, posts, and barns, and cast into the concrete railings of bridges or farm markers.

The patriotic appeal of the project—the binding together of the nation through automobile travel under the name of the preserver of the Union—evoked great public support. Farmers along the route set up concrete markers containing their own names and the name of the road and sometimes the "L" symbol or a bust of Lincoln. Similarly, businesses were named in honor of the road, as Lincoln Cafes, Lincoln Hotels, and Lincoln Highway Garages sprang up across the countryside, with exuberant signage beckoning passing motorists to stop.

Although the distinctiveness of the road lingered on for several years—due mainly to the efforts of local groups—the existence of the Lincoln Highway as a distinct entity was short. With the establishment by Congress of the numbered highway system in 1925, the Lincoln Highway was offi-

The red-white-and-blue official Lincoln Highway symbol was highly visible against the predominantly green landscape of the American heartland. It also expressed the patriotic spirit that was at the heart of the Lincoln Highway's appeal.

RIGHT: *Traveling Iowa's Lincoln Highway in the 1920s was a challenge to motorists. The rich black dirt, when soaked with rain or melted snow, became a highly unpleasant road surface: a thick mud, known locally as "gumbo," up to two feet deep.*

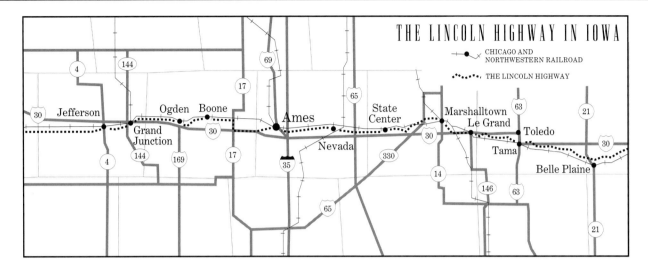

THE LINCOLN HIGHWAY IN IOWA

● CHICAGO AND NORTHWESTERN RAILROAD

●••• THE LINCOLN HIGHWAY

Jefferson · Grand Junction · Ogden · Boone · Ames · Nevada · State Center · Marshalltown · Le Grand · Toledo · Tama · Belle Plaine

LEFT: *The lighted Lincoln Highway bridge near Tama has been recently restored and is a state historic landmark. Although this bridge is unique to the Midwest, a second one similar in design was constructed along the Lincoln Highway route in Nevada.*

BELOW: *The most enthusiastic monuments to the Lincoln Highway are the work of individuals. This garage, owned by George Preston of Belle Plaine, is a local monument to the Lincoln Highway. Over the years, Preston has collected automobile and highway-related signs and other memorabilia, and, in the spirit of the Lincoln Highway, has transformed his repair garage and motel into a local tourist attraction.*

cially broken up into several numbered roads. The stretch passing through Iowa became part of U.S. 30, running from Philadelphia to Salt Lake City. By 1931, federal funds had transformed all but a few miles of what was once the Lincoln Highway into an improved, all-weather highway. The local character of the road gradually disappeared as the route became a straighter road with few steep hills. The automobile and the highway finally triumphed. But they did so by overpowering—rather than being a part of—the surrounding landscape.

■ MARY ANN BEECHER
Iowa State University

TOURIST ATTRACTIONS
Roadside Colossi in the Upper Midwest

In a nation endowed with natural marvels like Niagara Falls, Monument Valley, and the Grand Canyon, visitors have difficulty dealing with the consistent, uniform, quiet natural beauty of Wisconsin, Iowa, and Minnesota. Historian Karal Ann Marling, herself transplanted from the East, observed that midwesterners—particularly those in small towns—have attempted to relieve the monotony of so much opulent greenery with vertical "attractions." Her book *The Colossus of Roads* (1984) documents the monuments that dotted the space around her new home in Minneapolis.

The nineteenth-century settlers in this region at first depended on the less-than-spectacular natural offerings for weekend outings. The "Monument" halfway between the St. Croix River and River Falls, Wisconsin, was reputed to have been a sacred spot known as the Great Manito for both Dakota and Chippewa. This natural sandstone obelisk rising on a virtually treeless plain quickly became a popular tourist spot and, perhaps, the grandfather of modern roadside colossi. Today, the Monument has eroded to much less than its original imposing size. Nearby trees, highways, and buildings have caused it to dwindle further in the eyes of the beholder.

But the spirit of the "Great Manito" remains in various erections throughout the area whose purpose is to attract the curious and their commerce. What today's adventurer finds on both sides of the Mississippi in the northern part of the American heartland, in addition to abundant fishing, hunting, canoeing, hiking, and generally peaceful surroundings, are "attractions" of which the various Paul Bunyan effigies—some complete with full-scale models of Babe the Big Blue Ox and other animal sidekicks—are probably the epitome. Small-town Minnesotans, Iowans, and Wisconsinites have also erected statues of the world's largest Muskie, the world's largest Walleye, and Ole the Viking; and they have built smaller colossi to call attention to more modest commercial enterprises.

They've built pink elephants and orange stags to call attention to supper clubs and motels. They've built the world's largest cheese to promote Wisconsin cheese, and a Pillsbury Doughboy balloon to call attention to the Minnesota grain industry; a giant pelican for Pelican Rapids; a grandiose prairie chicken for Rothsay; and a colossal floating loon for a saloon in Virginia, all in Minnesota.

One of the newest midwestern colossi, and perhaps most indicative of the spirit behind such efforts, is the Coot at Ashby, Minnesota. The annual Ashby Coot Feed is a fundraising activity, not for commerce but for conservation, and the coot itself was not contracted to professionals but built by Ashby craftspeople volunteering their off-hours and their skills. Unusual though it is, it joins a worthy vertical tradition in a horizontal region.

Bemidji, Minnesota, is only one of several upper midwestern communities claiming an affinity with Paul Bunyan and displaying effigies of the lumberman and his blue ox. This c. 1930 photograph shows Babe being moved into position. (For another variation on the same theme, see the illustration on page 219.)

■ SUE BRIDWELL BECKHAM
University of Wisconsin—Stout

LEFT: *Few upper midwestern sites boast natural colossi. The sandstone "Monument" outside River Falls, Wisconsin, was one of the earliest vacation attractions in the area. Here, in an early-twentieth-century photograph, a group of tourists from Illinois poses by the Monument, providing scale and charm.*

ABOVE: *The giant "Coot" (a.k.a. mud hen) is one of the newest roadside colossi in the Upper Midwest. Built by volunteer craftspeople on time and under estimate, it took its place on the shore of Little Lake in Ashby, Minnesota (pop. 469), in the fall of 1991. An unabashedly created tourist attraction, the Coot was erected to raise funds for the preservation of local wildlife.*

The Fishing Hall of Fame in Hayward, Wisconsin, boasts the world's largest muskie—note the tourists standing in its mouth.

THE GREAT MIGRATIONS
African American Movement from Farms to Cities

All human inhabitants of the Western Hemisphere today are either migrants themselves or descendants of people who migrated to what we call the Americas from somewhere else in the world. Some came voluntarily, and others were brought here by force. Prominent among the enforced immigrants to the New World, of course, were captives from various parts of the African continent. Once the descendants of the African captives in the United States were liberated in the course of a bloody Civil War in which over 180,000 of them were soldiers, they were relatively freer to move about within the country of their birth in search of lands, jobs, and a better life. Much of that early post-emancipation movement, though, took place within the former Confederate States, and even as recently as the 1910 federal census, the overwhelming majority of Black Americans (nearly 90 percent) lived in the rural areas of the South.

But with the growth of the corporate empire in the early twentieth century, coupled with a drastic drop in European immigration to the United States during the First World War and the passage of legislation restricting immigration soon afterward, increasing numbers of black folk began packing their bags and moving to industrialized areas. Pushed by poverty, lynchings, legalized segregation, natural disasters, and farm mechanization, they moved. Pulled by industrial job opportunities, the right to vote, the urgings of such black-run publications as the NAACP's *Crisis* magazine and Chicago's *Defender* newspaper, and the bright lights of the cities, they moved. They moved massively from rural hamlets to cities (including, though it is sometimes overlooked, southern cities); from scattered settlements to high-density, and too often pathologically crowded, urban dwellings.

With the exception of a decline in black internal migration during the decade of the Great Depression, African Americans flocked to the cities in increasing numbers with each passing decade between 1910 and 1950. The new and growing con-

Most African American migrants to the industrial cities could take with them only what they could pack in suitcases tied to the top of cars or dragged along through train stations. In the tenements of northern cities, their lives would begin again.

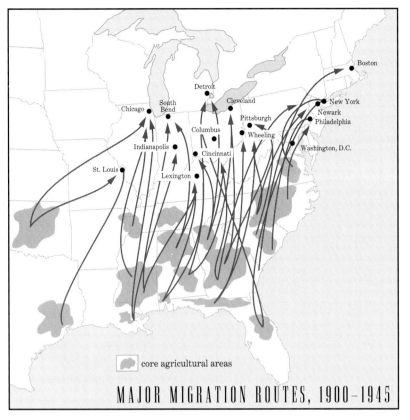

MAJOR MIGRATION ROUTES, 1900–1945

core agricultural areas

BELOW: *For many migrants, assembly-line labor took the place of agricultural work in the fields and packing houses of the South. Here a worker spray paints car bodies at the Ford Motor Company in Dearborn, Michigan.*

centrations of black urbanites in key cities of the North, West, and later the South gave black voters increasing political strength, especially in the most closely contested local and national elections. This highly visible and massive migration has had broad consequences for all Americans, transforming the black population from one of the nation's most rural to one of its most urbanized and bringing members of other groups into unprecedented levels of contact, competition, and cooperation with African Americans.

The social, economic, and policy consequences of such urbanization are profound and not fully sorted out, especially today, at a time when many of the corporations whose jobs initially attracted rural populations to America's cities coldly disavow any social responsibility to their workers and begin to migrate themselves.

■ ROBERT L. HALL
Northeastern University

BELOW: *The poverty, racism, and underdevelopment bound up with the system of tenant farming and intensive agriculture were important incentives to migration. This "typical cotton-picker's shack" was photographed by Dorothea Lange for the Farm Services Administration in July 1936.*

AT THE MOVIES: *Small-Town Movie Theaters*

For nearly half a century, from around 1905 to the mid-1950s, "going to the show" was a vital part of American social and cultural life. Virtually every community had its movie theater, ranging from small, unobtrusive buildings to ornate movie palaces boasting crystal chandeliers, marble-faced refreshment stands, and crimson plush seats. Movie palaces were rivaled only by churches for size and opulence—and in the American Protestant heartland, even the churches were often dwarfed by comparison. The local theater was a town focal point—perhaps even a shrine to the American Dream.

For several decades in the twentieth century—until television was widely accepted as home entertainment—small-town folk went to the movies every few nights. If they wanted to take the chil-

The Rohs Theatre in Cynthiana, Kentucky, retains some of its external grandeur. Once home to minstrel shows and small-town vaudeville as well as movies, it was relegated to use for Saturday matinees and community theater performances by the 1940s. The building, like many of its sisters around the country, has survived in a new guise. Haircut anybody?

dren, they went to the early show at 7:00 P.M. If they were courting and the young woman was lucky enough to have a late curfew, they went to the late show and strolled home after 11:00 P.M. The participants in this ritual paid their forty-five cents to see John Wayne win the West and Frank Capra heroes assure them that Americans were true and honest commoners. They greeted their neighbors as they went in, congregated at the refreshment stand for ten-cent unbuttered popcorn, and after the flick left the theaters chattering about what they had seen and where they would go next—often to the local drugstore for a soda.

The advent of widespread television in the early 1950s would change the face of the movie theater and the culture that went with it forever. New mall movie theaters that have appeared in recent decades are usually at the edge of town—never in the center—blending in with their mall settings, open from noon on with such varying schedules that movement in and out of theaters is indistinguishable from movement in and out of neighboring stores.

In many small towns across the country, early-twentieth-century Main Street movie theaters still stand, but few remain centers of the town's social or cultural life. Some of the structures have been converted to other uses: community theaters, storefront video arcades, or hair-styling salons. Or, like so many other main street businesses, they have closed their doors, boarded their windows, and replaced glittering marquee announcements with FOR SALE signs. The few Main Street theaters still operating struggle to attract enough movie lovers to pay the rent, and they count on three-dollar popcorn to make the profit. Ironically, these carefully preserved movie houses have themselves become part of the show—selling nostalgia for what now seems to have been a simpler time.

■ RICHARD H. BECKHAM
    University of Wisconsin—River Falls

■ SUE BRIDWELL BECKHAM
    University of Wisconsin—Stout

ABOVE, LEFT AND RIGHT: *Claimed to be the first "movie palace," the A. L. Ringling Theater in Baraboo, Wisconsin, was built in 1916 to serve as both a live theater and a movie house, functions it still serves today. The grand velvet-and-gold auditorium looks much as it did when the theater was new.*

ABOVE: *In Macomb, Illinois, the Art Deco Lark Theater—badly in need of refurbishing—continues to function as a picture show, but has dropped its prices to one dollar to compete with the video business.*

RIGHT: *Once the proud first-run house of Amory, Mississippi, the Varsity has joined many other Main Street buildings across America—standing empty while business has fled to the edges of town, where the parking is easier. Yet the Varsity is still distinguished by its broad brick front and the ornamental urns on the roof.*

PUBLIC ART
The Ideology of Post Office Murals in the South

POSTMASTER

Harold Egan's experiment in modern art for the people of Okolona, Mississippi, shown here in an early photo, is today buried under layers of paint. The mural purported to represent "The Abundance of the Soil"; the woman, Ole Miss—the Mississippi herself.

Between 1936 and 1942, during the Great Depression, the Federal government endowed about 1,150 new Federal buildings with works of art—most of them murals in small-town post offices and courthouses. The agency responsible for this massive gift of art was the Treasury Section of Fine Arts. While most Americans received the government's artistic largess with emotions ranging from mild gratitude to apathy, in the South, where regional feelings lingered in the aftermath of the Civil War and Reconstruction, anything the federal government did was suspect. As a result, citizens and communities were eager to make their views known about public art commissioned for them.

Thus when artists painted murals for southern post offices depicting southerners as happy, prosperous, and able to deal with their own problems, the local inhabitants were generally grateful and expressed satisfaction with government largesse. Doris Lee's painting for Summerville, Georgia, for example, depicted southern farmers, not poor or lazy or using outdated agricultural practices, but rather competent, egalitarian, well-dressed, and content.

In contrast, when Harold Egan painted a mural in the belief that the "Good People of Mississippi" would appreciate "modern" art once they were exposed to it, the experiment failed and the mural was quickly concealed under a layer of fresh paint. And when northerner Lee Gatch painted a mural for the post office in Mullins, South Carolina, that featured his own quite inaccurate depiction of the local tobacco industry, Mullins inhabitants, maintaining their politeness despite their displeasure at the artist's ignorance, left the mural on the wall for a number of years until it quietly disappeared.

Most of the southern post office murals remain on display—some moved to local museums, some in their original locations in buildings that have since been converted to libraries or offices. Reinterpreted by new generations, they remain part of a symbolic dialogue between private citizens and the federal government.

■ SUE BRIDWELL BECKHAM
University of Wisconsin—Stout

TOP: *A timid federal agency forced Doris Lee to make some slight changes in her lyrical and perfectly acceptable design for the Summerville, Georgia, Post Office, in fear that local residents would be offended by the lighthearted depiction of the Georgia countryside. The Washington bureaucrats vastly overestimated southern sensitivity. While southerners hated to be presented as poor, ignorant, or helpless, they did not fear genial caricature of prosperous farmers. The Lee mural was accepted in Summerville without objection.*

CENTER: *After being courteously detested for many years, the Mullins, South Carolina, mural of tobacco growing by Lee Gatch disappeared without a trace. The people of Mullins thought tobacco grown in a tent (Gatch's interpretation of tobacco canvas) represented no form of tobacco growing they had ever seen.*

LEFT: *A retired postal worker who officiated at the installation of Irving A. Block's mural "Peach Orchard" in the Batesburg, South Carolina, Post Office poses beneath the mural in 1987. While this work met the criteria for a popular southern mural, it was and is difficult to view—and to photograph—because of the vestibule that jutted out into the lobby and the awkward elevation.*

BILLBOARDS: *Woman, Mother, Machine*

Billboards mirrored the jolting transformation of the image of the American woman from Rosie the Riveter, darling of the World War II propaganda poster, to the "woman as mother and appliance" imagery that dominated the 1950s. Industry seemed as fecund as the mothers of the Baby Boom, as it churned out appliances and furnishings for suburban homes that embodied the postwar American Dream. In midwestern strongholds of heartland values, prosperity had to be imagined in terms that fit the cornucopia of goods into established traditions. Religion, cleanliness, family, and security were just such powerful concepts to help translate consumption messages into moral order.

From the Bible Belt to the Corn Belt, cleanliness and godliness formed a holy duo. The holy hygiene practiced by the good wife and mother in 1950s billboards sometimes provided surreal and even comic images. The Lewyt vacuum cleaner ad chopped off the diligent housewife at the waist, seeming to merge her with the appliance she ran. Yet her circle skirt and high heels hint at the sexual identity that enabled an appliance ad to hail the feminine woman in the domestic slave. Such messages with several angles enabled the symbols used on billboards to link woman-mother to appliance in 1950s ideology.

More often, womanliness spelled fertility, as in the double messages of the *Chick Startina* feed ad. Postwar America often looked back with nostalgia for the "good old days," even as daily life pushed on to modernity. Raising chickens and making pin money from selling eggs could seem romantically appealing: As farming itself declined, reminders of rural life grew in potency. In the Midwest, where agribusiness was gobbling up family farms, such imagery packed a powerful allure. Perhaps the image of women raising chicks simply helped grain companies sell products, but at the same time it evoked the security the human brood ought to feel in Mom's hands.

The needs of that brood in the suburbs that ringed the nation's cities created a new role for Mom: chauffeur. At first sight, the his-and-hers Fords garaged in the four-bedroom, three-bath dream house suggest a portrait of the idyllic life. But that station wagon functioned as a movable prison for Mom, the driver, as she shuttled each child around the miles of new suburban geography from football practice to ballet lesson to dentist.

Without intentional irony, a billboard that advised that "the family that prays together stays together" probably did capture a suburban family in a rare moment of togetherness—driving a car. Marketing prayer in the secular rectangle of a billboard blurred the lines between the sanctified and worldly spaces, gently universalizing the culture of selling.

■ KATHLEEN HULSER
New York University

In the 1950s, speed, power, and hygiene were the marks of modern housekeeping as much as the methods of the space race. With her hypermodern appliances, the housewife could keep her new home in a state of laboratorylike sanitation.

more power · lighter weight

LEWYT VACUUM CLEANER

NEW LOW PRICE

The Cult of Mom peaked in the 1950s. Purina feed ads just mirrored the ideology that women's fulfillment was in bearing babies, caring for their broods, and holding the family safe in motherly hands.

Ford's slick convertible for Dad and practical station wagon for Mom captured the gender identities of the 1950s. With family activities spread over miles of suburban sprawl, Mom, the chauffeur, might spend as much time behind the wheel as she did polishing the family home.

Keeping the family intact and the soul clean amid the distractions of an ebullient consumer economy took some reminding, as religious billboards scattered through the West and South testified.

CEMETERIES: *Living with the Dead*

We live each day of our lives surrounded by the dead. They lie in cemeteries and speak to us through the memorials that they or their kin erected. They hoped that these monuments would enter into a conversation with the living to perpetuate the beliefs they took to their graves. But the dead can only initiate the conversation; they cannot sustain it. Each generation reinterprets messages from the dead in terms of its own beliefs and time.

The earliest cemeteries in Broome County, New York, express the ideals of community that the deceased held in life. Graves were laid out in neat rows with relatively uniform white marble tablets, symbolizing a community of equality and harmony that the living could probably never have really obtained.

During the Victorian period, in contrast, cemeteries highlighted social differences, marking who was successful and who had failed in life. Each family built a prominent monument in a fenced plot, memorializing its most important patriarch. The largest and grandest monuments usually crowned the hill at the center of the cemetery, while those on the slopes were smaller, simpler, and less varied.

In the 1920s, Victorian burial customs were attacked as morbid and divisive. The cemetery increasingly denied or downplayed both social differences and the reality of death. The gravestones, now primarily family markers rather than monuments to patriarchs, became less varied and more uniform in size. Although members of certain ethnic groups—some established, some newly prosperous—continued to memorialize their most prominent members with ostentatious monuments, the overall impression of the cemetery was, through the 1930s and 1940s, of the basic equality of family groups.

After World War II, the extended family plot gave way to adjoining grave sites for husbands and wives, marked by a single headstone. The trend toward uniformity continued, both in cemeteries with standing headstones and in memorial parks with graves all marked with uniform, inconspicuous bronze tablets, flush with the earth. In the 1970s, many cemeteries added public mausoleums where the dead were stacked in identical cells.

Despite the general trend toward the symbolic equality of people in death, some ethnic groups in Broome County did not accept the dominant cultural forms of memorialization. For some, ostentatious monuments continued to be important; for others the extended family continued to be the common grave-site form. Yet whatever the particular expression, the modern American cemetery continues to symbolize the way people wish the world would be.

■ RANDALL H. McGUIRE
State University of New York at Binghamton

The most opulent Victorian memorials are private mausoleums, usually built in the image of Greek temples, like this family tomb in Floral Park Cemetery.

ABOVE: *The deemphasis of death and of social difference that began in the 1920s led to smaller and more uniform memorials, such as these from the 1940s in Riverhurst Cemetery. These monuments speak only to the intimate audience of family that seeks them out.*

ABOVE: *Binghamton, New York's early-nineteenth-century monuments, like this one from 1832, are often uniform white tablets, sometimes decorated with religious symbols and epitaphs that promise salvation in the afterlife.*

RIGHT: *One can barely tell that the modern memorial park is a cemetery at all. With its flush bronze markers and starkly modern public mausoleums, the Vestal Hills Memorial Park looks more like a golf course.*

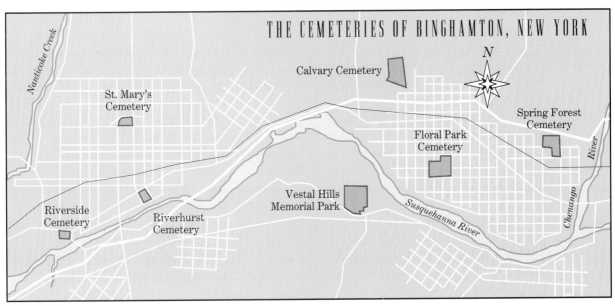

THE CEMETERIES OF BINGHAMTON, NEW YORK

Nanticoke Creek

Calvary Cemetery

N

St. Mary's Cemetery

Spring Forest Cemetery

Floral Park Cemetery

River

Riverside Cemetery

Riverhurst Cemetery

Vestal Hills Memorial Park

Susquehanna River

Chemango

SUBURBIA: *The Geography of Bel Aire Gardens*

A one-story ranch house built in the 1950s in Bel Aire Gardens. Single-story houses came into vogue among the middle class before 1890 and had great popularity in the form of the bungalow in the early twentieth century and the ranch house in the 1950s. Single-story homemaking was easier on the housekeeper, since it did away with stairs and required less furniture.

Most American cities after World War II gave birth to new suburbs to provide dwelling space to millions of new families. Lockport, New York's Bel Aire Gardens is an excellent example of characteristic 1950s development, since many features of the original landscape are intact today. The houses were built according to only a few plans; this kept costs down and achieved the homogeneity then seen as desirable. Modest variety was created by the houses' differing orientations, door placement, or siding materials.

Variety in the suburban streetscape is restricted to houses; no commercial, manufacturing, or institutional buildings are allowed to disturb the purity of the streets. The suburbs' strong appeal was based in part on their promises of a safe and healthy environment in which to bring up children. The only institutional buildings allowed in suburbs are schools and churches, and perhaps recreational buildings.

The street pattern of the post–World War II suburb features curving rather than straight streets. The taste for a curved street has its roots in English landscape gardening of the eighteenth century, which inspired gentlemen to improve the grounds of their country estates by creating little hills, dells, and meadows traversed by curving drives and foot paths. Embedding the family in a "natural" setting was believed to enhance its moral as well as physical health. The promise of health is also reflected in the extensive front, side, and back yards surrounding even moderately sized houses. Front yards continue a landscape tradition that dates from the mid-nineteenth century, when architectural handbooks promoted the marriage of nature and home to middle-class cottage and villa clients. On Eisenhower Drive, front yards continue to be the site of trimmed shrubs and well-kept ornamental plantings bordering a lawn. In the backyard landscape, where swing sets have been

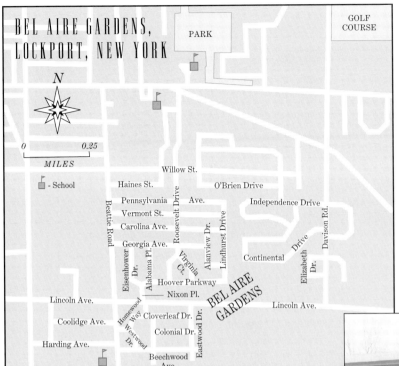

BEL AIRE GARDENS, LOCKPORT, NEW YORK

PARK

GOLF COURSE

N

0   0.25
MILES

▢ - School

Willow St.

Haines St.

Pennsylvania Ave.

O'Brien Drive

Independence Drive

Vermont St.

Carolina Ave.

Georgia Ave.

Roosevelt Drive

Beattie Road

Eisenhower Dr.

Alabama Pl.

Virginia Ct.

Alanview Dr.

Lindhurst Drive

Continental

Elizabeth Dr.

Drive

Davison Rd.

Hoover Parkway

Nixon Pl.

BEL AIRE GARDENS

Lincoln Ave.

Lincoln Ave.

Coolidge Ave.

Homewood Way

Westwood Dr.

Cloverleaf Dr.

Colonial Dr.

Eastwood Dr.

Harding Ave.

Beechwood Ave.

ABOVE: *Painted mailboxes, coach-and-horse silhouettes as door ornaments, and American flags were popular symbols for suburban residents. Seasonal decorations were one way for homeowners to express their individuality, and they sometimes served to distinguish the terrain of one ethnic or religious group from the next.*

RIGHT: *Although the suburban residential street was typically purged of all building types except for single-family houses, the elementary school was never far away. This school, built c. 1960 to serve the residents of Bel Aire Gardens, was a safe walking distance for even young children.*

installed, children at play are unimpeded by polite plantings.

Because suburban houses are often so much alike, house owners use their imaginations to ornament, paint, or decorate them with touches of individuality or symbols indicating character or belief. Some decorations remain all year and are part of the house: mailboxes, perhaps with painted ornament; lanterns reminiscent of bygone gas lamps; silhouettes of horse-drawn carriages used as door ornaments; shutters for a colonial effect beside the picture window. In Bel Aire Gardens, American flags are a favorite symbol. In other suburbs, religious statues predominate instead. At any rate, the slight touches of individuality are overwhelmed by the larger landscape of suburban conformity.

■ ELIZABETH C. CROMLEY
State University of New York at Buffalo

This split-level house has a two-car garage whose large doors function as the principal features of the facade design. Because suburbs are located on the periphery of city development, they are usually out of reach of convenient mass transportation. Developers assumed that every family would have to own a car to live comfortably in the suburbs, and most houses have built-in garages. Often the garage serves as a field for expansion when an extra room is needed.

HOME: *The Structure of Life on Eisenhower Drive*

Houses such as those on Eisenhower Drive in Bel Aire Gardens in Lockport, New York, represented the American "dream home" at minimum size and cost. Individualizing the house was a challenge. Interiors were specifically the responsibility of the woman of the house, who had to display her good taste but at the same time make the interior decor enhance family relationships and create settings in which children would thrive. The living room was the place where a family could make a statement about its tastes and social status. Here the homemaker displayed her talents in making slipcovers and pillows, or in selecting and displaying collections of glassware and figurines. Books placed in built-in bookshelves gave the room an atmosphere of cultivation.

Inside the house, the organization of space was carefully planned to segregate private areas from public and sociable spaces. Three bedrooms allowed Mother and Father to share a room and to give a room each to their son(s) and daughter(s). Each bedroom opened only onto a hallway—no communicating doors between the bedrooms disturbed the occupants' privacy. The bathroom too had only one door to the hallway. This crisp and uncompromising circulation pattern stood in contrast to early-twentieth-century arrangements in which bedrooms and bathrooms were often vulnerable to traffic through multiple doorways. The family members' private spaces were separated from the living-dining room and kitchen by a hallway, which buffered sound and suggested the clear separation of functions and turfs.

The kitchen was the most complex room in that it participated in three chains of circulation. One door led to the outside where the laundry could be hung to dry. This door allowed children to come in and out without tracking mud onto the living room carpet. Another kitchen door led to the hall and bedroom zone. A third led into the living-dining room to facilitate serving meals and entertaining guests. Such a small kitchen could barely accommodate three doors and still have the wall space needed for all its

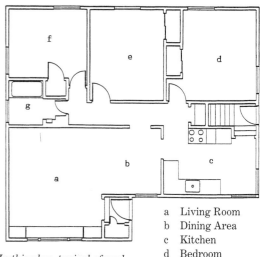

a   Living Room
b   Dining Area
c   Kitchen
d   Bedroom
e   Bedroom
f   Bedroom
g   Bath

Photo and plan of the 1950s-era house at 6 Eisenhower Drive in Lockport, New York. In this plan, typical of modestly priced and conservatively styled houses of the post–World War II suburb, one large social room encompasses the functions of both living room and dining room. A small kitchen is positioned so Mother can see what is going on in the living room while cooking. The loss of a separate dining room was interpreted in the 1950s as a sign of modernity and a device that encouraged family togetherness.

ABOVE: *The living room of 6 Eisenhower Drive was improved by following advice from women's magazines on how to personalize the minimally decorated rooms supplied by the house developer. The broad window is surrounded by built-in bookshelves, which also hold collections for display. Shutters provide privacy from passersby.*

BELOW: *The house was designed to make child-centered family life a reality. Little cowboys—as tidy and repetitive as their parents' houses—could dress in western outfits, as shown in the 1950 Sears Roebuck catalog, or decorate their bedrooms with Hopalong Cassidy paraphernalia.*

RIGHT: *The kitchen served as Mother's command post. From this room she kept tabs on all the other spaces in the house and on various family members; here she produced evidence of her care in daily meals and special desserts.*

appliances and cabinetry, but the kitchen's function as Mother's "command post" demanded such open access to all parts of the house.

For all its success, the small suburban home suffered from its size. Magazines suggested ways of expanding the house through additions, ways of decorating rooms to make the most of small spaces, and ideas for getting a room to do double duty (such as a dining and sewing room in one) with the help of clever storage arrangements. What seemed at first to be a "starter" home often became the family's permanent abode, one which only achieved the right size when the children grew up and moved out, leaving the parents to enjoy a house perfectly sized for a childless couple.

■ ELIZABETH C. CROMLEY
JAMES SMOKOWSKI
State University of New York at Buffalo

CIVIL RIGHTS: *New Heroes, New Monuments*

Protest runs deep in the African American experience. The civil rights movement has a history that reaches back to include the struggles of antebellum enslaved blacks, fugitive slaves, and their white allies against the hated institution of slavery. In fact, many of the activities of the civil rights movement after World War II can be viewed as a renewal of efforts to purge this land of the last vestiges of slavery. Beginning with an anti-segregation bus boycott in Baton Rouge, Louisiana, in 1953, the year before the Supreme Court's historic decision in the case of *Brown* v. *Board of Education*, the civil rights movement entered an era of activism that would dramatically focus attention on officially sanctioned racism in many parts of the United States.

Throughout the 1950s and 1960s, the nation's attention was riveted on the Montgomery Bus Boycott (1955); the Tallahassee Bus Boycott (1956); the Little Rock desegregation crisis (1957); sit-ins conducted by an NAACP youth group in Oklahoma City (1958); the Greensboro sit-ins (1960); the Freedom Rides; the Albany Movement (1961–1962); the Birmingham Movement (1963); the March on Washington and Dr. Martin Luther King, Jr.'s "I Have a Dream" speech (1963); the Jackson Movement (1963); Mississippi Freedom Summer (1964); the St. Augustine campaign (1964); the Selma-to-Montgomery March (1965); the Meredith March (1966); and the Memphis sanitation workers' strike (1968) during which Dr. King was assassinated.

The movement included many voluntary organizations—some of them national in scope, such as the Congress of Racial Equality; others local, such as the Montgomery Improvement Association. The

ABOVE: *Famed Civil Rights photographer Ernest C. Withers captured this historic moment in December 1956, when Dr. Martin Luther King and Reverend Ralph Abernathy boarded a municipal bus in Montgomery, Alabama, soon after a federal court ruling that ended racial segregation in the city's transit services. This victory had been won through the efforts of Montgomery's African American community and its supporters in organizing a widespread bus boycott that focused national attention on segregation.*

LEFT: *At the center of the civil rights movement was the struggle for recognition of the most basic human rights. Pictured here is a march of the striking Memphis sanitation workers in April 1968. This protest was to be the last in which Dr. Martin Luther King was a participant. He was assassinated in Memphis on April 4, 1968.*

ABOVE: *In the fall of 1961, after the harvest was gathered, dozens of African American tenant farmers in Fayette County, Tennessee—east of Memphis—were forced off their land as a result of their determination to register to vote. Local landowners were unable to prevent widespread voter registration; the new voters established a tent city once they had been forced out of their own homes.*

movement also gave rise to new leadership cadres that challenged the earlier styles of black leadership. New organizations such as the Southern Christian Leadership Conference (identified with Martin Luther King, Jr.) and the Student Nonviolent Coordinating Committee (which popularized the "Black Power" slogan in 1966) were formed.

The passage of the Civil Rights Act of 1964 was a clear victory of the movement in that it removed racial discrimination from the letter of the law, but voting rights violations persisted. These continuing forms of discrimination were dramatized by the Selma-to-Montgomery March in 1965, which undoubtedly hastened the passage of the Voting Rights Act of 1965. With these clear, if limited, victories behind them, civil rights activists struggled with one another and with the Federal government to decide how to address the deeper ills of African-American society: crime, malnutrition, and persistent poverty. Finding consensus on these matters has proved to be much more difficult than recognizing the right of a Black American man or woman to eat a hot dog or get a cup of coffee at a lunch counter . . . if they could afford it.

■ ROBERT L. HALL
Northeastern University

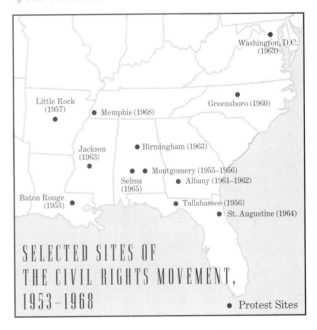

SELECTED SITES OF THE CIVIL RIGHTS MOVEMENT, 1953–1968

• Protest Sites

TEENAGERS: *Styles of Rebellion*

A journey in search of the landmarks of teenage rebellion will take us north from San Francisco, beginning with the North Beach coffee houses of the Beatniks of the 1950s. As the first youth subculture to "drop out" of mainstream America, the Beats ironically owed their existence to the abundance created by corporate capitalism. Middle-class youths could lead lives centered on art and soul-searching—away from the grind of production—because of the surplus of leisure time generated by modern technology. Society could support (and perhaps actually needed) a counterculture opposed to the dominant values to which the majority acceded out of economic necessity.

In the 1960s, a number of Beats moved to the Haight-Ashbury District and contributed to the birth of the largest youth counterculture ever witnessed. Economically, the United States could still afford the luxury of unproductive youth; ideologically, however, its political establishment could no longer tolerate the teens' message, especially as it became increasingly political. The Beats' cultural rebellion of art, music, and philosophy was succeeded by the Hippies' challenge to America's traditional sexual mores, economic values, and conventional lifestyles. Eastern religions beckoned as an alternative to established churches; marijuana, mescaline, and LSD were said to offer creativity and mystical insights in place of the boozy blurriness of earlier generations' whiskey and gin. Even more powerful was the impact of this counterculture in the anti–Vietnam War movement. Shock waves went across the country clear to the White House, and repression was meted out in undue proportion to the actual threat.

Haight Street is of course still there, presently lined with trendy boutiques, secondhand clothing stores, and the usual assortment of San Francisco characters. Though many artifacts and sites of the 1960s survive, they have become the drawing cards of a tourist attraction, not the focal points of a continuing counterculture. As the generations have aged and new teens have emerged to challenge, or at least question, American society's takens-forgranted, the image of the Flower Children of the 1960s has taken its place next to the Beats of the 1950s and the flappers of the 1920s as an icon of once-potent cultural rebellion that has been transformed into a harmless, nostalgic symbol of youth.

By the 1980s, the counterculture of American teens had become more difficult to define. Whether due to internal ideological consistencies, calculated

ABOVE: *Tibetan prayer painted on a cabin door taken from the Grateful Dead's country property in Marin County. The property is now a California State Historic Park. This door and other artifacts from the hippie period are preserved by state authorities.*

LEFT: *By the 1990s, English-made Dr. Martens boots—once worn only by British laborers—had become a mark of distinction in some circles. According to a California dealer, "If you're twenty-three and watch MTV, you know how hot these boots are."*

external oppression, or the country's continuing economic stagnation, youth culture became more fragmented, with groups arising all over the country, distinguished by music, dress, and symbols. The members of Generation X, raised in the 1970s and 1980s, were confronted with an unhealthy economy that could no longer support unproductive young people and that seemingly offered few prospects for success or fulfillment outside the path of conventional careers.

Yet for Generation X and the teens that have succeeded them in the 1990s, the youth counterculture survives. With the aid of inexpensive technology, young people across the country communicate with each other through computer networks, alternative "'zines" (self-published magazines), and demo tapes. Their messages are diverse and, like their predecessors of the 1950s and 1960s, these media raiders define a commercial milieu outside of corporate capitalism and the marketplace.

■ MARY PRAETZELLIS
Sonoma State University

▮ MARIA PRAETZELLIS
*Ursuline High School,
Santa Rosa, California*

ABOVE: *Underground 'zines of the 1990s sprang up and disappeared all over the country while conveying the shared countercultural messages, language, and images of its readers.*

FACING PAGE, LEFT: *The sparse accoutrements of Beat material culture, as seen in this photo (c. 1959), reflect the Zen influence also found in the writing of many Beat poets.*

FACING PAGE, RIGHT: *New American Gothic. A 1960s vegetable and marijuana garden behind an urban commune on Parker Street in Berkeley just up the block from the Brown House, where a red neon sign flashed "Smash the State" to passersby. Parker Street was the epicenter of urban communes.*

THE MYTHIC WEST

The images of the West that we derive from movies and television are mythic. They consist of cliched episodes—the gunfight in the street, the Indian attack on a stagecoach or train, the outlaw life that culminates in a violent end. These events transpire in an epic landscape that dwarfs the human actors: a landscape of long, barren vistas, breathtaking mountains, and deserts studded with cactus or covered with stark, towering crimson-and-purple mesas. The tales are built from a limited number of themes, parables about good and evil. Like all good myth, the mythic West combines reality, fantasy, and allegory.

The most common incidents of the mythic West were uncommon in the real West. Indian attacks on stagecoaches number in the dozens and only one time did Indians attack and stop a train. The dramatic face-off of quick-draw gunslingers in the street rarely happened, and notorious towns such as Tombstone and Dodge City were less violent than the cities of America today.

Perhaps the most famous gunfight in the West was the shoot-out at the O.K. Corral. The real gunfight occurred on October 26, 1881, as the result of a feud between the Earp Brothers and the Clantons. The action took place on Fremont Street, not a block away at the O.K. Corral. In sixty seconds of gunplay, three of the Clantons were killed or mortally wounded. Although the mythic West has made the Earps the white hats and the Clantons the black hats, both sides were nasty characters. The Earps may have gotten better press largely because Wyatt spent the last days of his life in Hollywood, hanging around the film sets and influencing directors of western pictures like John Ford.

The life of Billy the Kid is shrouded in mystery, as befits a legend. Historians cannot even agree on his real name. He earned his notoriety as a hired gun in a range war in southeastern New Mexico from 1877 to 1880. Yet he killed no more than six men in his entire career. Within a year after Pat Garrett shot him to death in Fort Sumner, New Mexico, he was immortalized in a dime novel, *The True Life of Billy the Kid*. Since that time, over six hundred items (novels, motion pictures, articles, biographies, and even a ballet) have been produced about him.

Most of the movies about the West have been made at a handful of locations, and these sites *are* the West in the minds of many people. John Ford chose the grandest of such locations, Monument Valley of the Navajo Nation in Arizona, to film ten of his most famous westerns from *Stagecoach* to *Cheyenne Autumn*. Today the valley is used primarily to film commercials. A quick look up might reward the lucky tourist with the sight of a car or a giant mockup of a toothpaste tube being helicoptered onto the top of one of the towering buttes.

■ RANDALL H. McGUIRE
State University of New York at Binghamton

Billy the Kid has become an icon in southeastern New Mexico. When you're in Las Cruces you can wet your whistle at the local Holiday Inn's Billy the Kid Saloon.

ABOVE: *The gunfight at the O.K. Corral sells products—and twentieth-century children's fantasies.*

LEFT: *John Ford's films made Monument Valley a backdrop for the collective daydreams of industrial America.*

FACING PAGE: *In the West you print the legend, and since the legend has it that the gunfight took place at the O.K. Corral in Tombstone, Arizona, this is the spot tourists flock to.*

NATIVE AMERICA IN THE TWENTIETH CENTURY

Indian country is anywhere there is a large resident Native American population. It is as much a state of mind as a specific place. Southwest Minnesota, southeast South Dakota, and northwest Iowa, often called Siouxland, is home to the Yankton Sioux, who have lived in the region since before 1700. Their problems and successes exemplify what it means to be Indian in twentieth-century America.

The core of Plains Indian life is spirituality. The people have a saying: *"Mitakuye Oyasin"*—"All my relations." That is, we come from the land and are part of it; all living things on it are related. Nowhere is this concept clearer than at Pipestone National Monument, five miles inside western Minnesota. At the monument, a soft red stone—thought of as the blood of Mother Earth—has been quarried for centuries by the Sioux. The stone continues to be carved into pipes, or "calumets," like that given to the people by the White Buffalo Calf Woman in Lakota mythology. To the Sioux, the pipe "religion" remains profoundly significant and an interpretive center at Pipestone National Monument highlights its cultural significance. Carvers often work in the center and quarry the stone outside. Yet outside the monument grounds, a locally produced Song of Hiawatha pageant, held annually in late July, is reviled by most Indians as pandering to stereotypes.

Establishing self-sufficiency is critical for Native American cultural survival. Many tribes have shifted to legalized gambling to bring in revenue and to provide jobs for tribal members. Stop at the new Fort Randall Casino recently built by the Yankton on state Highway 46 near Pickstown, South Dakota. Low-stakes gambling is the rule, with crowds coming from a four-state region.

Christian churches have been an integral part of Native American life since the reservation period. A county road heading south about seven miles west of Wagner, South Dakota, leads to the Yankton Sioux agency town of Marty. Catholic clergy had visited the Yankton since 1839 and in 1920 established the Marty Mission. St. Paul's Church, built in 1946 in Benedictine style of Indiana granite, dominates the mission. Behind the altar is a brightly

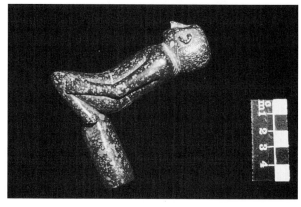

painted angelic choir in which all figures are Indian. Many other buildings, including the boarding school, were given over to Yankton control in 1975 and now serve as tribal headquarters.

Just about anywhere in Indian country during warm weather you can attend a *wacipi*, sometimes called a powwow. These are social occasions that reinforce Indian identity and cultural traditions. It is clear that Indians are not extinct, nor have they been assimilated into the American mainstream. The processes of colonialism threatened their cultures, and present-day Indians deal with that legacy every day. In spite of seemingly intractable problems, Indian culture has proven itself resilient, adaptable, and strong.

■ LARRY J. ZIMMERMAN
  KAREN ZIMMERMAN
  University of South Dakota

LEFT, TOP AND CENTER: *St. Paul's Catholic Church at Marty, South Dakota, completed in 1946, is typical of Christian structures on many reservations. The level of syncretism of Christian and traditional beliefs is variable, but clues are evident in the amount of Indian and Christian imagery inside the churches. The painting above the altar, entitled* Heaven and the Roads to Heaven, *depicts both European saints and Native American characters. This church is locally known as "The Queen of the Prairie."*

BELOW: *The Fort Randall Casino is an important local source of employment and tribal revenue. Most players are non-Indian locals from Nebraska and South Dakota.*

FACING PAGE, TOP: Wacipis *involve several generations, helping to provide cultural solidarity and continuity to the community. Special events are held for children, some of them dancing in their own costumes. Here, Samuel Necklace and Wakinya Thomas participate in an annual event at the University of South Dakota.*

FACING PAGE, BOTTOM: *Pipestone, sometimes called catlinite, is carved into pipe bowls. European-style elbow pipes were often carved into elaborate effigy figures of humans and animals. This pipestone effigy, from the early reservation period, circa 1880, seems to be a figure of a European.*

FAST-FOOD CULTURE: *The Archaeology of McDonald's*

The drive-in restaurant was not invented in southern California, but it may be said to have been perfected there. The warm climate, the distances of a far-flung city, and the general lack of encumbering historical traditions allowed experimentation with the ideal architecture for the new car culture. Out of that mix came one of the most vivid and successful icons of twentieth-century America: the golden arches of McDonald's, first seen in 1952.

By 1935, when architect Wayne McAllister designed Herbert's at Beverly Boulevard and Fairfax Avenue in Los Angeles, the new drive-in building type had evolved to a high degree of sophistication. Circular in plan so hamburgers could be delivered speedily by carhops from kitchen to customers' cars, its tall pylon with integrated neon sign beckoned hungry drivers by day or night.

When Richard and Maurice "Mac" McDonald revamped their struggling small-town hamburger stand at 1398 North E Street in San Bernardino in 1948, it was a simplified, vernacular version of the sleek big-city Herbert's stand. To gain a price advantage on competitors, they fired their carhops and introduced self-service: the customers would have to get out of their cars and walk up to the window to order and pick up their own food. The system clicked. By 1952, Dick and Mac decided to franchise their system as a small regional chain. To design the stand as part of a franchise package, they hired architect Stanley Clark Meston. Meston was familiar with the rules of the road when it came to architecture: He had worked with Wayne McAllister on Herbert's.

The result: two eye-catching 25-foot yellow neon-trimmed arches leaping over a small one-story stand. At roadside stood a third arch carrying a signboard and the chain's original mascot, a burger-faced baker named Speedee. The building itself (two sizes were available) was set back from the roadside so cars could park in front and to the side. A wedge-shaped roof jutted out over the order windows to shelter customers standing in line. With no indoor seating or counter space, the car was your dining

RIGHT: *Herbert's (1935) was typical of commercial drive-ins that evolved in the 1930s in Los Angeles. It is now demolished.*

FACING PAGE, LOWER LEFT: *Speedee, the original mascot, symbol, and watchword of the McDonald's chain, was dropped in 1962 when market research showed people identified McDonald's primarily with the golden arches. Ronald McDonald was introduced in 1963.*

room. The building was wrapped with red-and-white-striped ceramic tile and angled plate glass.

The end of the golden-arched stands began in 1968, when McDonald's Corporation abandoned the sleek 1950s image for a homely shingle-and-brick prototype. Though the original San Bernardino and Phoenix stands have disappeared, a few of the earliest stands have survived around the country in various states of remodel or ruin. The second stand, now the oldest in the nation, can still be found in Downey, California. In 1994, however, the McDonald's Corporation decided that the forty-one-year-old structure would be taken out of service and closed, despite the protests of local architectural preservationists. It nevertheless remains a significant historical monument. If and when this old drive-in gets a second chance, its red, green, and white neon trim (replaced on later McDonald's franchises by rear-lit plastic) will once again flash the staccato rhythms of the California commercial strip.

■ ALAN HESS
Rancho Santa Margarita, California

SKYSCRAPERS: *The Politics of Corporate Architecture*

William Penn, Philadelphia's founder, was surely displeased when, on May 13, 1985, developer Willard Rouse broke ground for a sixty-story office tower in Center City Philadelphia. Designed by Helmut Jahn, the tower is not tall by New York or Chicago standards, but its height created tremendous controversy because it would break an unwritten rule: No building in the city should climb higher than the statue of William Penn perched atop City Hall. Jahn's tower would be the tallest building in the city by more than two hundred feet.

The rule governing the skyline was not only observed out of respect for founding father William Penn; it represented an alliance between business and government that had developed in the decades after the Civil War. At that time, when Philadelphians moved their city hall from Independence Square to its present location at the intersection of Broad and Market streets, Philadelphia's captains of industry and commerce, eager to be close to the political center of the city, quickly built around the new City Hall.

Yet conservative Philadelphians were shocked in 1932, when the Philadelphia Saving Fund Society built its new headquarters a few blocks east of City Hall. Its horizontal strip windows and cantilevered tower mass gave America its first and arguably finest example of the International Style. Though the International Style sought a complete break with the past, the fourteen-foot neon "PSFS" sign remained respectfully below the brim of William Penn's hat.

The 1980s brought a new attitude toward the skyscraper that permitted William Penn to be dwarfed by new monuments. Fueled both by postmodern aesthetic interests and the desire to build spectacular edifices that would lure investors to the city, Philadelphia invited designs that would redefine its image. And if the new monument builders of the 1980s broke with the tradition of height, they did so by mining the familiar forms of the past. Through the postmodern architecture of their headquarters, Philadelphia-based corporations and firms echoed the styles of the most famous icons of corporate America. And though the new buildings are all considerably taller than City Hall Tower, these symbols of corporate power still cluster near William Penn.

The reshaping of Philadelphia's Center City has not been confined to the construction of new buildings. Nostalgia for the past—and the use of the past as an ornamental shell—also plays a significant role. The Mellon Bank took over the abandoned Lits Brothers Department Store Building, built in the nineteenth century, and converted it into stores and offices. And by recycling the old Reading Railroad terminal as part of their new convention center, the Philadelphia Convention Bureau, a partnership of government and private developers, is reaffirming the close relationship between political and economic power symbolized first by the statue of William Penn and now by the new corporate skyline of Philadelphia.

■ MAX PAGE
University of Pennsylvania

■ STEVEN CONN
Ohio State University

FACING PAGE: *As a postmodern monument to Philadelphia's civic aspirations to rival New York City as a center of investment and corporate power, the sixty-story Jahn Tower makes clear visual reference to Manhattan's Chrysler and Empire State Buildings.*

LEFT: *As the focus of Philadelphia's political and economic life for more than a century, the ornate, Second Empire–style City Hall, completed in 1901, and seen here at center, was surrounded by the major terminals of the Reading and Pennsylvania Railroads and John Wanamaker's immense department store. The tradition-bursting skyscrapers of the 1980s can be seen on the right.*

The Philadelphia Saving Fund Society headquarters (1932) is one of the earliest and finest examples of the International Style in America.

The Bell Atlantic headquarters' stepped vertical planes are reminiscent of the RCA building in New York's Rockefeller Plaza.

EPILOGUE

We close on the same note with which we began our examination of American history. We explore by means of history, space, and material culture what we are as a society and what we have become as a society. In exploring the American landscape for hidden histories, protesting voices, and disguised intentions, we can see that American history and culture are—to a degree not often appreciated—not an inevitable upward path of evolution but the result of the continual struggle between those who would dominate and those who would resist. As we've seen in so many cases throughout this book, our economic system and our culture have an enormous capacity to absorb other kinds of societies, other voices, other intentions and make them part of the mainstream. From the early contacts of European fur traders with the native peoples of the Northeastern forests, to the gradual incorporation of other native peoples into the Spanish mission system, to the enslavement of African peoples as plantation workers, through the nineteenth-century transformation of the population of the largely agricultural American colonies and states (not to mention millions of immigrants) into an industrial workforce, new groups with traditional or distinctive lifestyles have been brought into the service of a dynamic, private property–owning, profit-driven economy.

One of the most powerful characteristics of our system is that it can make daily life appear to be much different and better through the sudden availability of new consumer goods. But that is not all. These goods by their very nature can make their users ever more connected to the dominant economic system—to the point that they cannot live without them. Think back to the impact of brass kettles on the hunting patterns of native peoples; of newspapers on how colonial American people thought about their world; of clocks and watches on Americans' sense of time, work, and leisure; and the

enormous impact of the automobile. All these items of material culture promoted intensified consumption within a centralized, disciplined economy.

Today, the contrast between the skylines of the glass-and-steel cities seen from the automobile and the crime and grit surrounding them illustrate one of the most painful incongruities of modern corporate society: that the unregulated operation of the market produces dramatic inequality even in a democratic society. Since World War II, our society has focused mainly on external conflicts. Looming over domestic social problems has been the announced threat of nuclear annihilation and the expansion of a rival economic system in which no one was said to be free. Yet with the sudden collapse of state communism throughout Eastern Europe and the complete disintegration of the Soviet Union, the persuasive image of the great worldwide conflict—between Light and Darkness, Free and Slave—has become obsolete, and the contradictions of our own system must either be masked by some new ideology or faced directly.

In North America, the contradictions of our system are engraved throughout the continent along the highways. The autos and the roads and the products and ideas peddled along their routes are artifacts that provide clues about ourselves. And as with material culture in general, these things must be seen in use, or as they were used, in order to be understood as indexes to ourselves. They can't be read as though they were static, any more than our culture is. In the case of the highways, the clue is that they begin nowhere and end nowhere. Traveling, change, transport, and the idea of a new place are the objectives. And as a consequence, we have chosen to identify the combination of car and road as a modern source of continuous instability.

That instability, as we have defined it, has occurred throughout our history because Europeans considered land property, while Native Americans rejected that idea. Instability occurred because immigrants were led to expect wealth and the freedom it would buy when they came here, but found instead a class structure that made most of them into poor laborers. Instability occurred because the Revolution and Bill of Rights, for which many fought, benefited primarily the property owners—not very many people. Instability occurred because the Civil War, although it abolished slavery, in a broader sense freed almost no one at all, except perhaps northern industry—resulting in the strikes and labor unrest of the late nineteenth century and a great many disappointed people. Instability occurred because African Americans, Native Americans, immigrants, and women—by far the majority of the population—have experienced victimization, not equality, as their condition.

All this can be seen in the trade goods, maps, slave quarters, tenant farmhouses, workers' cottages, domestic environments, Wounded Knees, and teen paraphernalia we have presented. The historical landscapes—the American landscape of now nearly invisible places, people, and things— that we have surveyed delineate some of the outlines of a powerful economic and social system.

These patterns allow that system to function, and at the same time, they can also teach us about it.

If one underlying point can be made, it is that no particular constellation of social relations is inevitable, none inherently or necessarily "American." Our tradition consists of both the dominant trends and the voices of those who have proposed alternatives. History includes *both* the flow of events propelled by class and profit, and the quests for freedom and equality. We have tried to show that the social and economic relations of our nation have been constructed by people, not by destiny, nature, or progress.

In this book, we catch American history between two poles. One is the dynamic trajectory we have traced, which is composed of profit-making and the ideologies that assist it. The other is our common hope that liberty depends on our consciousness of the world around us. We believe that knowledge, understanding, experience, and thought can free us to see how the world works and can offer us a choice as to which voice we want to listen to, and thus which we will follow. So, we conclude, we can make the world.

PHOTO ACKNOWLEDGMENTS

The authors and contributors would like to thank the following institutions and individuals for permission to reproduce illustrations from their collections:

Title page: Photo by Janet E. Levy, University of North Carolina, Charlotte

1 HOW TO SEE THIS BOOK

Introduction

page 3: Osage Scalp Dance: National Museum of Art, Washington, D.C./Art Resource, New York, N.Y.
page 4: Colonial kitchen: Library of Congress
page 6: Virginia chart: I. N. Phelps Stokes Collection; Miriam and Ira D. Wallach Division of Art, Prints, and Photographs, The New York Public Library; Astor, Lenox, and Tilden Foundations
page 7: Three sisters: Museum of Fine Arts, Boston; bequest of Martha C. Karolik for the Karolik Collection of American Paintings
page 8: Greek Revival buildings: from Henry William Elson, *History of the United States of America* (1903)
page 9: Washington and feminists: Library of Congress
page 11: Man and woman eating: from Paul Hulton, *America 1585: The Complete Drawings of John White*, reproduced with permission of University of North Carolina Press
page 12: Ellis Island: National Park Service
page 14: Gravestones: drawing by Amy Elizabeth Grey
page 15: Garden plan: courtesy of Historic Annapolis Foundation
page 16: Excavators: courtesy of Historic Annapolis Foundation

The Ideology of Space

pages 18–19

Hartford: *Warren's Common School Geography* (1887)
Native American school scene: from the *Handbook of North American Indians* vol. 15, courtesy Smithsonian Institution
Pequot massacre: New York Public Library
Lyndhurst: Harris Brisbane Dick Fund, Metropolitan Museum of Art, New York

What Atlases Are

pages 20–21

Sunlit Globe: *Warren's Common School Geography* (1887)
Grizzly bear and Indian: *Warren's Common School Geography* (1887)

Crop maps: from Albert Perry Brigham, *Geographic Influence in American History* (1903)
Globe projection: drawing by Amy Elizabeth Grey, after Mark Monmonier, *How to Lie with Maps* (1991), reproduced with permission of University of Chicago Press

Travel Guides and Picture Books

pages 22–23

Chart of papal bulls: Drawing by Amy Elizabeth Grey
Monsters: Hartmann Schedel, *Liber Chronicarum* (1493)
Vespucci in America: Metropolitan Museum, New York
Tobacco: Historical Division, Cleveland Medical Library Association

The Search for Otherness

pages 24–25

All illustrations courtesy of Architect of the Capitol

Protesting Voices

pages 26–27

Nat Turner poster: Library of Congress
IWW symbol: Labadie Collection, University of Michigan Library
Suffragette placard: Library of Congress
From the Depths: Library of Congress

Space as Action

pages 28–29

Lowell, Massachusetts, plan: Lowell Town Plan (1852)
School: *Warren's Common School Geography* (1887)
Manufacturing village: *Warren's Common School Geography* (1887)
New Harmony: Collection of the New-York Historical Society

Folk Art as Consciousness

pages 30–31

Pottery maker: photo by Charles Zug
Man at forge: photo by John Michael Vlach
Iron fence: photo by John Michael Vlach
Man in boat: courtesy Maida Owens, Louisiana Folklife Program
Wood carvings: photo by Charles Briggs
Woman weaving wheat and woven wheat: photo by James Leary, Wisconsin Folk Art Survey of the John Michael Kohler Art Museum

Introduction

page 35: Sunwatch Hut: Dayton Museum of Natural History

page 37: Venetian map: Osher Collection, University of Southern Maine Libraries

page 38: Cahokia: Painting by L. K. Townsend, courtesy of Cahokia Mounds State Historic Site

page 40: Etowah mound: from William N. Morgan, *Prehistoric Architecture in the Eastern United States* (1980), reproduced with permission of MIT Press.

page 40: Chart: after Henry F. Dobyns, *Their Number Become Thinned: Native American Population Dynamics in Eastern North America* (1983)

page 41: Shell carving: Oklahoma Historical Society

page 42: Trash heap: courtesy Stanley South, South Carolina Institute of Archaeology and Anthropology at the University of South Carolina

page 43: Religious medals: courtesy of American Museum of Natural History, New York

page 44: Drake attack: St. Augustine Historical Society

page 45: Spanish fort: photo by Charles Ewen

page 46: Roanoke landing: from Paul Hulton, *America 1585: The Complete Drawings of John White*, reproduced with permission of University of North Carolina Press

page 48: Pocahontas: from John Smith, *The Generall Historie of Virginia, New England, and the Summer Isles* (1624)

The North Atlantic

pages 50–51

Pottery: courtesy James A. Tuck, Memorial University of Newfoundland

Map details: Osher Collection of the University of Southern Maine Libraries

Aerial view: photo by Faith Harrington

The Great Plains and the Northwest

pages 52–53

Buffalo jump site: drawing courtesy of Thomas F. Kehoe

Petroglyph: photo by Janet E. Levy

Dwelling plan: from the *Handbook of North American Indians*, vol. 8, neg. no. 93-4103, reproduced with permission of the Smithsonian Institution

Man and woman: from the *Handbook of North American Indians*, vol. 8, neg. no. 2854-G-5, reproduced with permission of the Smithsonian Institution

The Southwest

pages 54–55

Fallen wall: photo by Steadman Upham

Taos pueblo: photo by Adam C. Vroman, from the *Handbook of North American Indians*, vol. 9, neg. no. 1904-A, courtesy of the Smithsonian Institution

Pottery: courtesy Steadman Upham

Population graph: courtesy Steadman Upham

The Southeast

pages 56–57

Cahokia painting: by William R. Iseminger, courtesy Cahokia Mounds State Historic Site

Maize: Konrad Gessner (1516–1565), *Opera Botanica*

Anna and Winterville mounds: from William N. Morgan, *Prehistoric Architecture in the Eastern United States* (1980), reproduced with permission of MIT Press

Rattlesnake disk: Alabama Museum of Natural History

Clay pot: photo by Adam Taylor, Alabama Museum of Natural History

De Soto

pages 58–59

De Soto engraving: from Antonio de Herrera, *Historia de los hechos de los Castellanos en las Islas i Tierra Firma del Mar Oceano* (1601)

De Soto painting: Architect of the Capitol

Beads, bell, and halberds: courtesy Mississippi Department of Archives and History

Imperial Rivalries

pages 60–61

Fort Caroline: courtesy David Hurst Thomas

Drake portrait: St. Augustine Historical Society

Plan of Santa Elena: courtesy of Stanley South, South Carolina Institute of Archaeology and Anthropology at the University of South Carolina

Drake's attack: map by Baptista Boazio (1586), St. Augustine Historical Society

Spanish Florida

pages 62–63

Menendez portrait: from *Retratos de los Espanoles* (1791)

Chapel: courtesy Bonnie G. McEwan

Farmstead reconstruction: drawing by Charles B. Poe, courtesy Florida Bureau of Archaeological Research

Artifacts/drawings: courtesy Florida Bureau of Archaeological Research

The Caribbean

pages 64–65

Florida coast: photo by Charles Ewen

Pirate attack: from Theodore de Bry, *America* (1601)

Spanish coins: Florida Bureau of Archaeological Research

Hanging pirate: from Arthur L. Hatwood, ed., *A General History of the Robberies and Murders of the Most Notorious Pirates* (1926)

Spanish Missions

pages 66–67

All photographs and drawings courtesy of the American Museum of Natural History, New York

The Middle Atlantic

pages 68–69

Secotan and Roanoke chief: from Paul Hulton, *America 1585: The Complete Drawings of John White*, reproduced with permission of University of North Carolina Press

Death of missionaries: from Lewis and Loomie, *The Spanish Jesuit Mission in Virginia, 1570–1572*, reproduced with permission of University of North Carolina Press

CROATOAN carving: Courtesy North Carolina Division of Archives and History

The Great Lakes

pages 70–71

Longhouses: courtesy London Museum of Archaeology, University of Western Ontario

Trade kettles: courtesy Royal Ontario Museum

Champlain attacking village: Library of Congress

Southern New England

pages 72–73

Dutch ship: courtesy of the John Carter Brown Library, Brown University

Beaver: from Konrad Gessner, *Historia Animalium* (1558)

Aerial view: photo by Patricia Rubertone

Chief Ninigret: Museum of Art, Rhode Island School of Design; gift of Mr. Robert Winthrop

Virginia

pages 74–75

Living history: courtesy of the Jamestown-Yorktown Foundation

Powhatan's mantle: Ashmolean Museum, Oxford

Tobacco: Konrad Gessner (1516–1565), *Opera Botanica*

John Smith and Native American: from *The Complete Works of Captain John Smith*, Philip Barbour, ed. (1986), reproduced with permission of University of North Carolina Press

3 COLONIAL AMERICA, *1607–1780*

Introduction

page 79: Plimoth Plantation: courtesy of Plimoth Plantation

page 80: Derby House: courtesy Peabody and Essex Museum, Salem, Massachusetts/Essex Institute Collections

page 82: Mission: photo by Neil Silberman

page 83: Derby Estate (2 views): courtesy Peabody and Essex Museum, Salem, Massachusetts/Essex Institute Collections

page 84: Monticello garden: Coolidge Collection, Massachusetts Historical Society

page 85: Planting fields: photo courtesy Russell G. Handsman

page 86: Banknote: from Imogen Clark, *Old Days and Old Ways* (1928)

page 86: spoon: courtesy of Historic Annapolis Foundation

page 87: cup abd saucer: Wadsworth Atheneum, Hartford, Connecticut; bequest of Mrs. Gurdon Trumbull

page 87: plate: courtesy of Historic Annapolis Foundation

page 88: Indian attack: from John Deforest, *History of the Indians of Connecticut* (1856)

page 89: Slave life: Maryland Historical Society

page 90: Flintlock mechanism: courtesy of John Seidel

page 91: Minuteman engraving: from Henry Cabot Lodge, *The Story of the American Revolution* (1898)

page 92: William Paca portrait: Maryland Historical Society

A Crisis of Opportunity

pages 94–95

Bacon's Castle: Association for the Preservation of Virginia Antiquities

Godiah Spray plantation: Godiah Spray Plantation at Historic St. Mary's City, Maryland

Slave quarters: Colonial Williamsburg Foundation

Plan of Annapolis: Courtesy Historic Annapolis Foundation

Tribes, Trade, and Colonial Warfare

pages 96–97

Trade goods: Courtesy Mississippi State Historical Museum

Fort plan: from Marc de Villiers du Terrage, *Les Dernières Années de la Louisiane Française* (1904)

Choctaws: Peabody Museum of Archaeology and Ethnology, Harvard University

The Mission as Labor Camp

pages 98–99

Mission: photo by Helga Teiwes, Arizona State Museum, University of Arizona

1766 map: photo by Helga Teiwes, Arizona State Museum, University of Arizona

Heart medal: photo by David Tuttle, SUNY Binghamton

Church: photo by Randall H. McGuire

The Search for Philip

pages 100–101

Attack on swamp: from *Harper's New Monthly Magazine* (1857); photo courtesy Haffenreffer Museum of Anthropology, Brown University

Smith's Castle: courtesy of Cocumscussoc Association at Smith's Castle

Portrait: courtesy Haffenreffer Museum of Anthropology, Brown University

"Throne": from Samuel Drake, *Biography and History of the Indians of North America* (1834)

The Architecture of Power

pages 102–103

Drayton Hall: Drayton Hall, Charleston, South Carolina
Christ Church: courtesy Foundation for Historic Christ Church
Courthouse: courtesy *Gloucester-Mathews Gazette-Journal*, Tidewater Newspapers, Inc.
Gunston Hall: photo by Charles Baptie, courtesy Gunston Hall

Living Landscapes

pages 104–105

Map detail: Maryland Historical Society
Bolton Estate: Maryland Historical Society
Garden facade: Baltimore Museum of Art
Box Grove: Abby Aldrich Rockefeller Folk Art Center, Williamsburg, Virginia

The Control of Space

pages 106–107

Battle map: from Marc de Villiers du Terrage, *Les Dernières Années de la Louisiane Française* (1904)
North America: from Albert Perry Brigham, *Geographic Influence in American History* (1903)
Battle of Lake Champlain: Public Archives of Canada
Slave handbill: American Antiquarian Society

A Profitable World

pages 108–109

Shaving basin: courtesy of Winterthur Museum
Toothbrushes: courtesy Historic Annapolis Foundation
Clock: The Watch and Clock Museum of the NAWCC
Plate: Wadsworth Atheneum, Hartford, Connecticut, bequest of Mrs. Gurdon Trumbull
Fork: courtesy Historic Annapolis Foundation
Tea set: Yale University Art Gallery, Mabel Grady Garvan Collection

Colonial Childhood

pages 110–111

Gravestones: photo courtesy Robert Emlen
Mason children: The Fine Arts Museum of San Francisco, gift of Mr. and Mrs. John D. Rockefeller, 3rd.
Daggett sisters: courtesy Connecticut Historical Society, Hartford, Connecticut
Doll: Colonial Williamsburg Foundation

Ancestral Homelands, New Frontiers

pages 112–113

Wigwams: photo by Tim Johnson
Stone hoes: drawing by William Fowler, courtesy Massachusetts Archaeological Society

Waterfalls: State Archives, Connecticut State Library, Hartford, Connecticut
Portrait: National Gallery of Art, Washington, D.C.

The Pueblo Revolt

pages 114–115

Santa Fe plaza: photo by Randall H. McGuire
Excavation: from the Archives of the Museum of Indian Art and Culture, Laboratory of Anthropology, Museum of New Mexico
Hopi dolls: photo by David Tuttle, SUNY Binghamton
Indian dancers: Arizona State Museum, University of Arizona

"Class Warfare"

pages 116–117

Excavation: Colonial Williamsburg Foundation
Trenton barracks: courtesy Old Trenton Barracks Museum, Trenton, New Jersey
Louisbourg Fortress: courtesy Fortress of Louisbourg, Parks Canada
Minutemen: from Henry Cabot Lodge, *The Story of the American Revolution* (1898)

Military Industry in the New Nation

pages 118–119

All illustrations courtesy John Seidel

4 CHAOS AND CONTROL, *1781–1865*

Introduction

page 123: New Orleans street scene: The Historic New Orleans Collection, Museum/Research Center
page 125: Philadelphia street scene: courtesy Independence National Historic Park Collection, National Park Service
page 126: Textbook figures: *Warren's Common School Geography* (1887)
page 129: Tacoma house: photo by John Michael Vlach
page 129: Marden house: Library of Congress
page 129: Pocket watch: National Watch and Clock Museum of the NAWCC
page 131: Slave portrait: Peabody Museum of Archaeology and Ethnology, Harvard University
page 132: Factory life: *Warren's Common School Geography* (1887)
page 132: Rock crystals: courtesy Charles Carroll House of Annapolis, Inc.
page 132: Round barn: Hancock Shaker Village
page 133: Indian war: from *Warren's Common School Geography* (1887)
page 134: Springfield Armory: courtesy Springfield Armory National Historic Site
page 135: Railroad scene: courtesy Harpers Ferry National Historic Park, National Park Service

New Orleans

pages 136–137

All photos by Dell Upton

Philadelphia

pages 138–139

All photos by Dell Upton
U.S. Naval Asylum: Library Company of Philadelphia
Asylum plan: courtesy of Dell Upton

A Journey Embroidered

pages 140–141

Burr sampler: Museum of Art, Rhode Island School of Design
Stockton bedcover: New York State Historical Association, Cooperstown
Keys painting: Museum of Art, Munson-Williams-Proctor Institute, Utica, New York
Webb embroidery: Charleston Museum, Charleston, South Carolina

Gothic Revival Architecture

pages 142–143

Cottage drawing: Library of Congress
Merk House: Library of Congress
Ohio House: photo by John Michael Vlach
Missouri House: photo courtesy of Howard Wright Marshall

Greek Revival Architecture

pages 144–145

Virginia capitol: Library of Congress
Arlington House: Photo by John Michael Vlach
Alabama house plan: Historic American Building Survey, Library of Congress
New York farmhouse: photo by John Michael Vlach
Newton House: Library of Congress

Everyone Watches Time

pages 146–147

Clockmaking: mural by Suzanne and Lucerne McCullogh, 1939, in the Thomaston, Connecticut Post Office; photo by Russell G. Handsman
Clock: from *Illustrated Catalogue of Seth Thomas Clocks, Regulators, and Time Pieces* (1863)
Factory and Main Street: photos by Russell G. Handsman from the State Archives, Connecticut State Library, Hartford, Connecticut

Plantations and Reservations

pages 148–149

Middleburg Plantation: photo by David W. Babson
Indian school and classroom: Cumberland County Historical Society, Carlisle, Pennsylvania
Mistress and slaves: from Kate Pickard, *The Kidnapped and the Redeemed* (1856)

Landscapes of Slavery

pages 150–151

Green Hill Plantation: Library of Congress
Friendfield Plantation: courtesy of the Belle W. Baruch Foundation, Georgetown, South Carolina
Evergreen Plantation: photo by Sam Bowers Hilliard, Louisiana State University
Horses and fence: Library of Congress

Mass Production

pages 152–153

Factory: Manchester Historic Association
Boott Mills: Center for Lowell History, University of Lowell
Mill worker: from *Warren's Common School Geography* (1887)
Harpers Ferry: Harpers Ferry National Historic Park, National Park Service

African Religion in America

pages 154–155

Carroll House and excavated artifacts: Courtesy of Charles Carroll House of Annapolis, Inc.
Pottery sherd and symbol: courtesy of Leland Ferguson
Crystals: National Park Service, National Capitol Region Archaeology Program
Monticello finds: courtesy of William M. Kelso and Department of Archaeology, The Thomas Jefferson Foundation

Midwestern Utopias

pages 156–157

Zoar map: from *The Combined Atlas Map of Tuscarawas County, Ohio* (1875)
Hedge maze: courtesy of New Harmony State Historic Site, Division of State Museum and Historic Sites
Nauvoo: Edward E. Ayer Collection, The Newberry Library, Chicago
Big Brick: photo by Charles E. Orser, Jr.

The Cherokee

pages 158–159

Etowah mound: photo by Barbara J. Little
Sequoya: courtesy Smithsonian Institution

Printshop: photo by Paul A. Shackel
Cabin and beadworker: courtesy Cherokee Historical Association, Cherokee, North Carolina

The Civil War

pages 160–161

Harpers Ferry: courtesy of Harpers Ferry National Historic Site, National Park Service
African American soldiers: courtesy Department of the Army, U.S. Army Military History Institute, Carlisle, Pennsylvania
Antietam bodies: Library of Congress

Industrial Cleveland

pages 162–163

Houses: photos by Rob Brose/SubEtheric
Irishtown Bend map: courtesy of David S. Brose
Cleveland landscape: Western Reserve Historical Society

5 THE MAKING OF A MASS CULTURE, *1865–1917*

Introduction

page 167: Portraits: courtesy of Adrian and Mary Praetzellis
page 169: Silk workers: Passaic County Historical Society, Paterson, New Jersey
page 170: Saloon: photo from the collection of Frederick Charles Buckingham, Sr.
page 170: Tenant farmer shacks: photo by Marion Post Wolcott, Library of Congress
page 172: George Washington: courtesy of Mark Bograd
page 174: Row of houses: courtesy of the Leonia Public Library, Leonia, New Jersey
page 176: Beach tube: from *Scientific American* (1871)
page 176: Ladies' Mile: photo by Mette Munthe-Kaas
page 178: "The Last Yankee": Library of Congress
page 180: Little Bighorn marker: photo by Neil Silberman
page 181: Parade: from Mason A. Green, *Springfield, 1636–1886, History of Town and City* (1888)
page 182: Columbian Exposition: Library of Congress

Victorian Sacramento

pages 184–185

California capitol: courtesy California State Capitol Museum
Chinese New Year: Eugene Hepting Collection, City of Sacramento Archives and Museum
Tea set: drawing by C. Savitski, courtesy of Adrian and Mary Praetzellis
Historic district: photo by Adrian Praetzellis

The Northeast

pages 186–187

Button Room, Wrestler poster, and mangled hand: Scovill Collection, Mattatuck Museum, Waterbury, Connecticut
Scovill factories: Joseph Anderson, *The Town and City of Waterbury, Conn.* (1896)

The West

pages 188–189

Farmhands at table: photo from the collection of John Ferraro
Saloon, family group: photos from the collection of Frederick Charles Buckingham, Sr.
Highway view: photo by Margaret S. Purser

The South

pages 190–191

Waverly Plantation: photo courtesy William Hampton Adams
Millwood Plantation: photo courtesy Charles E. Orser, Jr.
Sharecroppers: photo by Dorothea Lange, Library of Congress
Laurel Valley Plantation: photo by Charles E. Orser, Jr.

Patent Medicines

pages 192–193

Labels and posters: Bella C. Landauer Collection, New-York Historical Society
Bottles: photo by Lynn Jones, courtesy Historic Annapolis Foundation

The Colonial Revival

pages 194–195

Mount Vernon postcard: courtesy Mark Bograd
Wallace Nutting photo: Library of Congress
Colonial Ball: courtesy Alexandria Library, Lloyd House
Domino's Pizza: Photo by Mark Bograd

Vaudeville

pages 196–197

Theater scene: Harvard Theatre Collection
Pat Rooney and Eva Tanguay: Billy Rose Theatre Collection of the New York Public Library at Lincoln Center
Jefferson Theater: photo by Robert Snyder

Old Suburbia

pages 198–199

All historic illustrations courtesy of Leonia Public Library
Modern town center: photo by Paul H. Mattingly

Public Art

pages 240–241

Post office interior: photo by Sue Bridwell-Beckham
Murals: National Archives

Billboards

pages 242–243

Vacuum: Farleigh-Dickinson University Archive
Chicks: courtesy of the Ralston-Purina Company
Fords: courtesy of the Ford Motor Company
Family: Farleigh-Dickinson University Archive

Cemeteries

pages 244–245

All photos by Randall H. McGuire

Suburbia

pages 246–247

Ranch house and garage: photos by Elizabeth Cromley
Decorated house and school: photos by James Smokowski

Home

pages 248–249

House and living room: photo by James Smokowski
Plan: drawing by James Smokowski
Cowboys: Sears Roebuck Catalog, Fall/Winter 1950–51, courtesy of Sears
Kitchen: Sears Roebuck Catalog, Fall/Winter 1946–47, courtesy of Sears

Civil Rights

pages 250–251

All photos by Ernest C. Withers, Memphis, Tennessee

Teenagers

pages 252–253

Beatniks: Robert Orlins Collection
All other photos by Adrian Praetzellis

The Mythic West

pages 254–255

O.K. Corral: photo by Pat Koester
Toy gun: photo by David Tuttle, SUNY Binghamton
Holiday Inn: photo by Thomas J. Caperton, New Mexico State Monuments, Museum of New Mexico
Monument Valley: photo by Neil Silberman

Native America in the Twentieth Century

pages 256–257

Children: photo by Mark Hennies
Pipe: photo courtesy of the University of South Dakota Archaeological Laboratory
Billboard: photo by Karen Zimmerman
Church exterior: photo courtesy Herbert T. Hoover
Church interior: photo courtesy of Sr. Madeleine, OSBS, St. Paul's Church

Fast-Food Culture

pages 258–259

Herbert's: Seaver Center for Western History Research, Natural History Museum of Los Angeles County
McDonald Brothers: photo by Ray Quiel
1950s McDonald's and Speedee: photos by Alan Hess

Skyscrapers

pages 260–261

City Hall and Jahn Tower: courtesy of City Representative, City of Philadelphia
PSFS tower: Temple University Urban Archives
Bell Atlantic tower and Philadelphia skyline: courtesy of Bell Atlantic

INDEX

Entries in *italics* refer to maps and illustrations.

B. Altman store, 202, 203
Baptism of Pocahontas at Jamestown, Virginia (painting), *25*
Baraboo, Wisconsin, *239*
Barrow, Alaska, 206
Basque, 37, 50, 188
Batesburg, South Carolina, *241*
Baton Rouge, Louisiana, 250
Batz, Alexander de, *97*
Beach, Alfred Eli, 200
Beach Pneumatic Tube, *176*, 200
Beads, *58*, 154, *159*
Beatniks, 10, 252, *253*
Beaux-Arts style, 203
Beaver pelts, 37–38, 72, *73*
Beckham, Richard H., 220, 238
Beckham, Sue Bridwell, 219–20, 222, 234, 238, 240
Becnel family, *151*
Beecher, Mary Ann, 218, 232–33
Beecher sisters, 127
Behavior
 and Civil War, 134
 ideology manifested as, 128
 and movies, 221
 and power on plantations, *148*
 and products, 87, 108, *108*, 177
 taught in childhood, 88
Bel Aire Gardens, 246–49, *246–48*
Bell Atlantic headquarters, *261*
Belle Plaine, Iowa, *233*
Belmont, August, 200
Belmont (estate), *105*
Bemidji, Minnesota, *234*
Berkeley, California, *253*
Berkeley, Gov. William, 94, 95, 116
Best & Co., 202
Bialystoker Synagogue, 205, *205*
Big Brick, *157*
Big Foot, chief, 209, *209*
Billboards, 222–23, *223*, 242, *243*
Billy the Kid, 254, *255*
Binghamton, New York, *224*, *245*
Birth(s)
 illegitimate, 124
 rates, 192
Bishop Hill, Illinois, *157*
Blackfoot people, *53*
Black Hills, 179, 208
Black Kettle, chief, 208
Black Muslims, 228
Black Panthers, 228
Blacksmiths, 31
Black stones, polished, 154
Blake, Eubie, 196
Blankets, 47, 48
Block, Adriaen, 72, *72*
Block, Irving A., *241*

Boarding School Site, *53*
Boardman, Daniel, *113*
Bograd, Mark, 10, 26–27, 172, 194–95
Bolton estate, *105*
Bonnet, Stede, *65*
Bontemps, Jean, 65
Bonwit Teller, 202
Boone, Daniel, *25*
Boone County, Illinois, *145*
Boott Cotton Mills, 152, *153*
Boston, Massachusetts, *8*, *110*, 175
Box Grove, *105*
Brainerd, Minnesota, *219*
Brecher, Jeremy, 168, 186–87
British (English), 15
 army, *117*
 blockade of Louisiana by, 96–97
 and Colonial Period, 79–80, 95
 early fishermen, 50, *51*
 first settlements of, 48–49, 74
 and formal gardens, 104
 and imperial rivalry, 44–45, 60–61, 65
 and Native Americans, *18*, *24*, *25*, *46*, 49, 74, *74*, *75*, 100–101
 retreat to Canada, 6
 and Spanish, 41, 81
Broadsides, 26, *26*, *107*
Brooklyn Rapid Transit Company (BMT), 200, *201*
Broome County, New York, 224, 244
Brose, David S., 37, 46, 47, 70–71, 135, 162–63
Broutin, Ignace François, *97*
Brown, John, 160
Brown University, *141*
Brown v. *Board of Education*, 228, 250
Buffalo (bison), 38, *53*, 208, *208*
Bunyan, Paul, 234, *234*
Burr, Cynthia, 140, *141*
Bus boycotts, 227, 250
Button manufacturing, 186–87, *187*
Buttons, 26

Caborca mission, 98
Cagney, Jimmy, 196
Cahokia, 39, *39*, *57*
California, 15, 52, 168, 188, 258–59
 State Capitol, *185*
Calvert House, *109*
Cameron site, *71*
Campbell County, Virginia, 150
Campbell estate, *105*
Canada, 6
Canned food, and Eskimos, 206
Cape Breton Island, 50, *51*, *117*
Cape Cod house, 226
Capellano, *24*

Capitalism
 and change, 125
 and clocks, 146–47
 and ideology, 221
 and utopianists, 156
 See also Corporate capitalism; Industrial capitalism; Mercantile capitalism
Capra, Frank, 221, 238
Caribbean, 6, 44–45, *45*, 64–66, *65*
 Treasure Fleet routes, *64*
Carlisle, Pennsylvania, Indian School, 148, *149*
Carroll Garden, 104
Cartagena, 64, *64*, 65
Carter, Robert "King," *103*
Carter's Grove, *95*, 104, *116*
Case, John, 188
Case, Leonard, Jr., *163*
Cassell, Mark S., 178, 206
Catholics, *31*, 62, 204–5
Cattle ranching, *63*
Causici, Enrico, *24*, *25*
Cemeteries, 224–25, 227, 244, *244*, *245*
Centerburg, Ohio, *143*
Central Pacific Railroad, 188
Champlain, Samuel, 70–71
Chapman, John G., *25*
Charles Carroll House, *132*, 154, *155*
Charlesfort colony, 60
Charleston, South Carolina, 102, *103*, *107*, 130, *140*, 148, 154
Charles V, king of Spain, 43
Chase factory, 187
Chattanooga Medicine Company, *193*
Cherokee nation, 133, 158, *159*
Cherokee Phoenix, 158, *159*
Chesapeake area, 91–92, 94, 104
Cheyenne, 179, 208, *208*
Cheyenne Autumn (movie), 254
Chicago, Illinois, 183
 World's Columbian Exposition (1893), *182*, 183, *203*, 212
Chicago and Northwestern Railroad, *218*, 232
Chickasaw, 96, *96*
 War, *97*, *106*
Children and childhood
 and cemeteries, *224*
 concept of, 7, *7*, 88, 110–11, *111*
 as inferior Other, 11
 and market, 88
 in South, 192
 and space in schools, *29*
 and suburbs, 226, *226*, 249, *249*
Chinese, 11, 16, 17, 184, *185*
Chinook (trade language), 38, 52
Chivington, 208

and ideology, 128–30, 230–31
and individualism, 93
and labor for profit, 87–88, 108
as means of conquest, 42, 43, 47
people tied to economic system by, 263
of postbellum plantation, 171
and Old Suburbia, 198
of recent protest, 10
Mats'a:ka (town), 54, *55*
Mattingly, Paul H., 174, 198
Mayflower Descendants, 173, 195
Maynard, John, *193*
Maynard-Burgess Houses, *193*
Meagher, Gen. Thomas Francis, 161
Mealtime behavior, *86*, 87, *87*, *109*, 128
Melendez, Doña Maria, 62
Mellon Bank, 260
Melting pot ideology, 135, 161, 178
Memphis, Tennessee, *251*
    sanitation strike, 250, *250*
Men
    and female artists 140, *141*
    and Greek Revival style, 127–28
    and patent medicines, 192, *192*
Men and Manners in America (Hamilton), 138
Menéndez de Avilés, Pedro, 41, 60–61, 62, *62*, *63*
Mercantile Capitalism
    and control, 106–7
    culture of, 86–88
    and personal identity, 108
Mercator projection, 21
Merchants, 13, 84, *123*
Meridians, 20–21
Merk House, *143*
Merwin, Henry, *163*
Meston, Stanley Clark, 258
Metacom (King Philip), 100–101, *100*
Metal goods and kettles, 47, 48, 50, 70, *71*, 263
Metichawon falls, *112*, 113
Mexico, 10, 25, 37, 38–39, 58, 66, 81
Michigan, 162
Middle Atlantic, 5, 68–69, 74, *75*, 142
Middleburg Plantation, 130, 148, *149*, 154
Middle class, 17, 153
    and consumer values, 177
    and department stores, 202–3
    and entertainment, 196
    and neighborhood segregation, 162
    and suburbs, 175, 198, *199*, 200, 226
    and subways, 200
Middleton estate, 104
Midwest
    billboards, 242

early trade, 70–71
highways, 232–33
houses, *143*, 144, *145*
industrialization of, 162
pageants, 210
tourist attractions, 234
utopian communities, 133, 156, *156*
Migrant laborers, 188, *189*
Milagros (medals), 99
Militia, 91–93, 102, *103*, 116–17, *117*
Millwood Plantation, *191*
Minnesota, 208, 234, 256
Minuteman image, 91–93, *117*
Minute Man of Concord (statue), *91*
Mississippian mound-building culture, 56, *57*, 70, 96, *211*
Mississippi Delta, 5, *191*
Mississippi Freedom Summer, 228, 250
Mississippi River, 58, 150, *151*
Mississippi Valley, 39, 40–41, 56, *59*
Missouri, 142
Missouri River, 52
Miwok people, *53*
Modernity, 135, 167–68, 174, 181, 223, *242*
Mohawk people, 70
Monk's Mound, *39*
Montgomery, Alabama, bus boycott, 227, 250, *250*
Monticello, *84*, 104, 154, *155*
Montpelier estate, 104
Monuments, 25, *25*, *105*, 204
Monument Valley, 254, *255*
Mormons, 10, 133, 135, *157*
Mortality rates, 80
Morven estate, 104
Mother at Home, The, 127
Mothers
    and billboards, 242, *243*
    role formalized, 127
    and suburbs, 248–49, *248*, *249*
Motion pictures, 197
Moundsville, Alabama, *57*
Mount Clare estate, 104
Mount Deposit, Baltimore, *105*
Mount Hope, 100–101, *101*
Mount Vernon, 104, 194, 195, *195*
Movies, 220–22, 238, *238–39*, 254
Mullins, Paul R., 87, 108
Mullins, South Carolina, 240, *241*
Museum of Man of San Diego, 183
Museums, 4, 134, 177
    and Colonial Revival, 195
    ethnological, 183
    and highways, 220
    and pageants, 210
Musket Factory at Harpers Ferry (painting), 152

Myths
    of citizen soldier, 117, *117*
    of Custer's Last Stand, 208
    of discovery of America, 49
    and inequality, 82
    of Jamestown settlement, 48–49
    of "Lost" Roanoke colony, 69
    mass-marketed, 171–73
    and pageants, 180–81
    of postbellum South, 169–71
    of West, *170*
    See also Ideology

NAACP, 250
Narragansett Bay, 72, *73*
Narváez, Pánfilo de, 41
Nash family site, *155*
Natchez, Mississippi, *57*
National Guard, 168
Native American Rights Fund, 230
Native Americans (Indians)
    and anthropologists, *126*
    in atlases, *21*
    "civilization of," 7
    and Civil War, 135
    in Colonial Period, 81, 94
    and conflict in West, *132*, 133, 167–68, 179
    control of, and reservations, 148–49
    cost of being "discovered," 46
    cultural destruction of, 9, 10
    before "discovery," 35–41, *37*, 50
    early trade, 38, 70–71
    English view of, *46*
    European conception of, 106
    forced to accept Euro-American culture, 148, *149*, 158, *159*
    and historical archaeology, 16, 17, 36
    and ideology, 13, 84
    and individualism, 92
    intermarriage with Spanish, 62–63
    and Jamestown colony, 6, 48–49, 74, *75*
    and King Philip's War, 100–101
    and land, 85, 88
    and mass-produced goods, 177
    and Middle Atlantic colonies, 68–69
    migrate to North America, 6
    and militias, *103*, 116
    and museums, 4
    and mythic West, 254
    and New Orleans, 123
    as Other, *23*, 24–25, *24*, *25*
    in pageants, *181*, *211*
    and Paradise Valley, Nevada, 188
    and patent medicines, 192
    and Plains Indian Wars, 208–9

Washington, George, *172*, 195, *195*
Wasserman, Suzanne, 178, 204–5
Waterbury, Connecticut, 186–87, *186*, *187*
Waverly Plantation, *191*
Wayne, John, 238
Wealth
 and cemeteries, 225
 extracted by Spanish, 81
 ideology of, 9, 88, 128
 and Mercantile Capitalism, 87
 and postbellum plantations, 171
 and suburbs, 175
 See also Inequality; Rich and poor
Wealthy planters
 and architecture, 102–3
 and formal gardens, 104
Weantinock planting fields, *85*, 112–13, *113*
Webb, Martha Cannon, 140, *140*
West
 early trade, 38
 Greek Revival style, 184
 and industrialization, 168–69
 movement to, 21, 168–69, 177, 188, *189*
 mythic, *170*, 229, 254, *255*
 and Native Americans, *132*
 and world's fairs, 213
West African tribes, 131, *155*
West Indians, 123, 154
West Indies, *44*
Whaling, 37, 50, *50*, 178–79, 206, *206*, *207*
Whiskey Rebellion, 116
White, John, *11*, *69*
"White City," *182*, 212
White-collar class, 168, 175
Whites
 males, control by, *153*

and postbellum plantation, 171
portrayals of, vs. Indians, *3*
southerners, 192, *192*
terrorist groups, 191
Wigwams, 113
"Wilderness"
 appeal of, 17
 depictions of, *25*
 ideology of, 10, 83–85, 104, 177
 "taming," and Plains Indians, 179
Williams, William A., 213
Williamsburg, Virginia, 82, *94*, *95*, 181, 194, 195, 210
Wine of Cardui, *193*
Winnemucca, Nevada, 188
Winterville ceremonial complex, *57*
Wisconsin, 234
Wishram people, 52, *53*
Withers, Ernest C., *250*
Wobblies (I.W.W.), 26, *27*
Wolcott, Marion Post, *170*
Wolstenholme Town, *116*
Women
 and billboards, 242
 and department stores, 177, *203*
 and dolls, *111*
 and domesticity, 125–27, 128, 140, 226
 and factory towns, 152, *153*
 in frontier literature, *25*
 and historical archaeology, 17
 and individualism and rights, 92
 as inferior Other, 11
 lower pay, *153*
 and market, 88
 in Native American societies, 38
 and patent medicines, 192, *193*
 "place is in the home" belief, 7
 and suburbs, 226, 248–49
 resistance to domesticity, 131, 140
 role of, in past, 4, 7

and space in plantations, 107
and strikes, 186
victimization of, 264
Women's movement, *9*, 10, *27*, 131
Wood carvers, *31*
Workers, *123*
 attitudes, 135
 and company towns, 130
 control of, 168, 183
 and highways, 219
 injuries of, *187*
 and movies, 221
 and residential patterns, 175
 resistance by, 10, 131
 segregation of, 162–63, *163*
 and space, *28*, 167
 and vaudeville, 173, 196–97
 See also Labor
Works Progress Administration (WPA), 222
World's Fairs, 167, 181–83, *182*, 212–13
World War I, 7, 210, 236
World War II, 223
Wounded Knee, 209, *209*

Yankton Sioux, 256
Yentsch, Ann E., *86*
Youth movement, 227, 228–29, 252–53
Ysleta, New Mexico, *114*
Yurok people, *53*

Zealy, J. T., *131*
Zen, *253*
Zimmerman, Karen, 179, 208–9, 229, 256
Zimmerman, Larry J., 179, 208–9, 229, 256
'Zines, 253, *253*
Zoar, Ohio, 133, *157*
Zuni, 114–15, *115*

973
Leo INVISIBLE AMERICA   30,123

DATE DUE

GAYLORD   PRINTED IN U.S.A.